Happy Hanukkah

This is something swell!

Love,
Mom

THE JEWISH BOOK OF
WHY

Also by Alfred J. Kolatch

Classic Bible Stories for Jewish Children
The Family Seder
The Jewish Child's First Book of Why
The Jewish Home Advisor
The Jewish Mourner's Book of Why
The New Name Dictionary
Our Religion: The Torah
The Second Jewish Book of Why
This Is the Torah
Who's Who in the Talmud

THE JEWISH
BOOK OF
WHY

by

Alfred J. Kolatch

 Jonathan David Publishers, Inc.
Middle Village, New York 11379

THE JEWISH BOOK OF WHY

Jonathan David Publishers, Inc.
68-22 Eliot Avenue
Middle Village, New York 11379

39 41 43 44 42 40 38

Library of Congress Cataloging in Publication Data

Kolatch, Alfred J., 1916-
  The Jewish book of why.

  Bibliography: p.
  Includes index.
  1. Judaism—Customs and practices. I. Title.
BM700.K59   296.7   81-3274
ISBN 0-8246-0256-0   AACR2

Printed in the United States of America

For
DR. MAX ARZT
of blessed memory
Friend, Rabbi and Scholar,
who thought this book
needed to be written
and who first suggested its title

In Appreciation

Thanks are due to many colleagues and associates for their help in preparing this manuscript. The task was far greater than it seemed at the outset, and without their advice and assistance this book could not have been published.

Particular thanks are due my son Jonathan for his probing questions and keen insights and observations. And to my son David, for his critical comments and unceasing insistence on clarity in answering all questions, my most profound thanks and appreciation.

To my secretaries, Florence Weissman and Mary McGee, for typing and retyping the many drafts of the manuscript, my thanks.

Contents

General Introduction

I

Over the years, many books describing Jewish life—its laws, its customs, its ceremonies—have appeared. Practically all are devoted to a recitation of rules of conduct, but few if any devote themselves to an explanation of *why* specific laws, customs, and ceremonies have evolved.

The Jewish Book of Why does not advise Jews how to conduct their lives. It is not a book of *halacha*—of Jewish law. Orthodox, Conservative, and Reform scholars, rabbis, and religious associations have made their views and attitudes clear. This volume is designed only to explain the reasoning behind the practices that are followed.

If Jews go to a stream or to a river or to the oceanfront on the afternoon of the first day of Rosh Hashana to cast crumbs into the water—a ceremony called *Tashlich*—this book does not concern itself with whether this custom should be retained. It simply explains *why* the custom is practiced.

If Jews leave stones on a tombstone when visiting the cemetery, or if a mirror is turned around to face the wall in a house of mourning, this book does not judge the value of the custom. It simply explains *why* it is followed.

If the groom breaks a glass at a wedding, or if the bride, under the canopy, marches around the groom three times or seven times, this book does not evaluate the merit of the practice. It merely explains *why* it evolved and discusses what its significance might be.

Needless to say, the number of questions that might have been included in this book is limitless, and only those thought to be uppermost in the mind of the layman are treated. A full bibliography is included for the reader interested in delving more deeply into the subject. *The Second Jewish Book of Why* likewise provides more information on many of the subjects discussed in this volume.

* * *

To understand *why,* it is important first to understand how, when, and where. How, when, and where did the mass of Jewish laws and customs develop?

Were a Jew of the generation of Moses or Solomon or Judah the Maccabee alive today, he would be quite confused as he observed our religious conduct. He would look at the *talit* (prayershawl) or *kipa* (skullcap) that we wear and ask, "Why do Jews wear them? What are they for?" He would notice the *gartl* (girdle) and *shtreiml* (fur hat) worn by the *chassid* and be puzzled by this special garb.

Were one of our ancestors of the biblical era to join us at a Seder, he would wonder about the types of food served. He knows the Bible, and the Bible refers only to the Paschal lamb and the *matza* that the Jews of Egypt ate during those last hectic days of enslavement. He would also wonder where the narrative and songs of the Haggada originated.

A Jew of those early years would also wonder about our Sabbath observance. He would surely question why there are so many dos and don'ts. He would wonder why some Jews observe holidays for longer periods than others, and why the *shofar* is not sounded on the Sabbath, which it was in biblical times.

And were he to think of Israel Isserlein (1390-1460), the fifteenth-century German Talmudist who was described by his students as wearing a *geriffete,* a fur-lined mantle with ruffles around the neck, similar to a garment worn by women at that time, he would be quite confused. And were he to note modern-day Jews on the streets of Jerusalem or Tel Aviv wearing *yarmulkes* (skullcaps) that are held to their heads with ladies' bobby pins or hair clips, he would be dismayed. Why, he would wonder, are they not observing the explicit commandment of Deuteronomy 22:5: "A woman shall not wear a man's garment, neither shall a man put on a woman's garment; it is an abomination before God."

To understand contemporary Jewish observance, our visitor from the past would have to learn that the laws of the Bible, although primary and central, are not the only source of Jewish practice. Jewish law has never been static; it has continued to change and grow with each passing generation. While on the one hand strict adherence to biblical and Talmudic prescriptions has always been expected, rabbinic authorities have also expressed their awareness of the influence of local custom in shaping Jewish conduct.

The Talmud (Baba Metzia 86b) emphasizes the point: "When you come to a town, follow its customs, for when Moses went up to heaven, he refrained from food for forty days and forty nights. And when the angels came down to visit Abraham, they partook of his meal, each one submitting to the custom of the place."

Should a custom *(minhag)* conflict with some established law *(halacha),* the custom frequently takes precedence (Soferim 14:18).

*   *   *

Almost 1,000 years passed from the time the last book of the Bible was admitted to the canon and the editing of the Talmud was completed. It is easy to overlook the dramatic changes that took place within Judaism during that period. What was a strong, united nation under King David and his son Solomon became a divided nation. The kingdom of the North (Samaria), consisting of ten of the Twelve Tribes of

Israel, and the kingdom of the South (Judea) became two distinct monarchies, both of which were eventually destroyed by hostile neighbors. The northern monarchy was destroyed by the Assyrians around 700 B.C.E., and the Ten Tribes were dispersed. The southern kingdom came to an end in 586 B.C.E., when the Babylonians destroyed the Temple that had been built by Solomon 500 years earlier. The inhabitants of the southern kingdom were, for the most part, exiled to Babylonia.

Seventy years later, after Persia defeated the Babylonians, Jews returned to Palestine and the Temple was rebuilt. Then the Greeks defeated the Persians and the Romans defeated the Greeks. Under the Romans the Second Temple was destroyed in the year 70 C.E.

Despite the upheaval, Jewish life was not static. In bustling academies of learning there was constant studying, interpreting, and reinterpreting of the Bible. Scholars did not always agree. The two rival schools of the first century (during the reign of Herod), the disciples of Hillel and the disciples of Shammai, differed on hundreds of points of Jewish law, even on such minor matters as whether the Chanuka lights should be kindled from left to right or right to left. So far apart were the schools in their thinking and observance that the Talmud (Sanhedrin 88b) expresses the fear that there was danger that the one Tora might end up as two Torot.

During the first five centuries of the Common Era, scholars in the academies of learning in Babylonia and Palestine were busily engaged in explaining and interpreting the words of the Bible. The first group to do this was the *tannaim* (singular, *tanna*), scholars of the first and second centuries who continued the debates begun by Hillel and Shammai, whose successors included Rabbi Akiba and Rabbi Ishmael. Finally, by about 220 C.E., the debates and decisions were summarized and edited by Rabbi Yehuda Hanasi. This body of literature is called the *Mishna,* which, once edited, was considered final. It became the authoritative source of *halacha* (Jewish law), second only to the Bible itself.

The period that followed the tannaitic period, extending

from approximately 220 to 470 C.E., was called the amoraic period. During this time, scholars known as *amoraim* (singular, *amora*) studied the text of the Mishna and added their comments and interpretations. No *amora* had the right to take exception to the opinion of a *tanna* unless he could find support for his view from another *tanna*. The discussions and laws of the Babylonian *amoraim*, together with the Mishna itself, were finally collected in what is known as the Babylonian Talmud. The views and opinions of the Palestinean *amoraim*, together with the Mishna itself, were collected in what is known as the Jerusalem (Palestinean) Talmud. Because the Babylonian Talmud was finalized at a later date than the Jerusalem Talmud, its decisions are generally the more accepted ones.

The geonic period followed this talmudic period. *Geonim* (singular, *gaon*) were distinguished scholars in the great academies of Babylonia (Sura and Pumpedita) who succeeded the *amoraim*, and their interpretations and opinions became paramount for centuries to follow. Despite the "closing" of the Talmud by the *amoraim* Rabina and Ashi around the year 470, the *geonim* and later scholars introduced *takanot* (rulings) on matters not specifically treated in the Talmud itself.

In the sixth century and later, as groups of Jews settled further away from the centers of Jewish learning in Babylonia and Palestine, old customs changed and new ones came into being. Local customs varied, and they had the power of law. Even the *geonim*, who were very influential with the Jews of the Diaspora between the seventh and eleventh centuries, refused to tamper with local customs. They went so far as to support the retention of local practices of which they personally did not approve.

Throughout the Middle Ages scholars such as Rashi (1040-1105), in France, wrote commentaries on the Bible and Talmud, and their writings were used as a basis for interpreting the law in order to arrive at practical decisions. Questions of law were addressed to scholars on issues where the Talmud did not offer direct or complete guidance. The responses (Responsa) to these questions, depending on the locality from which they were issued, were often different, but they became the basis for new codifications of the *halacha* (Jewish law).

By the twelfth century, many authorities were extremely worried about the effect of the diversity of opinion and interpretation of Jewish law, and the effort to create uniformity began. In France in the twelfth century, Rabbenu Jacob Tam, the grandson of Rashi, condemned the proliferation of individual customs. Playing on the word *minhag* (custom), he inverted the Hebrew letters and referred to *minhag* as *gehinom,* meaning "hell." He considered the differences in local custom detrimental to Jewish unity. By the fifteenth century, with the appearance of the German Rabbi Jacob Levi Mollin (the "Maharil"), some of the diversity was restrained. The Maharil wrote a book, published after his death (1427), that established standards for synagogue practices and community conduct.

The effort undertaken by the Maharil continued and reached its climax with the appearance a century later of the *Shulchan Aruch (Code of Jewish Law),* which was prepared by Joseph Caro, a sixteenth-century Spanish scholar. To this day it is the authoritative code of Jewish law. At first, the *Shulchan Aruch* was not accepted by all of Jewry because it did not represent the attitudes of German and Polish Jews, who constituted a major portion of the world Jewish population. But the problem was remedied when Moses Isserles of Cracow wrote his famous notes to the *Shulchan Aruch* (known as the *Mappah*), which took German-Polish opinions and practices into account.

Despite the primacy of the *Shulchan Aruch,* other influences were felt by Jews. Jews were people of the world. Jewish communities existed in Asia, Africa, and Europe, each with its own character and dress, each with its local foods and eating habits, each with its own language. And the laws, customs, and ceremonies observed by each local Jewish community—each with its distinctive cultural background—prevailed even when they did not coincide precisely with the *Shulchan Aruch.*

With the advent of the modern age and the growth of the

Conservative and Reform movements in the United States and elsewhere, new attitudes and customs began to emerge. These liberal movements introduced the Bar Mitzva, Bat Mitzva, and Confirmation ceremonies. They took issue with many observances, particularly those connected with the nature of "work" as reflected in Sabbath observance. Their committees on Jewish law often issued opinions and directives which did not conform to the accepted Orthodox interpretation. The reasons for these new practices and attitudes are treated in this book as well.

It should also be noted that Jewish conduct has always been greatly influenced by the practices of the outside world, particularly the Gentile world. For example, the Talmud (Taanit 22a) suggests that Jews in mourning not wear black shoes because this was a distinctly Gentile practice. What prompted Jews to require the wearing of a headcovering at religious services was an aversion to the Christian practice of keeping heads uncovered during worship. And even though the *Shulchan Aruch* (Yoreh Deah 178:1) warns against mimicking "the ways of the heathen," it does contain many laws which carry on ancient heathen or Gentile practice. For example, the Roman superstition of putting on the right shoe first when dressing became the basis for the prescription that a Jew put on his right shoe first in the morning, although a new Tora-based reason was found to justify the action.

II

The Jewish Book of Why covers all aspects of Jewish life—including marriage, death and mourning, dietary laws, synagogue ritual—with much concentration on the holidays in the Jewish calendar. Because it is virtually impossible to fully understand the holidays without some knowledge of the Jewish calendar, some basic information is presented at the outset.

THE JEWISH CALENDAR

The Jewish calendar was put in its present form over 1,600 years ago. Until 359 C.E. the Sanhedrin functioned in Jerusalem as the supreme judicial body in Jewish life. It was the Sanhedrin, through a special Calendar Council called *Sod Ha-ibur* (literally, "secret of the calendar intercalation"), that decided when a leap year would occur and whether the months Cheshvan and Kislev should have twenty-nine or thirty days.

The process of intercalating (adding to the calendar extra days or months) was necessary in order to harmonize the Jewish calendar with the Civil (Gregorian) calendar. The Jewish calendar being a lunar calendar with 354 days in its year, and the Civil calendar being a solar calendar in which there were approximately 365 days, there is an eleven-day discrepancy.

The Calendar Council of the Sanhedrin, headed by its president, Patriarch Hillel II, was concerned with synchronizing the two calendars for the simple reason that the Jewish holidays were based on the solar cycle and had to be observed at their "appointed times" as specified in the Bible. Passover, for example, had to be celebrated in the spring. If adjustments in the calendar were not made, the biblical command to observe the holiday at that time of year would be violated, for if allowed to fall behind by eleven days each year, in a short time Passover would be observed in the winter months.

The annual eleven-day discrepancy between the Jewish and Civil calendars was reconciled by adding an extra month (Adar II) every two or three years (seven times in nineteen years). In addition, each year a day was added or subtracted from the months Cheshvan and Kislev, as required. These were the "swing" months: in some years they would have twenty-nine days, in some years thirty days.

Exactly how the calendar calculations were arrived at was a closely-guarded secret of the Sanhedrin. This was one of the ways in which the Sanhedrin managed to hold onto its power, which it did until the year 359, after which its influence waned and the Jewish community in Babylonia (where the great Babylonian Talmud was being composed) became dominant.

Up until the year 359 the arrival of the New Moon was announced by the Sanhedrin each month, based on the testimony of two eyewitnesses who appeared before the Sanhedrin and were questioned about the crescent of the New Moon that they reported having observed. If the Sanhedrin was satisfied with the integrity of the witnesses and their testimony, it then checked that testimony against its own (secret) calculations, which had been worked out in advance using mathematical and astrological knowledge. If everything harmonized, the Sanhedrin would send torch signals from mountaintop to mountaintop to notify all communities that the New Moon had officially been sighted. At a later date, the Sanhedrin decided to relay the information by messenger rather than by signalling with torches because dissidents such as the Samaritans, who did not accept the authority of the Patriarch and his Sanhedrin, were known to send up false flares in order to confuse the message being transmitted.

When the Romans who ruled Palestine had begun to deny the Patriarch some of the freedom he and his court had enjoyed for many years, and the situation had become generally grave for the Jewish community in Palestine, Hillel II decided to publish the calendar for distribution to all communities. By this action, the official day(s) of Rosh Chodesh (beginning of the new month) and each of the Jewish holidays was fixed; the testimony of witnesses was no longer required.

IMPORTANT FACTS PERTAINING TO THE CALENDAR

• According to the Civil calendar, a new day begins at midnight and extends for twenty-four hours. In the Jewish calendar, the day begins and ends at sunset. Therefore, according to the Jewish calendar a person born at nine P.M. on Thursday night, January 1, 1981 is considered to have been born on Friday, January 2. His Jewish birthday is Friday, 26 Tevet 5741, which corresponds to January 2, 1981. By the same token, according to the Jewish calendar one who died on Thursday night, January 1, 1981 is considered to have died on Friday, 26 Tevet 5741. In future years the *Yahrzeit* (anniversary of death) of that person must always be observed on the Jewish date: 26 Tevet.

• The following months in the Jewish calendar always have twenty-nine days: Iyyar, Tammuz, Elul, Tevet, Adar.

• The following months always have thirty days: Nissan, Sivan, Av, Tishri, Shevat.

• Cheshvan, sometimes called Mar-Cheshvan (*mar* means "bitter, sorrowful") because no Jewish holidays fall in this month, and Kislev are "swing" months. They may have twenty-nine or thirty days, the number depending on whatever adjustments are required.

• In a leap year (which occurs seven times *every* nineteen years), a second Adar is added to the calendar, making a total of thirteen months in the year. In a common (nonleap) year, Adar has twenty-nine days; in a leap year, Adar I has thirty days and Adar II has twenty-nine days.

• Following are the holidays of the Jewish year, broken down month by month. An asterisk after the name of the holiday indicates that it is of biblical origin. The date it commences and the number of days it is to be observed are stated in the Bible.

It is important to note that whereas Israeli Jews observe all biblical holidays for the number of days indicated in the Bible, in the Diaspora only Reform and some Conservative congregations follow this practice. Most Conservative and all Orthodox congregations in the Diaspora observe Passover, Shavuot, and Sukkot for an extra day because of the uncertainty of the calendar in early times. (See page 185.)

Nissan

*Passover,** on the fifteenth day of the month, for seven days.

Iyyar
> *Lag B'Omer,* on the eighteenth day, for one day.

Sivan
> *Shavuot,** on the sixth day, for one day.

Tammuz
> *Shiva Asar B'Tammuz,* on the seventeenth day, for one day.

Av
> *Tisha B'Av,* on the ninth day, for one day.

Elul
> No holidays.

Tishri
> *Rosh Hashana,** on the first day of the month, for one day (but the holiday is observed for two days both in the Diaspora and in Israel, as explained in the body of the book).
> *Fast of Gedaliah,* on the third day, for one day.
> *Yom Kippur,** on the tenth day, for one day.
> *Sukkot,** on the fifteenth day, for seven days.
> *Hoshana Rabba,** on the twenty-first day, for one day.
> *Shemini Atzeret,** on the twenty-second day, for one day.
> *Simchat Tora,* on the twenty-third day, for one day.

Cheshvan
> No holidays.

Kislev
> *Chanuka,* on the twenty-fifth day, for eight days.

Tevet
> *Asara B'Tevet,* on the tenth day, for one day.

Shevat
> *Chamisha Asar B'Shevat,* on the fifteenth day, for one day.

Adar
> *Fast of Esther,** on the thirteenth day, for one day.
> *Purim,** on the fourteenth day, for one day.
> *Shushan Purim,** on the fifteenth day, for one day.

PRONUNCIATION AND TRANSLITERATION

The pronunciation of the Hebrew words used in this volume is that used in modern Israel. The system used to transliterate these words is the one currently used in most scholarly books. Exceptions to this rule were made when it was felt that a person unfamiliar with Hebrew might be more likely to mispronounce a word if it were presented in the established manner. Consequently, the guttural **ch**, as in Chanuka or *challa,* is spelled with a **ch**, not with an **h**. The final **h**, in words like Tora and *challa,* has been dropped in keeping with the system established by the *Jerusalem Post.* Other minor deviations have also been introduced, but always for the purpose of helping the reader to come closer to the true pronunciation of the Hebrew words.

ALFRED J. KOLATCH

Chapter 1

The Early Years

INTRODUCTION

Judaism is more than a religion. It is a way of life. Over the centuries it has created standards of practice, most of which have been codified in the *Shulchan Aruch (Code of Jewish Law)*, referred to in the General Introduction. These laws spell out what the conduct of the Jew should be from the moment he opens his eyes in the morning until the moment his head touches the pillow at night.

The *Shulchan Aruch* forbids one from walking more than "four cubits" upon arising in the morning until he has poured water three times (from a pitcher kept in readiness) upon the fingers of each hand alternately (so as to rid the body completely of the evil spirits that entered the body upon going to sleep at night). Although some Jews still follow these prescriptions, most are unaware that Jewish law even makes these demands. Obviously, then, it will not occur to most Jews to ask questions about practices of this kind.

Many of the questions posed by the modern Jew about the early years of the life cycle relate to rites of circumcision *(brit)* and Redemption of the First Son *(Pidyon Haben)*.

The modern Jew is also deeply concerned about the naming of children. When, where, and how is the child to be named? Are there any restrictions imposed upon the name selection? These questions, in addition to questions about the Bar Mitzva, Bat Mitzva, and Confirmation ceremonies, are treated in this chapter.

Why is the religion of the mother the primary factor in determining the religion of the child?

Jewish law considers a child Jewish if the mother is Jewish. A child is considered non-Jewish if the mother is non-Jewish, regardless of the father's religion. The rule was established because one can be sure who gave birth to the child, whereas the paternity is sometimes questionable.

In March 1983 the Reform rabbinate, by a majority (three to one), recognized the validity of patrilineal descent, by which the child of a non-Jewish mother and a Jewish father is to be considered Jewish if that child is reared as a Jew and is identified formally and publicly with the Jewish faith. (See *The Second Jewish Book of Why* for further discussion.)

Why is the child of a Jewish woman who converts to another religion still considered Jewish?

A child born of a Jewish mother is considered Jewish regardless of the future actions of the mother or father. The child's Jewishness is considered his or her natural right, one that cannot be denied by the action of either parent.

Why is a celebration held on the Friday night following the birth of a boy?

The celebration called *Shalom Zachar* ("welcome to the male child") or *Ben Zachar* is of kabbalistic origin. During this ceremony of welcome to the newborn boy, relatives and friends gather in the home of the child's parents to socialize.

Among the foods served are cooked legumes (beans, peas, etc.), which are believed to be an effective charm against spirits and demons that might harm the child.

Among Sephardic Jews the *Shalom Zachar* is held on the night before the circumcision. They believe that the presence of a group of people will deter Satan, who is eager to prevent Jews from observing the rite of circumcision. The Ashkenazic community, which does not share this belief, observes the *Shalom Zachar* celebration on the Friday night following the child's birth.

Why is a Jewish male child circumcised?

Biblical law requires that every son of a Jewish woman be circumcised on the eighth day after his birth.

The word for circumcision in Hebrew is *brit,* which means "covenant." This refers to a pledge God made to Abraham (Genesis 17:2), in which He promised to bless Abraham and make him prosper if Abraham, in turn, would be loyal to God ("Walk before Me, and be thou wholehearted"). This covenant was entered into and sealed by the act of circumcision, called in Hebrew *ot brit,* "sign of the Covenant." Genesis 17:11 records the agreement in these words: "And ye shall be circumcised in the flesh of your foreskin; and that will serve as a sign of the Covenant between Me and you." This section in Genesis ends with these words: "And the uncircumcised male . . . that soul shall be cut off from his people; he hath broken my commandment."

Why is the circumcision performed by a *mohel*?

The person who "cuts away" the foreskin is called a *mohel* in Hebrew. Although any qualified Jew who is proficient at the surgical procedure and is able to recite the appropriate blessings may perform the circumcision, the *mohel* is a specialist who is able to execute the procedure as efficiently as any surgeon. If the father is able to perform the circumcision, it is his duty to do so; he is not permitted to delegate the function to anyone else.

Why are women traditionally not permitted to perform a circumcision?

Originally, it was the father's obligation to circumcise his child. The first instance was Abraham, who circumcised Isaac when he was eight days old (Genesis 21:4). Later, the function was assumed by a professional *mohel,* who was in effect a surrogate of the father, hence he had to be a male.

In the case of Zippora, wife of Moses, who undertook to circumcise her son with a polished stone (Exodus 4:25), the Talmud (Avoda Zara 27a) claims that she did not complete the circumcision, that Moses did. This detail, not mentioned in the Bible, is the rabbinic way of declaring that the obligation to circumcise belongs to the father and should not be performed by a woman. However, later rabbinic authorities declared that a woman is permitted to perform the circumcision if a competent Jewish man is not present.

In recent years the Conservative and Reform rabbinates have certified women to serve in the capacity of *mohel.*

Why do most people prefer to have a *mohel* rather than a doctor perform the circumcision?

Although a *mohel* is not a medical doctor, he is a trained specialist with wide experience in his field, much more than any doctor or surgeon is likely to have.

In England, the Royal House had a long tradition, dating back to Queen Victoria (1837-1901), requiring that all royal male children be circumcised by the Jewish *mohel* of London. The tradition has not been followed in recent decades, and the younger members of the British royalty have not been circumcised.

Why does a *mohel* sometimes place the scalpel under the baby's pillow the night before the circumcision?

Originally, a scalpel was placed under the baby's pillow only on Friday, before dark, for a Sabbath morning *brit*. Because it is forbidden to carry on the Sabbath, the *mohel* left his scalpel there for safekeeping.

In the sixteenth century the practice of leaving the scalpel under the pillow was extended to all circumcisions, even those to be performed on weekdays. It was instituted by kabbalists (mystics) who believed that demons attack newborn infants but are scared off by knives and similar objects.

This practice is not common today.

Why is a circumcision allowed to take place on the Sabbath or on Yom Kippur?

Circumcision is considered more important than any other commandment. The Rabbis state in the Talmud that circumcision outweighs all other commandments in the Tora; consequently, no deviation from biblical law is permitted. Circumcision must be performed on the eighth day following a male child's birth, be it Sabbath or Yom Kippur, unless a postponement is necessary because of the ill-health of the child.

Why are some circumcisions held *after* the eighth day following birth?

When a child is not in perfect health or was born prematurely, the circumcision is postponed until the child is in good health, when there is absolutely no danger to his person. After his recovery, seven days must elapse before the rite is performed, for as the Talmud points out, the day of his recovery is considered to be his day of birth (Yevamot 88).

Why do some adults undergo circumcision?

Jews not circumcised as children are obligated to be circumcised at a later date if they wish to be considered part of the Jewish community in every sense of the word. Males wanting to convert to Judaism are also required to be circumcised.

Why do some Jews oppose circumcision?

In the nineteenth century a group of Reform Jewish leaders advocated the abolition of circumcision on the grounds that it was antiquated and barbaric, but the prospect of abolition was vigorously opposed by the Reform movement as a whole. Today, all Jewish religious groups accept circumcision as an important religious rite, although there are individuals who still oppose it on the grounds that it is a traumatic experience for the child. Few medical authorities agree with this contention, citing the tens of millions of Jews and non-Jews who have been circumcised without ill effect.

Why is a vigil kept around the baby's crib on the night before the *brit*?

On the night before the *brit* it was customary in many European communities to conduct a vigil, called *Wachnacht,* a German word meaning "night of watching." Schoolchildren would be invited to surround the crib and recite the *Shema* prayer along with adults, who then spent the night in study. This circle of protection is of kabbalistic origin and, as is true of many other Jewish customs where encirclement is practice, its original purpose was to ward off evil spirits.

Why is a *sandek* present at a circumcision?

Before the tenth century the circumcision was held in the home, and the two major participants were the *mohel* and the father. Thereafter, the ceremony was held in the synagogue after the morning service and in the presence of the entire congregation. At this point, to honor a close friend or relative, a third person joined the father and *mohel* as an active participant: the *sandek,* a title derived from the Greek word meaning "godfather." The *sandek* was the assistant to the *mohel,* and it was his task to hold the child on his lap during the circumcision. He is also called the *baal brit,* "master of the circumcision ceremony," because of his central position in the ceremony.

Why are the *kvater* and *kvaterin* present at the circumcision ceremony?

In the Middle Ages, in addition to the father, the *mohel,* and the *sandek,* two other personalities were honored by being invited to participate in the circumcision ceremony: the *kvater* and the *kvaterin,* usually a husband and wife or a brother and sister. Being assistants to the *sandek,* they are also thought of as godfather and godmother to the child.

The word *kvater* has been explained as being composed of the Hebrew letter *kaf,* meaning "like" when used as a prefix, and the German word *Vater,* meaning "father." Undoubtedly, the original form is the German *Gevatter,* meaning "godfather." *Kvater* and *kvaterin* are Polish-Yiddish corruptions.

During the circumcision ceremony, the *kvaterin* takes the child from the mother and hands it to the *kvater.* The *kvater* hands the child to the father. The father hands the child to the *sandek,* who is seated in the special chair prepared for him. These intermediary steps are required because the husband is not permitted to take the child from the mother, since she is still in a state of impurity from childbirth (as explained in the Book of Leviticus 12:1-5).

Why is a Chair of Elijah provided at a *brit*?

During the circumcision ceremony, a chair is placed next to the seat reserved for the *sandek*. This chair, which remains unoccupied, is reserved for the prophet Elijah, who according to tradition attends every *brit* to protect every infant from danger.

In some synagogues, especially in Oriental communities, there is a permanent Chair of Elijah, which always remains empty. To make sure that no one sits in this Chair of Elijah, the chair is sometimes placed high on a wall.

Why is a *Pidyon Haben* ceremony held?

According to the Book of Exodus (13:1-3) the firstborn of a mother belongs to God or, to be more precise, to the *Kohayn* (the Priest), who represents God. To free a firstborn male Israelite from the obligation of dedicating his life to the service of God, it was necessary to redeem him through the payment of five *shekalim* (which we today consider the equivalent of five silver dollars) to the *Kohayn*.

The redemption ceremony, which is still held today, is called a *Pidyon Haben* "redemption of the firstborn son"). It must take place when the child is one month old, on the thirty-first day after birth (the day of birth is counted as the first day), unless the thirty-first day falls on a Sabbath or Jewish holiday, in which case it is postponed to the next day. The thirty-first day was selected because it was considered likely that once the child survived the first month of life, his chances for good health were assured.

Why is a *Pidyon Haben* not required for the first-born male child of a *Kohayn* (Priest) or *Layvee* (Levite)?

The original purpose of the redemption ceremony *(Pidyon Haben)* was to exempt the firstborn male of an Israelite *(Yisrael)* family from dedicating his life to Temple service. Since Priests and Levites were obligated to serve in the Temple (and could not be exempted), the *Pidyon Haben* ceremony did not apply to them. The redemption tradition is still followed today.

Why is a *Pidyon Haben* not held on the Sabbath or on major holidays?

Since a money transaction is conducted between the Priest *(Kohayn)* and the father (the father paying five silver *shekalim* for the redemption of his son) during a *Pidyon Haben,* this ceremony cannot be performed on the Sabbath or on a holiday when business transactions are prohibited.

Why is a *Pidyon Haben* not required if the child was delivered by Caesarean section?

The law requires that for a *Pidyon Haben* to be celebrated, the child be naturally born. It must exit naturally from the womb *(peter rechem),* as prescribed in Exodus 13:1. Caesarean births do not meet this requirement.

Why is a *Pidyon Haben* not required for a first-born male if the mother had earlier suffered a miscarriage?

For a child to be considered a firstborn *(peter rechem)* in the biblical sense, it must be the first fetus to have exited the mother's womb.

Why is a *Pidyon Haben* not required for some orphans?

If the father dies before his firstborn male child is born, and if the mother is in financial straits, it is considered unfair to impose upon the mother's household the payment of the five *shekalim* (silver dollars) required for the *Pidyon Haben*. She is therefore not obligated to redeem her son. According to some authorities, the boy is obligated to redeem himself at a future date.

Why is a girl named in the synagogue whereas a male child is named at the *brit*?

The *brit* is the most important religious event in the life of a Jewish boy, and it is appropriate that his naming take place during the circumcision ceremony. For girls, the first opportunity for naming is at the Sabbath service immediately after birth, for then a *minyan* is assembled. On that occasion, the father is honored with an *aliya,* after which the baby girl is named. The naming can also take place at the morning service on a Monday, Thursday, or on Rosh Chodesh (New Moon) since the Tora is read on those occasions as well.

In the naming of boys and girls, the name of the newborn is mentioned in the blessing recited, together with the name of the father. Today, the name of the mother is sometimes mentioned at the ceremony as well.

Why are Jewish children usually not named after living relatives?

Not naming a child after a living relative is common primarily among Ashkenazic Jews, who identify the name more closely with the soul than do Sephardic Jews. Ashkenazic Jews believe it would rob a person of his full life if another member of the family were to carry his name in his lifetime.

Sephardic Jews (from Spain, North Africa, and the Middle East) do not share this belief and do name offspring after living relatives.

Why was a more intensive Jewish education traditionally given to boys than to girls?

Traditionally, the religious obligations of the woman centered about the home and family, and she was exempt from observing many of the commandments *(mitzvot)* a man was obligated to carry out. She did not have to don *tefilin* (phylacteries), wear a *talit* (prayershawl), attend synagogue services regularly, etc., because these might conflict with her home duties. For similar reasons, the education of girls did not include the study of Bible and Talmud and was limited to learning the practical aspects of Jewish living.

Why is the Bar Mitzva celebrated at age thirteen, while the Bat Mitzva is celebrated at or after age twelve?

Girls generally mature earlier than boys, and this fact is reflected in the religious life of the Jew.

Why does the Bar Mitzva boy receive the *maftir aliya*?

The *maftir aliya* is the last *aliya* awarded each Sabbath morning. The person honored with *maftir* also recites the *haftara,* a portion selected from one of the prophetic books of the Bible.

The *maftir aliya* was assigned to the Bar Mitzva because it was an additional *aliya,* beyond the prescribed seven *aliyot* given out on the Sabbath. (The words *maftir* and *haftara* are probably derived from the Hebrew root meaning "additional" or "left over.") The custom of assigning this additional *aliya* to the Bar Mitzva began in the fourteenth century, when many rabbis feared that an *aliya* might be given to a boy who had not yet reached his thirteenth birthday. The Rabbis ruled that only the *maftir aliya,* not one of the prescribed seven *aliyot,* could be given to the Bar Mitzva.

In many congregations today the *maftir aliya* is given to the Bat Mitzva.

Why has the Bat Mitzva observance become popular in recent years?

The observance of Bat Mitzva for girls was introduced by the Reconstructionist movement (Society for Advancement of Judaism) in 1922, whereas the Bar Mitzva dates back to the fourteenth century. Until recent times the role of women in Jewish life was limited to the home; conferring upon them a full education was never considered mandatory. In recent years this attitude has changed, and with it a Bat Mitzva ceremony was introduced into synagogue life primarily in the Conservative movement. Some Orthodox and a larger number of Reform congregations also honor the girl of Bat Mitzva age.

Why are some Bar and Bat Mitzva ceremonies held on days other than the Sabbath?

The essence of the Bar Mitzva and Bat Mitzva ceremonies is the call to the boy and girl to recite the blessings over the Tora. This can be accomplished any time the Tora is read: on Mondays, Thursdays, Rosh Chodesh (the beginning of the Hebrew month), on the Sabbath, and on holidays. Observant Jews often schedule a Bar and Bat Mitzva on weekdays to accommodate relatives and friends who do not travel on the Sabbath.

Why is Confirmation celebrated?

In the nineteenth century the Reform congregations in Germany substituted a ceremony they called Confirmation (probably inspired by the practice of the Christian Church) for the Bar Mitzva ceremony. They contended that the age of thirteen, when the Bar Mitzva was celebrated, was too early an age for a Jewish boy to be ushered into the Jewish fold. They felt that at age sixteen or seventeen a teenager was better equipped to understand Judaism.

In the United States in modern times, Confirmation is held in Reform and most Conservative congregations. The age has been reduced to about fifteen. The Confirmation ceremony, in which boys and girls participate, is generally held on Shavuot, the holiday associated with the giving of the Tora on Mount Sinai.

Chapter 2

Marriage and Divorce

INTRODUCTION

The Talmud records a conversation between Rabbi Jose ben Halafta, a second-century scholar, one of the disciples of Rabbi Akiba, and a Roman matron:

"What has your God been doing since He finished making the world?" she asked.

"He has been matching couples," the rabbi answered.

"That isn't so difficult," said the woman. "I can do as much."

"You may think it is simple," said Rabbi Jose, "but it is as difficult as the splitting of the Red Sea."

Unmoved by the rabbi's argument, the Roman matron set out to prove her point with an experiment. She took one thousand male slaves and one thousand female slaves, lined them up in rows, separated them into couples, and joined the couples' hands in matrimony. The next morning they descended upon her in droves, one with a broken head, another with gouged-out eyes, a third with a broken leg. The couples demanded that the marriages be annulled.

The matron conceded the point to the rabbi.

In Judaism, marriage has always been considered a sacred institution. From the days of the prophets, it has been viewed as a holy covenant between man and woman—with God as the intermediary.

Holiness, or *kedusha,* is the term with which marriage has always been associated. In Maimonides' classification of the laws, marriage is grouped under "Holiness," while to Nachmanides a treatise on love and marriage merited the title "Sacred Letter." The very term by which the marriage ceremony is called—*kiddushin*—is indicative of the high esteem in which the institution is held.

The Tora allows for divorce when marriages do not succeed. In the Bible, the first reference to divorce is in Deuteronomy 24:1:

> When a man marries a woman in whom, after a time, he is displeased because he has discovered something unseemly about her, he may write a document of divorce and give it to her. . . .

According to the Tora, the man has the right to issue a divorce, not the woman. Later, however, Jewish courts ruled that under certain conditions the husband could be forced to issue a divorce.

In this chapter we address ourselves to the great variety of customs, ceremonies, and laws that people ask about these two important aspects of life.

Why is marriage such an important institution in Jewish life?

In Jewish tradition matrimony is an expression of the fulfillment of the divine plan to propagate the human race: "Be fruitful and multiply and fill the earth" (Genesis 1:28). So important was the fulfillment of this commandment that the Rabbis ruled (Ketubot 17b) that even the study of Tora may be suspended in order to rejoice with, and bring joy to, a bride and groom.

In addition, Judaism sees marriage as an institution basic to healthy living, an antidote to loneliness: "It is not good for man to be alone; I will make for him a companion" (Genesis 2:18). The Talmud says: "One who does not have a wife lives without joy, without bliss, without happiness" (Yevamot 62b).

Why were early marriages once encouraged?

In talmudic times eighteen was considered the proper age for marriage (Ethics of the Fathers 5:21). When the economic situation of Jews was good (as in Babylonia of the early centuries), youthful marriages were common. When conditions were poor (as in Palestine of that same period), young people waited until they could afford to marry.

In the Middle Ages girls were betrothed as young as age twelve. In Russia of the late nineteenth and early twentieth centuries, child marriages were common so that boys would not have to serve in the military.

Why was a matchmaker (shadchan in Hebrew) a very important person in Jewish communal life?

Since earliest times the matchmaker has held an honorable position in the Jewish community. Jewish tradition pictures him as doing "God's work." Although in more recent times the shadchan has been thought of disparagingly, marriage brokers were traditionally an asset to the Jewish people because Jews as a whole were so often denied mobility. The matchmaker was permitted to move around and thus was able to bring together people from various communities who might otherwise have never met. Some of the most illustrious rabbis and scholars (for example, the fifteenth-century Jacob ben Moses Halevi Mollin, the Maharil) made their living as *shadchanim* (plural of *shadchan*).

Why do some men avoid marrying a woman whose first name is identical to that of their mother?

Rabbi Yehuda He-chasid (1150-1217), author of *Sefer Chasidim*, believed that if a man marries a woman with exactly the same name as his mother, it might lead to the embarrassing situation of the mother answering when the man was actually addressing his wife. In Jewish tradition, to address a parent by their first name is a sign of disrespect.

Generally, in the naming of children, Ashkenazic Jews (unlike Sephardim) are averse to using the names of living relatives. Therefore, if a man were to marry a woman with the same first name as that of his mother, and his mother were to die, the man would not be able to name his future child after her because his wife (still living) carried that same name.

Why are some marriages classified as incest?

The Bible contains a long list of prohibited marriages between blood relatives. (The list was later expanded upon by the Rabbis of the Talmud.) The only explanation for these prohibitions, which are classified as incest, is that they were practiced by idolatrous cultures and therefore forbidden to the Children of Israel. Leviticus 18:3 explains: "After the doings of the Land of Egypt, wherein ye dwelt, shall ye not do; and after the doings of the Land of Canaan, whither I bring you, shall ye not do."

Why can't a *Kohayn* (a member of the Priestly Family) marry a divorcee or a convert?

The marriages prohibited to a *Kohayn* are based on the effect such marriages would have on the status of the children of the union. Just as the sacrifice brought by the Priest in the Temple had to be pure (could have no blemish), so the Priestly stock had to remain pure. The offspring of the marriage of a Priest to a divorcee, a convert, and several other categories of women are, in Jewish law, considered ritually impure (*chalalim*), unfit to carry out Priestly duties. Marriages between a *Kohayn* and a divorced or converted woman are therefore prohibited.

Why is intermarriage forbidden?

Since biblical days intermarriage has been considered a practice that weakens the essential core of Judaism. Hence, it has been opposed. In earliest times the rationale for the opposition was: "Lest you take wives from among their [heathen] daughters for your sons, their daughters will lust after their gods and cause your sons to lust after their gods" (Exodus 34:16). In modern times experts have advanced the argument that intermarriage by and large leads to a breakdown of the family structure—the primary institution in Jewish life.

Why is a bridegroom sometimes showered with nuts following his *aliya* on the Sabbath before his wedding?

The groom is generally called to the Tora on the Sabbath before his wedding. The occasion is designated by the Yiddish word *aufruf*, which means "calling up." As the groom returns

to his seat after the *aliya,* he is showered with nuts. The custom, not widely observed in America, evolved because the
numerical value of the letters in the Hebrew word *egoz* (nut)
were found to be equal to the value of the Hebrew word *tov*
(good). Both equal seventeen. The *aufruf* ceremony symbolizes entry into a new phase of life which, it is hoped, will be
good and wholesome. In some communities, raisins and
other sweets are thrown at the bridegroom, thus expressing
the hope that his new life will be sweet and fruitful.

Why does the bride often present the groom with a *talit* before the wedding?

The custom of the bride presenting the groom with a *talit*
is based on an interpretation of two biblical verses. Deuteronomy (22:12) states, "You shall make fringes on the corners of
your garments," which is the basis for the creation of the
talit. This verse is immediately followed by the verse, "If a
man takes a wife. . . ." The inference is drawn that a *talit*
must be presented to the groom by his bride.

In talmudic times married men covered their heads with
their *talitot* (plural of *talit*) during prayer, an indication that
they were married. Unmarried men did not. In later years it
became the practice for single men not to wear *talitot* at all.
This practice is still followed in many Orthodox congregations.

Why is Tuesday a favorite day for marriage among some Orthodox Jews?

Tuesday is favored for marriage in some Orthodox circles
because the Bible repeats the words *ki tov,* "[and God saw]
that it was good" (Genesis 1:10-12), in referring to the third
day of Creation. Tuesday is the third day of the week.

Why are weddings prohibited between Passover and Shavuot?

The seven-week period between Passover and Shavuot is considered a time of semimourning, and weddings are prohibited. Many theories have been advanced to explain why.

One theory, advanced by students of folklore, is that the *Sefira* period (see page 208) falls in the month of May, and that the wedding ban can be traced to a Roman superstition against celebrating marriages in May. Romans believed that during this month the souls of the departed return to earth and disturb the living.

Modern scholars have advanced the theory that in 134 or 135 C.E., between Passover and Shavuot, the soldiers of Bar Kochba, many of whom were students of Rabbi Akiba, suffered a serious defeat in their rebellion against the Roman forces occupying Palestine. Because of this defeat (referred to as a plague in the Talmud [Yevamot 62b]), in which thousands of Bar Kochba's soldiers lost their lives, the seven-week period became a time of mourning, and weddings were banned.

Why are weddings permitted on Lag B'Omer?

According to the Talmud (Yevamot 62b), a plague that had spread among students of Rabbi Akiba between Passover and Shavuot abated on Lag B'Omer, the thirty-third day of the Omer. (*Lag* is the Hebrew numerical equivalent of thirty-three.) To commemorate that happy day, weddings were permitted, but they were not allowed during the other *Sefira* days, which continued to be observed as days of mourning. In time, the law was relaxed and weddings were permitted on other special days during this seven-week period. (See the next question.)

Why are weddings held in some communities at various times during the *Sefira* period?

There are varying opinions as to which of the *Sefira* days are to be observed as days of mourning.

All agree that on festive days such as Lag B'Omer (the thirty-third day of the Omer), the New Moon of Iyyar, and from the New Moon of Sivan until Shavuot marriages may be performed. But not all agree on which of the other days between Passover and Shavuot weddings may be held.

In some communities, with the exception of the semiholidays mentioned above, weddings are totally banned. The Sephardim ban weddings from Passover to Lag B'Omer but permit them thereafter. In other communities, weddings may be held during the first two weeks of *Sefira* (from Passover until the New Moon of Iyyar), but weddings are prohibited from that time until the New Moon of Sivan. And in still other communities weddings may not be held for the first two weeks after Passover, but they may be held after Rosh Chodesh Iyyar.

Why are weddings rarely performed between Rosh Hashana and Yom Kippur?

Although there is no explicit prohibition against holding a wedding between Rosh Hashana and Yom Kippur, weddings traditionally are not performed during this time. The ten-day period between Rosh Hashana and Yom Kippur is a time for serious introspection. The spirit of fun often manifested at wedding celebrations, some Jews believe, is not appropriate during this rather somber period in the Jewish calendar.

Why are weddings not permitted during a three-week period each summer?

For a three-week period each summer, beginning with the

seventeenth day of Tammuz and extending to the ninth day of Av, marriages are banned. It was during this three-week period in 586 B.C.E. that the walls of Jerusalem were first breached and the Temple finally destroyed. Because of these disastrous events, the three weeks prior to Tisha B'Av have been observed as a period of mourning in the Jewish calendar.

Why do the bride and groom often fast on their wedding day?

Because marriage represents "a new beginning" for the bride and groom, it became traditional to enter this new phase with fasting and prayers for the forgiveness of past sins—much in the manner of Yom Kippur. The origin of the custom of fasting on one's wedding day can be traced to the Jerusalem Talmud, where the opinion is ventured that the sins of a king, a prince, and a groom are forgiven on the day they enter their new lives.

While in some communities both bride and groom fast on their wedding day, in others only the bridegroom fasts. Some Jews believe that if the groom were not required to fast, he might join his friends in the prenuptial celebration and become inebriated, placing him in poor condition to carry out the legal formalities involved in the wedding ceremony. Since it is considered less likely that the bride's friends will imbibe, or that they will induce the bride to imbibe, the demand that she fast is not made.

If the ceremony is held at night, the fast is broken when the first stars appear. Fasting is not observed on Rosh Chodesh, Purim, Chanuka, and several other minor holidays.

Why is the wedding ceremony held under a *chupa?*

A *chupa* is a wedding canopy—usually a large piece of decorated material (silk, satin, or velvet)—supported by four firm poles.

The origin of the *chupa* has been explained in a variety of ways. Some believe it is a vestige of the ancient tent-life of Israel. It has been pointed out that even to this day Bedouin tribes construct a special tent for the bride and groom.

Some scholars regard the *chupa* as symbolic of the laurel wreath worn by the bride and groom during the marriage ceremony in talmudic times. The original meaning of the word *chupa* is "to cover with garlands."

Other authorities believe the *chupa* is a reminder of the room in the groom's house to which the bride was brought at the end of the betrothal (engagement) period and where the couple cohabited, thus consummating the marriage. This aspect of the ceremony, called *yichud,* was considered to be of the essence.

During the Middle Ages, when marriages were performed in the synagogue, it became customary to erect the type of *chupa* still in use today.

Why is a *talit* sometimes used as a *chupa?*

The use of a *talit* as a *chupa* dates back to seventeenth-century Germany and France, where the groom spread his *talit* over the bride's head as a symbol of protection. German Jews based this custom on an interpretation of a verse in Ezekiel: ". . . Your time was the time of love, and I spread my mantle over you . . ." (16:8). French Jews based it on the words of Ruth to Boaz: "Spread . . . thy cloak over thy handmaid, for thou art a near kinsman" (Ruth 3:9). In Israel today, at weddings of soldiers the *chupa* is often a *talit* held up by four rifles.

Why does a groom wear a *kittel* (a simple white robe) under the canopy?

In ancient times, the *kittel,* a white robe symbolizing purity, was worn in the synagogue on some holidays and at home during the Passover Seder. Many Jews still follow this practice today.

Among some segments of the Orthodox community, it is customary for the bridegroom to wear a *kittel* under the wedding canopy as a reminder that the new life on which he is about to embark must be pure and clean.

Why is the marriage ceremony sometimes held outdoors?

In some Jewish circles, particularly ultra-Orthodox and *chassidic,* the marriage ceremony is performed at night in the open, under the stars. This custom probably developed because the stars are associated with God's assurance to Abraham: "I will bless thee . . . and multiply thy seed as the stars of heaven and as the sand of the seashore" (Genesis 22:17).

Why is a bride's face covered with a veil?

There is an old tradition in Jewish life that is known in Yiddish as *badekn die kalla,* which means "covering the bride" with a veil. This is usually done in the bride's dressing room prior to the marriage ceremony. The groom drops the veil over the bride's face, at which time the rabbi or cantor chants: "O sister! May you be the mother of thousands of myriads" (Genesis 24:60).

The custom is said to be related to the incident in the Book of Genesis where Abraham's servant, Eliezer, is sent to find a wife for Isaac, and he finds Rebecca. When Isaac comes to meet her for the first time, Rebecca says: "Who is this man who walks in the fields to meet us?" And the servant replies: "It is my master, Isaac" (24:65). Whereupon Rebecca takes her veil and covers herself.

Students of Jewish folklore believe the use of a veil by a Jewish bride may be an adaptation of Roman custom. Among Romans the bride wore a full-length veil, which was later used as her burial shroud.

Among Oriental Jews, the bride's veil is made of opaque material. It is so designed to serve as testimony that the bride (who is led to the canopy, in effect, blindfolded) has complete faith and trust in the man who is about to become her husband.

In some communities it is the custom for the groom to cover the bride with the veil immediately before the wedding ceremony begins. In others, when the groom is brought to the bride before the ceremony, it is the marriage performer (the clergyman) who covers her with the veil.

Why is a ceremony involving a handkerchief conducted before the wedding ceremony?

In its earliest form the concept of marriage was one in which a man "acquired" a woman with a fee paid by the father or the guardian of the girl. In Jewish law, one way to confirm a purchase or transaction was *kinyan sudor,* meaning "agreement by handkerchief."

During the nineteenth century, and to a limited extent today, after a marriage had been agreed to, a date was set for stipulations *(tenaim)* to be executed in writing. (In German and Yiddish the writing ceremony is known as *knas mahl.*) When the agreement was finally set down, it was symbolically affirmed by the marriage performer (or some other person) holding up a handkerchief, with a representative of the bride holding one end and a representative of the groom holding the other.

Since the *tenaim (knas mahl)* ceremony is no longer very

common, the handkerchief ceremony (also known as *kabalat kinyan,* literally "receiving the acquisition") is held today privately before the wedding ceremony is conducted. The two witnesses to the *ketuba* are present in addition to invited guests. The bridegroom indicates his agreement to fulfill the obligations of the *ketuba* by taking hold of a handkerchief or piece of cloth held up by the officiating rabbi. The groom raises the handkerchief and then returns it to the rabbi. Witnesses sign the *ketuba,* and the groom is then escorted to the bride's chamber, where the veiling ceremony takes place.

Why are lighted candles sometimes carried by the escorts of the bridegroom?

Various interpretations have been advanced for this custom. The commonly held view is that the carrying of lighted candles by the groom's escorts is related to the giving of the Ten Commandments by God (the bridegroom) to Israel (the bride) at Mount Sinai: "There were voices and lightning and a thick cloud on the mountain" (Exodus 19:15). The candles are reminders of the lightning that appeared when Israel (the bride) accepted God (the bridegroom).

An essential feature of marriage among the Romans was the passing of a torch. (Light was a symbol of purity.) Among the Jews of the first century, the bride was received by bridesmaids, who carried torches.

Why does the groom approach the marriage canopy before the bride?

One explanation relates this tradition to the giving of the Ten Commandments at Mount Sinai. Just as God (the bridegroom) came forth to receive Israel (the bride) so should the groom take his place under the canopy first, ready to receive the bride as she walks down the aisle.

Why does the bride, followed by her parents, circle the groom at many wedding ceremonies?

Although many interpretations have been advanced, the origin of the bride circling the groom during the wedding ceremony is probably based on the belief that evil spirits seek to deny a newly-married couple the fulfillment they seek. The bride, by walking around the groom seven times, or three times as is the practice in some communities, protects the husband from demons assigned to harm him. (Demons are unable to penetrate circles.)

This concept is reinforced by the view that a bridegroom is like a king. Just as a king has his soldiers who encircle him and protect him, so does the bridegroom.

The idea of circling the groom *three* times is based on the verses in Hosea (2:21-22) in which God, the groom, speaks to Israel, the bride, and says: "And I will *betroth* you unto Me forever; and I will *betroth* you unto me in righteousness, and in justice, and in lovingkindness, and in mercy; and I will *betroth* you unto me in faithfulness, and you shall know the Lord." Use of the word "betroth" three times is the basis for the encirclement of the groom three times.

Those who believe the encirclement should be seven times consider seven a holy and significant number: there are seven days in the week; seven *aliyot* are distributed on the Sabbath; Sabbath is the seventh day of the week; and most particularly, on Hoshana Rabba, in Temple days, a procession circled the altar seven times *(Hakafot)*.

Why does the bride stand to the right of the groom during the wedding ceremony?

The positioning of the bride on the right side of the groom is based on an interpretation of a verse in Psalms (45:10): "The queen stands on your right hand in fine gold of Ophir." In Jewish tradition the bride is a queen and the groom is a king.

Why is the *ketuba* (Jewish marriage contract) read under the canopy?

Created by Simeon ben Shetach in 80 B.C.E., the *ketuba* is the legal document which attests to the marriage. Written in Aramaic (the language of the masses and of all legal documents of that period), it spells out the legal obligations of the husband to the wife should he die or divorce her. The obligations of the wife to her husband are not spelled out in the *ketuba*. These have always been taken for granted.

Why can't a relative of the bride or groom sign the *ketuba* as a witness?

As in all legal matters, witnesses must not be related to the parties involved. This rule is an extension of Deuteronomy 24:16, in which it is stated that a father cannot be put to death based on the testimony of his son. From capital cases, this practice was extended to include civil suits, and then to include all relationships.

Why are two separate cups of wine drunk from during the wedding ceremony?

According to one interpretation, the two cups symbolize the joy and sorrow the couple may encounter in life. By both parties sipping from both cups, they are expressing their willingness to face life's vicissitudes as equal partners.

The more likely explanation is that the wedding ceremony is an outgrowth of two separate and distinct ceremonies that were, in the beginning, celebrated as much as one year apart—one year if the bride was a virgin, and one month apart if she was a widow.

The first ceremony was called *erusin* (later called *kiddushin*), and the second was called *nisuin*. The *erusin* was the betrothal, the equivalent of our engagement ceremony, and on this occasion prayers were recited and a cup of wine was shared by the bride and groom. The second ceremony was the *nisuin,* the actual marriage ceremony, and here blessings were also recited over a cup of wine from which the bride and groom drank. The practice of reciting blessings over two separate cups of wine continued even when the two ceremonies were incorporated into one.

Why is the *ketuba* read after the first cup of wine is drunk?

As explained above, the present wedding ceremony is an outgrowth of two independent ceremonies. The *ketuba* is read after the first cup of wine is drunk, marking what was once the end of the first ceremony.

Why does the groom place a ring on the bride's finger during the wedding ceremony?

In its earliest form, the marriage was essentially a business transaction: the bridegroom "acquired" a bride, and the transaction was sealed by the payment of a silver or gold coin that had a determinable value of not less than one *peruta,* the smallest denomination of currency in talmudic times.

Probably as the result of Roman influence, a ring was substituted for the coin. In ancient Egypt and in ancient Rome the ring was a sign of authority. The Bible tells how Pharaoh placed his ring on Joseph's finger when he gave him authority to rule Egypt (Genesis 41:42).

Yemenite Jews still use a coin at the wedding ceremony, during which the groom says to the bride, "Behold thou art consecrated unto me with this coin."

Why must the ring given to the bride be simple, without jewels or ornaments?

The ring the groom gives the bride must be of determinable value. The value of a ring containing diamonds, rubies, or ornamentation cannot be easily appraised by an inexperienced person. If given a jewelled or otherwise ornamented ring by her groom, a naive bride might erroneously think she is receiving something of great value. Judaism protects the bride by suggesting that a simple, unadorned ring be used.

Why is the ring placed upon the forefinger of the bride's right hand?

The index finger of the right hand, which is used for pointing, is the most prominent digit. The ring is placed on that finger so that witnesses to the ceremony can see very clearly that the bridegroom is placing a ring on the bride's finger. After the ceremony the ring is transferred to the traditional fourth finger of the left hand. (This is based on an ancient belief that a vein runs directly from this finger to the heart.)

The origin of the practice of placing the ring on the forefinger of the bride's right hand is attributed to Rabbi Moshe Mintz, a fifteenth-century German rabbi.

Why does the groom break a glass at the end of the marriage ceremony?

Several reasons have been suggested for having the groom break a glass at the end of the ceremony. In every case the underlying purpose is the creation of noise.

The popular, traditional explanation is that the breaking of a glass represents an expression of regret and sorrow over the destruction of the Temple in Jerusalem. The shattering noise of the glass is a stark reminder of the traumatic loss of Jewish national independence suffered at the hands of the Romans in 70 C.E.

Another explanation is that the noise is a warning to man that he must temper life's joyous moments (such as the celebration of a wedding) with sober thoughts: that life is not all joy; that the happiness of the wedding day will not continue indefinitely; and that the young couple should be prepared for all of life's eventualities. This reasoning became popular as a result of the talmudic story in which the great scholar Rabbina surprised the guests at his son's wedding during a moment of hilarity by smashing a valuable white porcelain vase before their eyes. His action reflected the ancient belief that it is wise to dampen enthusiasm so as to forestall misfortune.

Most probably the real explanation for the origin of the custom is to be found in the realm of superstition. In the Middle Ages it was customary for the groom to taste of the wine after the seven wedding benedictions had been recited. He would then let his bride taste of it as well, after which he would turn to the north wall and throw the glass against it. In the world of Jewish magic and superstition it was believed that evil spirits came from the north. (This belief was popular in biblical times. The prophets often spoke of the evil enemy as descending upon Israel from the north.) And it was believed that the most effective deterrent to evil spirits and demons is noise, including that made by breaking a glass.

The kabbalistic explanation for the breaking of the glass is similar. The kabbalists believed that demons are intent upon disturbing the happiness of the new couple and that by smashing and destroying a glass the evil spirits will be satisfied.

The practice of throwing a glass against a wall has long been abandoned, and today, instead of using the glass from which the wine was drunk, a separate glass is prepared for the ceremony and is crushed under foot.

It should be pointed out that in many cultures and civilizations noise was considered an antidote to the influence of evil spirits. Church bells were originally rung to ward off evil spirits. The same is true of the noise caused by the smashing of a bottle against the hull of a ship before it is launched.

Why is a light bulb instead of a glass often broken at the wedding ceremony?

Since the main purpose of breaking a glass is to create noise, as explained above, some rabbis prefer that a light bulb be used instead: it is easier to break and usually makes a louder noise.

Why are the phrases *mazal tov* and *siman tov* shouted at the end of the wedding ceremony, after the glass is broken by the groom?

As far back as the Middle Ages, two types of congratulations were shouted at the bride and groom at the conclusion of the wedding ceremony. Ashkenazim used the words *mazal tov* and Sephardim *siman tov*. Both have ancient roots.

In biblical and talmudic times, the word *mazal* referred to a star, a constellation of the zodiac, and also a planet. In those days it was widely believed that man's fate depended on the position of the stars. *Mazal tov,* "good star," later took on a secondary meaning, "good luck."

Siman tov, meaning "good omen," is of talmudic origin. The term has been retained by the Sephardic community as a way of expressing "congratulations."

Why are rice and nuts thrown at the couple at the end of the wedding ceremony?

In some cultures, rice and nuts are considered symbols of fertility. By throwing these items at the couple, those in attendance at the wedding are expressing the hope that the couple will "be fruitful and multiply," as commanded in the Book of Genesis (1:28).

Why do a bride and groom go into a private room to be alone immediately after the wedding ceremony?

Spending a period of time alone in a private room after the ceremony is known as *yichud,* meaning "union, joining." The bride and groom may eat there in privacy. As explained above, the room is a vestige of Jewish life of early times when the marriage ceremony was not held under a *chupa,* as it is today. Then, the bride was brought to the groom's house, and it was there, without formality, that the marriage was consummated.

Why is a honeymoon sometimes postponed or delayed?

One tradition declares that marriages are to be celebrated for seven days, since Jacob was required to work for seven years for each of his wives, Leah and Rachel. How did this evolve? The Bible (Genesis 29:27) says, "Fulfill the week of this one [Leah], and we will give thee the other [Rachel] also for the service which thou shalt serve with me for seven more years." In this verse the word "week" is used as a synonym for the word "year." The Rabbis interpreted this to mean that the wedding celebration should last for a whole week.

Beginning with the first meal after the wedding ceremony, the seven blessings that were earlier recited under the canopy are repeated. And for seven days afterwards, a *minyan* gathers each day with the bride and the groom present to hear these seven blessings *(Sheva Berachot)* again. The honeymoon takes place after these seven days have passed.

If one marries a widow or a divorcee, the celebration is held only for three days, and the *Sheva Berachot,* the Seven Benedictions, are recited only on the first day.

Why was a loaf of bread traditionally given to the couple upon their return from the honeymoon?

So that bread may never be lacking in their home, the couple was traditionally met at the door of their new home by friends and family, who gave them a loaf of bread.

Why is divorce discouraged?

Judaism looks with disfavor upon divorce. The Rabbis of the Talmud considered marriage a holy contract, and the dissolution of marriage an unholy act. They quote the prophet Malachi: ". . . the Lord has been witness between you and thy wife of your youth against whom you have dealt treacherously, though she is your companion, the wife of your covenant" (2:14). And they add (Sanhedrin 22a): "Even the altar [God] sheds tears when anyone divorces his wife."

Why can't a woman initiate a Jewish divorce?

The Bible (Deuteronomy 24:1) speaks only of a man divorcing his wife. This became the basis for the law that only a man can initiate a divorce, an action that may be taken even without the wife's consent.

About 1,000 years ago, the highly respected rabbinic authority Rabbenu Gershom ben Yehuda (965-1028) decreed that it would no longer be permissible for a husband to divorce his wife without her consent. This decision *(takana)* was accepted as binding by European Jewry.

A Jewish religious court can *compel* the husband to grant a divorce when there is just cause, such as when a husband refuses to have marital relations, when he does not provide adequately for her support, when he is unfaithful, when he is a wife-beater, when he has a loathsome disease (leprosy, for example), etc.

Why is a *get* issued when a couple is divorced?

Get is the Hebrew word for "divorce document." According to some authorities it is derived from the Akkadian word which means a "court writ." Since a Jewish marriage is entered into by the issuance of a legal contract between husband and wife, it can be terminated only by the issuance of a legal writ nullifying the original contract.

It should be noted that the issuance of a *get* is not a substitute for securing a civil divorce. Reform Jews believe that a civil divorce is sufficient for remarriage and have therefore abandoned the practice of issuing a *get*.

Why does a *get* have to be handwritten?

Based upon the statement in the Book of Deuteronomy (24:1) which states that when a man wants to divorce his wife "then let him write her a bill of divorcement," the Rabbis conclude that the document must be handwritten by a scribe for the occasion. The written document was required so as to nullify the *ketuba* (marriage contract) which was also—originally—a handwritten document.

It is important that both the writing of the document and its delivery be properly witnessed.

Why is the *get* written in Aramaic?

Aramaic was the everyday language of the masses in countries outside of Palestine, particularly in Babylonia, where large numbers of Jews lived. All legal documents (such as the *get*) of the mishnaic and talmudic periods were written in Aramiac.

Why is the *get* cut after it is written?

The custom of cutting the *get* with a scissor or knife after it is written began during Hadrian's rule over Palestine (117-138 C.E.), when all legal authority was denied the Jewish community. During that time, Jewish courts continued to function secretly. When a *get* was issued, the document was cut so that if it were discovered by Roman authorities, the Jews could always deny that the document was legal. After the cut *get* was returned to the Jewish court by the wife, the court presented her with a document verifying the divorce.

Chapter 3

Death and Mourning

INTRODUCTION

Just as there is a Jewish way of life, there is a Jewish way of death.

Two basic considerations come into play when death strikes and the laws of death and mourning become applicable. One consideration involves the principle of *kevod ha-met*, treatment of the deceased with reverence and respect. The other involves the principle of *kevod he-chai*, concern for the welfare of the living. These two principles provide the basis for many of the laws and customs pertaining to death and mourning.

It is in accordance with the principle of respect for the dead that Jewish law looks askance at cremation. A ban has been imposed upon cremation not only because of the biblical concept that the body must revert to its original state and be buried in the earth from which it came, but because cremation is considered an unnaturally speedy way of disposing of the body of a person who was once a beloved member of a family group.

Jewish law also looks with disfavor upon embalming,

unless extenuating circumstances exist. Embalming sometimes involves mutilation of the body, an act of irreverence
toward the dead.

Jewish law and custom mandate that the feelings of the
survivors of a deceased never be ignored. Their anxieties
must be eased. It is therefore required that burial take place
promptly—that is, within three days of death, unless there is a
compelling reason for delay. This same regard for the feelings
of mourners is expressed in the way they are treated upon
returning from the burial service. Neighbors traditionally prepare a Meal of Condolence for the bereaved, who otherwise
might not bother to prepare food for themselves. Visitors are
urged to refrain from paying a condolence call until the third
day after burial to give mourners the chance to express their
grief privately and to collect their thoughts.

Finally, the concept of resignation plays an important role
in the practices and liturgy of the period of death and mourning. The advice of the Psalmist (Psalms 90:12), "So teach us
to number our days that we may get us a heart of wisdom," is
usually quoted to drive home the point that despite the great
loss the mourner has suffered, he must carry on. Death is
beyond man's control, but the pursuit of life is not. The liturgy
recited at the cemetery and in the house of mourning emphasizes this point.

The *Tziduk Hadin* and the *Kaddish,* two prayers recited
during the mourning period, accentuate the concept of resignation. The *Tziduk Hadin,* recited during the funeral service,
begins with the words from Deuteronomy 32: "Our Rock
[God], His actions are perfect. All His ways are just . . ." Thus
God's will is justified, and man accepts his fate. And the *Kaddish,* too, is an expression of the mourner's adoration of God
and acceptance of His will, even while the mourner finds
himself greatly traumatized, unable to rationalize his sorrowful condition.

These are the basic concepts and considerations that un-
derscore most of the Jewish laws and practices relating to
death and mourning.

Why do Jews treat the dead with great care and respect?

In Jewish tradition the sacredness of the human person does not end with death. The laws and customs connected with death and mourning, even those that are clearly offshoots or adaptations of practices commonly followed by primitive societies, are geared to promoting the dignity of the human spirit.

Why do some Jews follow the custom of placing the deceased on the floor and of then pouring water on the floor?

In biblical times the pouring of water was a way of expressing a person's or a nation's sense of guilt. It was a way of acknowledging God's displeasure with man's actions (Judges 20:26) or of expressing remorse at a time of calamity (Joel 1:14).

Although no longer widespread, the practice of pouring water on the floor where a deceased lay is considered by many a way of notifying people who enter a room that a death has occurred. It originated in the Middle Ages, when it was common belief that the ghost of the dead was present after death and was dangerous to ungrateful relatives. This custom, in a variety of forms, was practiced in many cultures. Primitive man believed that spirits could not cross bodies of water and that the ghost, if it made such an attempt, would fall in.

Why is the body of the deceased never left unattended?

Jews today consider leaving the body of the deceased unattended a sign of disrespect. Until burial, someone must be present at the side of the deceased, standing guard and reciting Psalms. This individual is called a *shomer* (or *shomeret*, the feminine form), meaning "one who watches." In early times, Jews, like other peoples, took pains to guard the deceased from being harmed by ghosts and spirits (as described above).

Why is Jewish law opposed to conducting an autopsy in most cases?

Jewish law forbids mutilating the body; hence, autopsies may be performed only when absolutely essential. In cases where a death is the result of homicide, or where there is suspicion of homicide, most religious authorities allow an autopsy to be performed.

Autopsy is also sometimes permitted when it is thought that as a result of the procedure man's scientific knowledge might be enhanced and lifesaving discoveries eventually might be made.

In Israel, autopsy has been the subject of much controversy. The current law limits the freedom of doctors to perform autopsies and organ transplants by requiring them to respect the wishes of relatives of the deceased when they oppose operations on the cadaver.

Why is embalming forbidden in Jewish law?

In embalming, the blood is drained from the body and discarded. Jewish law regards the blood as part of the body; it must not be removed from the deceased.

The embalming of Jacob and Joseph, mentioned in the Bible, was an Egyptian custom. Embalming was not a prevalent practice among Jews, although it was still carried out in Second Temple times, as we are informed in the writings of the first-century Jewish historian Flavius Josephus.

Embalming was forbidden by the Rabbis of the Talmud not only because it shows disrespect for the dead, but also because it retards swift decomposition of the body and its return to the earth from whence it came.

Why are Jews buried in simple shrouds?

Eighteen hundred years ago Rabbi Gamaliel instituted the

practice of burying all Jews in the same type of garments, thereby indicating that rich and poor are equal before God. Shrouds (*tachrichim* in Hebrew) consist of seven separate garments in which the deceased is dressed, all made of simple, inexpensive muslin, cotton, or linen material. The outer garment is a large white sheet in which the entire dressed corpse is wrapped.

Why are shrouds made of white material?

White is a symbol of purity. It has been referred to as the national color of the early Jews.

Originally, there was no preferred color for shrouds. Although white was commonly used, black, red, and other colors have been used in the course of history. From the third century on (in the talmudic and post-talmudic period) we find scholars expressing a variety of preferences. After the sixteenth century white became the accepted color for shrouds.

Why are some Jews buried in a *kittel*?

A *kittel* (pronounced *kitl*) is one of the seven garments in which a deceased is usually dressed. A man distinguished for his piety is often buried in the *kittel* (robe) that he wore in his lifetime during High Holiday services and at the Passover Seder.

Why do shrouds have no pockets?

Shrouds are made without pockets to symbolize that none of man's material possessions can be taken with him after death, a view not shared by Egyptian and other early civilizations. These people, who were as preoccupied with death as with life, filled their tombs with precious stones, utensils, and provisions for a new life after death. Some cultures (Apache, for example) still bury a person with his belongings. Jews believed that "in the hour of man's departure from this world, neither silver nor gold nor precious stones nor pearls accompany him, but only Tora and good works" (*Pirke Avot* 6:9).

Why is Jewish tradition opposed to viewing the body before the funeral ceremony?

Viewing the remains before burial is a recent American-style custom. This practice was rarely followed in Europe except for the lying-in-state of royalty and other notables. Jewish tradition regards viewing as incompatible with *kevod ha-met,* the principle of showing "proper respect for the dead."

The concept of a "wake," which is common among Christians, is alien to Jews.

Why are coffins used?

In very early times coffins were not used. In the Bible, the phrase "Joseph was put in a coffin in Egypt" (Genesis 50:26) refers to an Egyptian custom, not a Jewish one. In talmudic times the attitude towards the use of coffins changed; it was regarded as a dishonor to be buried without a coffin. By the Middle Ages there was no accepted rule, and a variety of customs prevailed. In Spain coffins were not used; in France they were. In the sixteenth century, the kabbalists considered it better for the dead body to make direct contact with the earth, and coffins were not used. This is the common practice in Israel today. In Western countries local law generally demands the use of coffins.

Why must coffins be made of wood?

In the Talmud, Rabbi Levi explains that the origin of the custom of using coffins made of wood can be traced to the Garden of Eden. He says that the fact that Adam and Eve were hiding among the *trees* when God called to them (Genesis 3:8) indicated that when a person died, his body should be placed in a wood coffin.

The kind of wood used was of little consequence, but over the years inexpensive soft woods (especially pine) have been preferred primarily because it was thought that they decompose more rapidly than hardwoods such as oak. A metal casket, which is slow to decompose, is not traditionally used because, if it were, the biblical commandment, "Unto dust shalt thou return" (Genesis 3:19), would not be easily fulfilled.

Wood is also preferred over metal because the latter is a symbol of war. Burying a loved one in a metal coffin would not be in keeping with the idea of "resting in peace."

Finally, the use of wood—preferably unpolished wood—for the coffin is seen by the Rabbis of the Talmud (Moed Katan 27a and Ketubot 8b) as a reminder that ostentatious funerals are to be frowned upon, and that Jewish tradition favors modesty and simplicity in its treatment of the dead.

Why do some Jews insist on drilling holes in the bottom of a casket?

This practice is followed by Jews who feel strongly that drilling holes hastens fulfillment of the commandment "Unto dust shalt thou return" (Genesis 3:19). If holes are drilled, air and moisture are better able to penetrate the box, and the body will decompose much sooner.

Why is earth from the Holy Land often placed in the coffin?

There is a strong belief, shared by many Jews, that when the Messiah appears there will be a resurrection of the dead and that those who lived a pious life will roll underground to the Holy Land to be resurrected. In preparation for that trip, earth from Israel is sometimes placed in the coffin. The earth from the Holy Land is considered to possess atoning power (Ketubot 111a).

Why do some Jews wish to be buried in Israel?

As mentioned in the preceding answer, some Jews

believe that when the Messianic Age comes, the pious dead will roll underground (*gilgul mechilot*) until they reach the Holy Land, and they will then rise again to life *(techiyat ha-maytim)*. To avoid the difficulties that may be encountered in such a journey, arrangements are made for burial in Israel, regardless of where the death occurs.

The hope that the Messianic Age will come soon is the reason why the phrase, "May the Lord comfort you with all the mourners of Zion and Jerusalem," is mentioned as a greeting to mourners at the end of the funeral service.

Why is the coffin covered with earth immediately after it is placed in the ground?

The custom of covering the coffin and filling the grave immediately is connected with the primitive concept of guarding against the return of the ghost of the deceased, who may want to harm one of the living whom it considers an enemy. In the Middle Ages belief in the power of ghosts was popular among Jews, which explains why Jews (as well as other peoples) threw sticks, stones, and clumps of grass on graves.

Why is it forbidden to bury a suicide next to other members of the family?

In Jewish tradition the taking of one's life is considered a serious offense against God and man. Those who have committed suicide (and who have been acknowledged to have been sane at the time the act was committed) are buried separately, near the outer limits of the cemetery, at least six feet from other Jewish dead.

Today, however, it is more acceptable to all Jewish denominations to consider a suicide a "distressed person" (*anuss* in Hebrew), one acting under an uncontrollable compulsion and hence not responsible for his or her actions. Consequently, most suicides are now treated like all other deceased persons.

Why is cremation prohibited according to Jewish law?

In the Bible, God said to Adam (the first man): "For dust thou art, and unto dust shalt thou return" (Genesis 3:19). Judaism regards interment in the earth as essential. When cremation is performed, the body is usually not returned to the earth, that is, the ashes are not buried. They are usually scattered or placed in an urn, which is kept in the home or in the crematorium. Cremation, therefore, is not recognized as a legitimate form of burial.

A second view explaining Jewish opposition to cremation is that the resurrection of the dead will not be possible in the future if a body has been destroyed through fire.

Why does Jewish law require that burials take place within twenty-four hours of death?

This is based on two biblical commandments, both found in Deuteronomy 21:23:

1. "Thou shalt surely bury him the same day."
2. "His body shall not remain all night."

Based on these positive and negative statements, Jewish law demands that burial take place within twenty-four hours after death. When circumstances dictate, such as when it is necessary to await the arrival of very close relatives, or when a government regulation so requires, funerals are delayed, but never for more than three days.

Why are some Jews not permitted to attend funerals?

The Priestly Family (Kohanim), which was responsible for the conduct of religious activities in the Tabernacle in the desert and later in the Temple in Jerusalem, was required to remain in a state of purity. Since contact with the dead placed one in a state of impurity, Priests were forbidden to be in close proximity to a corpse.

A *Kohayn* (member of the Priestly Family) is not permitted to attend a funeral unless it is that of a member of his immediate family. If a *Kohayn* wishes to attend the funeral service of friends or strangers, he usually remains a distance from the area where the service is being conducted.

Why are some funerals held on holidays?

The Rabbis regarded the second day of a holiday as a semiholiday insofar as burial of the dead is concerned. Although funerals may not take place on the Sabbath or on Yom Kippur, they may be held on the second day of Passover, Shavuot, Sukkot, and Rosh Hashana. This makes it possible for loved ones to comply with the requirement that the deceased be buried as soon as possible. Additionally, the holding over of the dead for an extra day before burial would necessitate the use of spices and perfumes to remove unpleasant odors. This was a non-Jewish practice, and a basic rule of Jewish life was to avoid imitating the customs of non-Jews.

Why is it required that a *minyan* (a quorum of ten adults) be present at a funeral and at an unveiling?

A *minyan* is required so that the mourners are able to recite the mourner's prayer *(Kaddish)*. If a *minyan* is not present, a service may be held, but the *Kaddish* may not be recited.

Why are people discouraged from sending flowers to Jewish funerals and to houses of mourning?

According to the Talmud, the purpose of flowers, like

spices, was to offset the odor of a decaying body. The practice of sending flowers to funerals was common among non-Jews, who kept their dead for longer periods before burial. Jewish law demands immediate burial, at most within three days. To encourage a distinction between the Jewish practice and the non-Jewish practice, flowers are not encouraged at funerals, but they are not forbidden by Jewish law. In Israel today, placing flowers on graves, particularly in military cemeteries, is considered acceptable.

Why do mourners tear their garments before the funeral service?

The custom of tearing the garment of a mourner (called *keria* in Hebrew) is of biblical origin. When Jacob saw Joseph's blood-stained coat of many colors, he was told by his sons that Joseph was killed by a wild beast. Jacob reacted by tearing his garment.

The Bible also describes how David tore his clothes when he heard of the death of King Saul. In the Book of Job, Job is described as tearing his mantle when he begins to mourn the loss of his children.

Why is a garment torn on the left side for a mother and father, but on the right side for other close relatives?

For parents the left side of a garment is torn *(keria)* because the left side is closest to the heart, and parents are closest to the heart of a child. For a son, daughter, brother, sister, and spouse *keria* is made on the right side of the garment. Strict observance demands that the tear effected for the parents be done by hand.

Why are ribbons used for *keria*?

Although strict observance demands that the actual tear

be made in the garment itself (a woman's dress and a man's vest or jacket), the fact that this often makes it necessary to discard an otherwise good garment has led to the custom of using a ribbon.

Why do mourners have to stand when *keria* is performed?

Jewish law requires that mourners be in a standing positon when *keria* is performed. The Rabbis considered this to be biblically mandated, citing the posture of Job when hearing of the death of his family members: "Job stood up and tore his clothes" (Job 1:20).

Why is it Orthodox practice for women to perform *keria* on other women?

Generally, the officiating rabbi performs the *keria* on all mourners. In Orthodox circles, however, where it is considered an act of immodesty for a man to touch a strange woman, one of the women present who can lead the mourner in the *keria* prayer performs *keria* on the womenfolk.

Why is a bride or groom not required to tear his or her clothing if a close relative dies within seven days after marriage?

In Jewish tradition no commitment is more sacred than marriage, and nothing may intrude upon the joy of the occasion. Although a bride or groom feels intense grief upon hearing of the death of a close relative, he or she is not permitted to take on the role of mourner until after the honeymoon period (the seven-day period following marriage). *Keria,* the tearing of clothes, is therefore delayed for a week (or until bride and groom return from the honeymoon), at which time *Shiva* begins.

Why are the words "Blessed is the Righteous Judge" pronounced when *keria* is performed?

By reciting the blessing containing these words at a moment of intense grief, the mourner is bearing testimony that he does not blame God for his misfortune and that he accepts the judgment of the Righteous Judge (God) as part of life.

Why do mourners sometimes follow the hearse for a block or two immediately after the funeral service at the chapel or synagogue?

Halvayat ha-met ("escorting the dead") is an old Jewish tradition. Family and friends show their respect for the deceased by an action indicating their unwillingness to abandon their loved one. In solemn procession they escort the body for a short time after the funeral ceremony. This tradition is adhered to today only by ultra-Orthodox Jews.

Why are there periodic pauses in the procession to and from the grave?

The pauses, considered symbolic today, are an expression of man's unwillingness to take leave of the deceased. There are various procedures in this regard.

While carrying the coffin *to* the grave, some follow the practice of pausing three times, some seven—until the burial site is reached. The origin of the practice of pausing during the procession *leaving* the gravesite was indicated by the Gaon Sar Shalom, the ninth-century head of the great academy in Sura. In his day the procession paused seven times to shake off evil spirits that clung to those returning from a funeral. With each stop, one of these spirits would disappear. Scholars in subsequent centuries (Rashi, Isserles) repeated this explanation for the practice of halting the procession on the way to and from the grave. Other scholars believe the custom of halting seven times stems from the seven references to the vanity of life mentioned in the Book of Koheles (Ecclesiastes).

Why do those who attend a funeral wash their hands after the burial?

This custom is connected with the ancient practice of purification through washing after being in close proximity to the dead. It is also connected with the ancient belief that demons follow the dead and hover around graves, so that those who have followed the cortege must purify themselves after having been in close proximity to the unclean demons.

The hands are usually washed upon returning from the cemetery and before entering the home. A pitcher of water is left at the front door by friends or neighbors. Washing may also be performed before leaving the cemetery, but since water is not always available there, it is most often done upon returning home.

Why is the first meal after the funeral prepared for mourners by neighbors?

Preparation by neighbors of the first full meal eaten by mourners after returning from the funeral is a very old Jewish tradition. The Rabbis of the talmudic period reprimanded neighbors who were so callous that they did not prepare food for neighbors who were burying their dead, thus displaying a lack of concern for the grief of others. The importance of preparing such a meal is evident from the name given to it: Se'udat Havra-a, meaning "Meal of Condolence" or "Meal of Healing." Psychologically, it is of great help in assuaging grief and helping in the process of recovery from a painful loss.

Why does the Meal of Condolence (Se'udat Havra-a) generally include rolls, bagels, and hard-boiled eggs?

The menu for the first meal upon returning home from the cemetery was designed to include symbols of eternal life. The round rolls, the round bagels, and the oval eggs are all symbolic of the cyclical, eternal, and continuous nature of life.

A second interpretation is that round foods, particularly eggs, are served at the Meal of Condolence because these items have no mouth, that is, they have no opening. They represent the mourner, still in shock, who has no words for anyone.

Of course, other foods can be served to mourners in addition to these.

Why is the initial period of mourning, known as Shiva, set for seven days?

The establishment of seven days (shiva means "seven" in Hebrew) as the first and most intense stage of mourning is based on an interpretation of a verse in Amos (8:10): "And I will turn your feasts [which usually lasted seven days] into mourning. . . . " The Rabbis ruled that just as the major festivals are celebrated for seven days, so should the initial period of mourning be seven days. They also noted that Joseph mourned for his father, Jacob, for seven days (Genesis 50:10).

So that a mourner will have ample time to adjust to the loss just suffered, the Rabbis prescribed that three additional weeks beyond the Shiva period be set aside for grieving. This total of thirty days is known as the Sheloshim period, sheloshim being the Hebrew word for thirty. An even longer period was prescribed for children mourning parents: one full year, known in Hebrew as Yud Bet Chodesh, or Twelve Months (of mourning). For additional information, see The Second Jewish Book of Why.

Why do mourners sit on low stools during the first week of mourning (Shiva)?

This ancient custom, according to some scholars, is based on the Bible's description of Job. When Job suffered his misfortunes, he was comforted by friends who sat with him on "the earth." Mourners today do not sit *on* the earth; rather, they sit as close to the earth as possible, usually on a wooden stool or a hassock. Jewish law merely demands that the mourner not sit on chairs of normal height, to symbolize the mourner's awareness that life is not the same, that he or she wants to stay close to the earth in which his or her loved one is now buried.

Why are the mirrors covered in a house of mourning?

Many reasons have been advanced for this practice. The most popular explanation is that mirrors are associated with personal vanity. During a period of mourning, it is not appropriate to be concerned with one's personal appearance.

The covering of mirrors has also been explained as an expression of the mourner's belief that despite the great loss just suffered, he refuses to blame God. To see himself in a sorry state, as a grieving mourner, is not a compliment to God, since man was created in the image of God.

Another reason given for the covering of mirrors is that prayer services are held in the house of mourning, and it is forbidden to pray in front of a mirror. (Synagogues are not decorated with mirrors.)

Finally, the practice of covering mirrors or of turning them to face the wall, which was common among early cultures, has been explained as part of man's primitive belief that a man's soul was his image or shadow. The soul was reflected in a mirror (and in water). Since it was feared that when the soul of man is projected in a mirror the ghost of the deceased might snatch it away, pains were taken not to allow man's image or shadow to make an appearance, and mirrors were therefore covered.

Why is a memorial candle lighted in a house of mourning?

In Jewish tradition the candle is symbolic of the body and soul. The flame is the soul, which reaches ever upward. By lighting a candle and keeping it burning throughout the Shiva period, it is believed that the soul of the departed is aided in its journey heavenward.

Burning a candle in the house of mourning for seven days is a custom first mentioned in the Jewish literature of the thirteenth century.

Why was a towel and a glass of water once placed near the memorial candle in a house of mourning?

Sometime after the thirteenth century it became customary to place a towel and a glass of water near the memorial candle. According to popular belief this would appease the Angel of Death, who might want to wash his sword in the water and dry it with a towel. There also existed the belief that man's soul returned to cleanse itself in the water. Nineteenth-century scholars condemned this practice and forbade it.

Why does one refrain from shaving or taking a haircut during the week of Shiva?

Remaining unshaven and not meticulously groomed is a sign of social withdrawal. It is an expression of one's grief and lack of concern with social amenities.

Remaining unshaven does not carry the same message in all societies. In the Bible, Jeremiah (41:5) described the people of Shechem as having come "with shaven cheeks and rent clothing." At that time, in that locale, unlike today, to shave one's hair was a sign of mourning.

Why is bathing not permitted during the week of Shiva?

A distinction is made between bathing for cleanliness and bathing for comfort. Bathing for mere pleasure, namely bathing in hot water for an extended period, is definitely considered improper in Jewish law. However, bathing for basic cleanliness is considered proper.

Why do some mourners place a bit of sand or earth in their shoes if they must leave the house during Shiva?

The discomfort of feeling the sand or earth will remind the mourner of his status—that he is still in mourning—and that he must return to the house as soon as the urgent business that brought him out is concluded. "Urgent business" generally includes matters that must be attended to in order to prevent irreversible financial loss (such as distributing perishable goods that would be unusable if not sold that week).

Why are mourners not permitted to wear leather shoes while sitting Shiva?

Denying oneself the pleasure of comfortable footwear is an expression of grief. (On fast days it is common practice not to wear comfortable leather shoes.) It reminds the mourner of the sad state of his present condition. A mourner is permitted to wear shoes made of materials other than leather, since leather is generally equated with luxury.

Why is it considered an obligation to pay a condolence call to mourners during the first week of mourning?

Paying a condolence visit is an act of compassion often theologically connected with God's message to the Jewish people as expressed by the prophet Isaiah: "Comfort ye, comfort ye, my people" (40:1). The condolence call during the *Shiva* period helps the mourner work through his initial period of depression and loneliness.

Why is it improper to greet a mourner during *Shiva* in the normal fashion?

It is self-evident that a mourner is not in the best state of mental health at this point in his life, and to pretend to be casual about his situation is considered an affront. The Bible states that God said to Ezekiel, "I sigh in silence." Rabbis cited this statement to support the position of Jewish tradition that idle chatter be avoided when visiting mourners. This includes refraining from uttering customary greetings such as "hello," "good morning," and "how are you?"

Why is it considered proper Jewish etiquette to refrain from undue conversation when visiting a mourner during *Shiva*?

One's mere presence in the house of mourning is most important. This is felt and appreciated more than words. The Bible, in describing Job—considered the classic mourner—

tells us that when Job was visited by his three friends, they sat with him for seven days and no one uttered a word. The Talmud adds: "The greatest reward is bestowed upon all who know how to be silent in a house of mourning." This does not mean that one should remain totally silent in the company of a mourner, but it does suggest that the visitor choose his or her words carefully.

Tradition advises that the visitor be prepared to respond rather than to initiate conversation.

Why is it recommended that one delay the *Shiva* call until the third day after burial?

This custom developed because it was evident that grief is most intense during the first two days of mourning. Tradition dictates the advisability of allowing mourners time to be alone with their thoughts and with members of their immediate family, and it suggests waiting until the third day of *Shiva* before paying a condolence call. However, if one will have no other opportunity, he may visit a mourner early in the *Shiva* period.

Why is mourning not observed on the Sabbath?

The Sabbath is a day of delight *(oneg)* in Jewish tradition. Isaiah said, ". . . and you shall call the Sabbath a delight" (58:13). Tradition demands that Jews express joy and fulfillment on the Sabbath (and holidays), and this makes it mandatory that there be no intrusion, not even because of a death. Therefore, mourning is suspended for the duration of the Sabbath and holidays (although it is counted as one of the seven days of mourning). On these days a mourner dresses up, attends synagogue, and carries on somewhat normally until nightfall, at which time he resumes mourning.

Why do some mourners stop *Shiva* for the Sabbath at noon on Friday, while others wait until an hour before sundown?

Mourners are obliged to sit *Shiva* until about one hour before sundown on Fridays. The exact time varies with the time required by the individual to prepare food and dress for the Sabbath (or for holidays). That *Shiva* is suspended at noon on Fridays is a widespread misconception.

The same rule applies to holidays.

Why does the *Shiva* period end early on the morning of the seventh day?

In Jewish tradition part of a day is considered equal to a whole day. If a mourner sits *Shiva* for as little as one hour on the day of the funeral, that is considered as one full day of *Shiva*. The same is true if a mourner sits *Shiva* for only an hour on the seventh day: it is considered a full day. Generally, on the seventh day mourners sit on their stools after the morning service and receive words of consolation from those present. With this action, the *Shiva* period is considered ended.

Why do mourners sometimes walk around the block at the end of the *Shiva* period?

This is a custom followed by some Jews. They all walk together for a short distance (usually around the block) to symbolize their return to society and the real world from which they have withdrawn for a week.

Why, at the Friday evening service attended by a mourner during the *Shiva* week, does the congregation greet the mourner when the last stanza of the *Lecha Dodi* hymn is recited?

This is a symbolic gesture by the community, which says

to the mourner, who is waiting at the rear door, we understand that you are in emotional distress during this period of
Shiva, and we accept you back into the community of people.
The mourner walks down the aisle and joins the congregation
while the last verse of the Lecha Dodi hymn is chanted.
However, to indicate that there has been a momentous
upheaval in his life, the mourner does not occupy his usual
seat.

Why is a mourner not given an *aliya* during the week of *Shiva*?

The blessing a person recites when he receives an aliya
(is called to the Tora) expresses a feeling of good fortune. For
the mourner, this is a sentiment not truly in keeping with the
reality of the moment. However, if the mourner is (improperly) called to the Tora, he must accept the aliya, for to do otherwise would be an affront to the holy scroll.

Why do some Jews mourn (sit *Shiva*) when a child of theirs has abandoned the Jewish faith or intermarried?

The abandonment of one's faith is considered a total
betrayal of one's heritage. Some Jews mourn for a child who
has defected, because they feel that the child is now lost to
them; they consider that child dead. Such action, however, is
not demanded by Jewish law, which considers a Jew, even if
he has defected, to be a Jew forever.

Why is the *Kaddish* recited by mourners?

The Kaddish (mourner's prayer) is an ancient Aramaic
poem that is recited during synagogue services. It is an expression of faith on the part of the mourner that although he
is distressed, he still believes in God and in the worthwhile-
ness of life. The Kaddish has been called an echo of the Book
of Job. Job said, "Though He [God] slay me, yet will I trust in
Him."

The earliest reference to the *Kaddish* as a mourner's prayer is in a book (*Or Zarua*) by Rabbi Isaac ben Moses of Vienna (1180-1260). The *Kaddish* declares man's submission to the will of God. It makes no direct reference to God, but infers, as the Talmud (Berachot 60b) points out, that when a man's heart is filled with grief and sorrow, he lays his burden in the lap of God by uttering the *Kaddish,* which begins with the words, "Magnified and glorified is His great name." This implies that whatever God decides is good.

Originally, only a son was obligated to say *Kaddish,* and only for his parents. Gradually, this practice was extended, and today *Kaddish* is often also recited by daughters for parents. *Kaddish* is also recited by members of the immediate family for a brother, sister, son, daughter, and wife. For relatives other than parents, *Kaddish* is recited for thirty days, a period of time called *Sheloshim* in Hebrew.

Why is the language of the *Kaddish* Aramaic rather than Hebrew?

Aside from the final verse, "May He who makes peace in His high places make peace for us and for all Israel, and say ye, Amen," the language of the *Kaddish* is Aramaic. For nearly a thousand years, from the time of Ezra in the fifth century B.C.E. until well after the end of the talmudic period, Aramaic was the vernacular of the Jewish masses in Babylonia and Palestine. As such, the *Kaddish* was composed in the everyday, spoken language of the masses, a language (unlike Hebrew) that was widely understood.

Why must *Kaddish* for parents be recited for twelve months according to some authorities and for eleven according to others?

The primary *Kaddish* obligation belongs to sons, who are required to recite the prayer for deceased parents for an entire year.

The stipulation of a twelve-month period for parents is derived from the Talmud, which states (Berachot 58b), "The

memory of the dead grows dim after twelve months." However, the belief was prevalent in talmudic times that the wicked
are consigned to hell (*gehenna* or *gehinnom*) and are subject
to punishment for a maximum of twelve months. To avoid the
possibility of people thinking that the parent for whom *Kaddish* was being recited (for a twelve-month period) was
wicked, scholars of the caliber of Rabbi Moses ben Israel
Isserles (c. 1525-1572) of Cracow reduced the requirement
for the recital of the *Kaddish* for parents to eleven months. By
ruling that *Kaddish* for a parent should not be recited for
more than eleven months, Rabbi Isserles was removing all
possibility of ascribing wickedness to the parent. Even when
the Jewish year has thirteen months, as in leap years, *Kaddish,* according to Isserles, should be recited only for eleven
months.

Most Jews follow the ruling of Isserles.

Why does one who is reciting *Kaddish* take three steps backwards when reciting the last verse?

The last verse of the *Kaddish* is a quotation from the
Book of Job which beseeches God, "Who makes peace in
the heavens," to bring peace to all mankind. With the recitation of this verse the mourner concludes his "audience" with
God, who in Jewish tradition is portrayed as the King of
Kings. Just as one who has had an audience with a king takes
short steps backwards to mark the conclusion of his audience,
so does the mourner, after concluding his prayers of supplication, retreat respectfully. After the retreat, the mourner returns promptly to his original position.

Why is a sexton sometimes engaged to say *Kad-dish* for a deceased person?

Out of respect for the dead, in cases where there are no
surviving children or relatives capable of saying *Kaddish,* the

synagogue sexton (or any stranger) is sometimes engaged to say Kaddish. It is, however, considered inappropriate for the person engaged to be reciting Kaddish for more than one mourner at a time, as is sometimes the case.

Why are women mourners not required to say Kaddish?

According to Jewish law the obligation to say Kaddish for a parent falls upon the sons of the deceased. Even in the absence of sons, daughters are not required to say Kaddish. Orthodox practice suggests that a daughter who wishes to honor her departed father or mother should satisfy her need by listening attentively as others recite the Kaddish and by responding "Amen" at the proper time. Such attentiveness of the daughter is considered equivalent to her personally reciting the Kaddish.

Several authorities, however, see no objection to the recitation of Kaddish by daughters. The famous chassidic woman rebbe, the Maid of Ladamir (1815-1892), an only child, recited Kaddish for her father Monesh Werbermacher. Likewise, Henrietta Szold, founder of Hadassah, recited Kaddish for her father, Rabbi Benjamin Szold. But this is an uncommon practice among Orthodox Jews. Women in Conservative and Reform congregations do stand with all mourners to say Kaddish.

Why do some members of the congregation (who are not in mourning) stand when mourners recite the Kaddish?

The general rule is that only the mourner is required to stand when reciting the Kaddish. In most communties the congregation remains seated, but there are congregations that evolved the custom of standing because they considered the Kaddish an important declaration of faith that all members of the congregation should join in reciting.

Why is the *Kaddish* recited by all mourners in unison in some congregations?

The practice of having all mourners recite the *Kaddish* in unison developed in Sephardic congregations, which generally chant prayers in unison. After the custom was approved by Rabbi Jacob Israel Emden (1697-1776), the foremost authority of his age, it was accepted and followed by a majority of congregations in all communities.

Why is a tombstone erected over the grave of a deceased?

According to scholars, this practice dates back to biblical times. When Rachel died on the road to Bethlehem, Jacob "set up a pillar (*matzayva*) upon her grave" (Genesis 35:20).

There are several other reasons given for the erection of a tombstone. First, it is considered a symbol of respect for the deceased. Second, it marks a place that Priests (*Kohanim*) should avoid. (Priests, according to biblical law, are rendered impure if they come in contact with the dead.) Third, it is an indication to all relatives and friends who want to visit the grave that this is the place of burial of the deceased.

There is a theory among scholars that the first tombstones were erected in the Middle Ages, when many people believed in ghosts. A grave was promptly filled with earth so as to contain the ghost of the deceased who might otherwise harm his enemies. And the tombstone was originally employed for the same purpose. Later, the tombstone took on new meaning and began to reflect affection for the deceased.

The erection of a tombstone is not mandatory.

Why does one usually wait twelve months before erecting a monument (tombstone) over the grave of a deceased?

Most authorities agree that a monument (*matzayva* in Hebrew) may be erected at any time, even immediately after *Shiva*. The reason usually given for waiting a full year is that since the deceased is well remembered for the first year after death (when family members say *Kaddish* for him or her), there is no need to erect a tombstone as an additional reminder.

A more practical reason for waiting a year before erecting a monument is to give the earth a chance to settle, preventing the heavy tombstone from sinking into the ground.

Why is it recommended that the tombstone selected be simple and inexpensive?

Expensive stones are considered ostentatious. Scholars urge that headstones be very simple to reinforce the words of the Book of Proverbs: "The rich and the poor meet together [in death]. The Lord is Maker of them all" (22:2). Some people in Orthodox circles believe that an ostentatious tombstone undermines belief in the coming of the Messiah and the resurrection of the dead.

Why do some tombstones have two hands engraved on them, and others a cup or a laver?

Graves of a *Kohayn* often have tombstones engraved with outstretched hands. These represent the conferring of the Priestly Benediction. Tombstones on the graves of Levites often have a laver or cup engraved on them, which symbolizes a function of the Levites: to pour water on the hands of the *Kohayn* before he offers the Priestly Benediction.

Why do we find an *ohel* (a tentlike structure) erected over the graves of some outstanding religious leaders?

The burial place of a Jewish notable often became a place of pilgrimage for his disciples, and a canopy was usually erected over the grave. This practice, common to many communities, was inspired by the desire to bestow royal treatment upon leaders of great merit.

The cemetery in Tiberias, Israel, has a very elaborate *ohel* for Moses Maimonides.

Why are unveilings held?

The unveiling, a service of commemoration, has become the formal way of dedicating the monument that has been erected. The practice was instituted toward the end of the nineteenth century both in England and the United States. The British call the ceremony "tombstone consecration." There is no religious obligation to hold an unveiling.

Why is a veil (a piece of cloth) draped over the stone at an unveiling?

The words inscribed on the stone are usually covered so that a member of the family will have the honor of unveiling it "officially," at which moment the inscription will be seen for the first time by the public. The unveiling is a strictly ceremonial act.

Why is it unnecessary to have a rabbi recite the prayers at an unveiling?

It is not necessary for a rabbi to be present at an unveiling or at a funeral. Anyone able to recite the prescribed psalms and to deliver a eulogy (if one is desired) may officiate.

Why do some people drop clumps of grass on the grave or monument when visiting a gravesite?

Some scholars believe that this custom, which originated in medieval times, is connected with the belief in ghosts and evil spirits. Grass was considered a safeguard against evil spirits.

Why do some people place stones on the tombstone when visiting the gravesite?

This is a symbolic act indicating that members of the family and friends have not forgotten the deceased. The final scene in Steven Spielberg's movie *Schindler's List* (1993) portrays scores of survivors, and relatives of survivors, one by one placing a stone on the tombstone of Oskar Schindler, who saved over 1,100 Jews from extinction during the Holocaust.

Why do many people bring food to the cemetery, which they serve after the unveiling service?

This practice may have started many years ago when visiting the cemetery, because of its distance from cities, was a full day's activity. After hours on the road, mourners and their friends were offered wine and cake, and sometimes even more elaborate food, to ease their discomfort. Today, this need does not exist, and many people think it undignified to bring food to the gravesite.

Why is *Yahrzeit* observed?

Observance of the anniversary of a death *(Yahrzeit)* began in talmudic times. Death anniversaries of parents and teachers were observed as a sign of reverence for the deceased.

The observance is old, but the word *Yahrzeit* was not used before the sixteenth century. Derived from the German

Jahrzeit, it was used in the Christian Church to denote the occasion for honoring the memory of the dead.

Some people fast on the day of *Yahrzeit,* and many visit the graves of their departed relatives.

Why do some people observe *Yahrzeit* on the anniversary of the date of burial?

Yahrzeit is usually observed on the actual anniversary of death. The only exception is in cases where burial took place three or more days after the day of death. Then, on the first anniversary only, *Yahrzeit* is observed on the date of burial. In subsequent years, however, *Yahrzeit* is observed on the date of death.

Why is a *Yahrzeit* candle lighted on the day *Yizkor* is recited?

In Jewish tradition the candle and its flame symbolize the essence of man. This is generally based on the idea expressed in Proverbs 20:27: "The spirit of God is the lamp of the Lord." And so, on all occasions when the dead are remembered, candles are lighted. Today, for safety reasons, an electric bulb is sometimes used instead of a candle. It is not necessary to light more than one *Yahrzeit* (or *Yizkor*) candle per household.

Why are *Yahrzeit* candles lighted on the night *before* the actual day of the anniversary of death?

The *Yahrzeit* candle must burn for a period of twenty-four hours. In the Jewish calendar, a day begins after dark on the day preceding it. The full twenty-four-hour *Yahrzeit* period therefore begins with nightfall on the day preceding the actual anniversary of death and concludes with twilight on the following day (the actual anniversary of death).

Why must a widow wait for three months after the death of her husband before she can remarry?

After three months it can be definitely determined whether or not the widowed woman is pregnant. Should she remarry earlier, the paternity of the child might be in doubt. However, under exceptional circumstances, where it can be definitely ascertained that the woman is not pregnant, the woman may be granted permission to remarry immediately after the *Shiva* period.

Why must a widower wait for the passing of the three major festivals (Pesach, Sukkot, and Shavuot) before he can remarry?

This tradition took root because it was felt that if the widower waited for a cycle of three separate holidays to pass, he would not hastily enter into a second marriage, which he might later regret. However, according to law a widower may marry immediately after the thirty-day period of mourning (called *Sheloshim* in Hebrew) has passed.

A widow was permitted to remarry much sooner than a widower because, in the opinion of the Rabbis, the unmarried lifestyle is much more difficult for a woman than for a man.

Why is the grave not visited during the first year of mourning?

Grave visitation during the first year of mourning is considered psychologically undesirable. Mourners often experience unwarranted feelings of guilt after the death of a loved one, and to establish a habit of visiting the grave too early and too often might deepen that feeling. Although there is no ban on visitations during the first year, mourners generally wait until a tombstone is erected before beginning regular visitations.

Why do Jews traditionally visit the cemetery before the High Holidays?

Visits to the cemetery, especially during the month of Elul (the month preceding Tishri, the month of the High Holidays), are common. During this month it is traditional to start preparing for the Days of Awe: Rosh Hashana and Yom Kippur. Part of that preparation consists of readying oneself for the fast day of Yom Kippur, the culmination of the Days of Awe. In talmudic times it was customary for people to visit graves on all fast days.

Why do Jews traditionally visit the cemetery between Rosh Hashana and Yom Kippur?

The period from Rosh Hashana through Yom Kippur is known as the Ten Days of Repentance *(Aseret Yemei Teshuva)*. According to tradition, the fate of man is judged between Rosh Hashana and Yom Kippur. During this time, to influence the Heavenly Tribunal to act favorably upon man's petitions for a New Year of goodness and health, the individual Jew sometimes turns to his departed and asks them to testify in his behalf. This is accomplished by cemetery visitations.

Why was the *Yizkor* service introduced into the synagogue service?

Scholars believe that *Yizkor* was introduced as a formal

part of the prayer service during the Crusades of the eleventh century, when many thousands of Jews were murdered indiscriminately by Christians who made their way to the Holy Land to wrest it from the Moslems. The *Memorial Prayer* (*Yizkor* in Hebrew) expressed the hope that the deceased would intervene with God and bring about the amelioration of suffering.

Originally *Yizkor* was recited only on Yom Kippur, but later its recitation was also included in the synagogue service on Passover and Shavuot as well as on Shemini Atzeret, the holiday after Sukkot. *Yizkor* is generally recited by family members only for the deceased members of that immediate family.

Although the earliest reference to the *Yizkor* service is found in the eleventh-century *Machzor Vitry* (composed by Rabbi Simcha ben Samuel of Vitry, a pupil of Rashi), some scholars believe that the service is much older. It was first introduced, they believe, in 165 B.C.E. in the Maccabean period, when Judah Maccabee and his soldiers prayed for their fallen comrades and brought sacrifices in the Temple of Jerusalem to atone for the sins of the dead (II Maccabees 22:39-45).

Why was there opposition to the introduction of Yizkor into the synagogue service?

Hai Gaon (939-1038), the most eminent Babylonian scholar of the eleventh century, together with his prominent pupil Nissim ben Jacob, opposed the custom of praying for the dead on festivals and on Yom Kippur. They also opposed donating charity in memory of the dead, as the *Yizkor* prayer requires. These scholars believed that the only things important to God are the good deeds an individual himself actually performs in his own lifetime. He cannot be saved through the good deeds of his parents.

The attitudes of Hai Gaon and his disciple did not find favor with the masses, who wanted to maintain strong links to their deceased parents. The observance of *Yizkor* therefore continued to spread.

Why is *Yizkor* recited on Passover, Shavuot, and Sukkot?

As mentioned above, *Yizkor* was originally a memorial prayer recited in the synagogue only on Yom Kippur. It was later also recited on the three major holidays: Passover, Shavuot, and Sukkot (actually Shemini Atzeret). On these three pilgrim festivals, a section from Deuteronomy was read to the pilgrims who had made their way to Jerusalem. In this section, Jews were admonished not to enter the Temple empty-handed: "Each man shall give according to his ability" (Deuteronomy 16:16). Since giving charity was an integral part of the *Yizkor* service, it was natural to extend the practice of reciting *Yizkor* to include these three major festivals when Jews brought offerings (charity) to the Temple.

In many Reform congregations *Yizkor* is recited only on Yom Kippur and on the last day of Passover.

Why is *Yizkor* not recited during the first year following the death of a person?

This is a widespread fallacy. Although many Jews are under the impression that *Yizkor* may not be recited during the first year, no such prohibition exists, Actually, *Yizkor* may be recited beginning with the very first holiday following the death of a loved one. Since *Yizkor* is a positive statement of faith in God and love for a departed relative, there is no valid reason to postpone its recital for an entire year.

Why do some Jews believe that one may not recite the *Yizkor* prayer at home?

Although it is considered preferable to recite the *Yizkor* prayer at a public service in the synagogue, where a *minyan* (a quorum of ten adults) is present, it is also permissible to recite the prayer at home in privacy. The *Kaddish,* however, may not be recited unless a *minyan* is present.

Why do some people leave the synagogue when *Yizkor* is recited?

Although there is no requirement that one leave the synagogue if he or she is not required to recite *Yizkor,* many people believe it would tempt fate to be present. Others feel it might be distracting to those who are required to recite *Yizkor.* Those reciting *Yizkor* might feel envious or uncomfortable to see worshippers sit in silence while they stand, express grief, and perhaps shed a tear.

Why are Tora scrolls, prayerbooks, and other holy articles buried in cemeteries?

Burial of religious articles is an expression of respect and adoration. In ancient times religious books and articles that were no longer usable were stored in a back room of the synagogue. This was called *geniza,* "hiding." The most famous *geniza* was discovered in the synagogue of Fostat, Cairo (Egypt), built in 882. Its large store of manuscripts was first noticed in 1763.

Today, Scrolls of the Law and other holy articles are buried in a cemetery with the same dignity and care as a departed human.

Chapter 4

The Dietary Laws

INTRODUCTION

One of the great misconceptions under which many of us labor is that the Jewish dietary laws (the laws of *kashrut*) were instituted for health reasons.

The Bible (Leviticus 11:44-45) explains the reason for the imposition of dietary regulations in simple, direct language:

> For I am the Lord your God! Therefore, sanctify yourselves and be holy, for I am holy. . . For I am the Lord that brought you up out of the land of Egypt to be your God. You shall therefore be holy.

Over the centuries, individuals have advanced what they have considered logical practical reasons for the institution of these laws. Many have suggested that the use of certain meats was prohibited because they were considered unwholesome, because they were thought to carry disease.

If Jews derived any health benefits from observing the dietary laws (such as a lower incidence of trichinosis, which can be traced to the eating of pork products), those have been unexpected. Studies have shown that the life span of the Jew is not affected by the observance of the dietary laws, nor is his general health improved.

The Rabbis of the talmudic and later periods were quite content in going no further than the Bible in explaining the purpose of the dietary laws. They classified these laws as *chukim,* mandatory statutes, which must be obeyed even though the reason for them is beyond man's understanding.

Despite the willingness of the observant Jew to accept the dietary laws, the propensity to question persists. And from this questioning have come some fascinating answers.

Maimonides, seeking a meaningful reason for the dietary laws, concluded that they "train us to master our appetites; to accustom us to restrain our desires; and to avoid considering the pleasure of eating and drinking as the goal of man's existence."

One additonal value of the dietary laws is reflected in attitudes of the early Rabbis. They believed that the secret of Jewish survival was separatism. Holiness means being separate. Being a holy people, to them, meant being a people apart.

Adhering to the dietary laws keeps the observant Jew apart from those who have rejected him. He cannot mingle freely because socializing together often means dining together. And the Rabbis, taking this point to its outer limits, noted, in effect, that "if we cannot eat with them, our sons will not marry their daughters and Judaism will be preserved."

Why are the kosher dietary laws (laws of *kashrut*) observed?

Observance of the laws of *kashrut* has been a unifying factor for the Jewish people throughout the ages, continually serving to remind Jews of their roots.

The primary dietary laws are set forth in the Book of Leviticus, where a list of kosher and nonkosher animals is given. The rationale for these laws is not elucidated. The

Bible merely states that the laws be observed because "I am the Lord that brought you up out of the land of Egypt, to be your God. Ye shall therefore be holy, for I am holy" (Leviticus 11:44).

Holiness is the only reason given in the Bible for the observance of the dietary laws.

Orthodox and Conservative Jews subscribe to the dietary laws (although there are varying degrees of observance.) Reform Jews, by and large, do not, although many refrain from eating pork or pork products.

Why was the idea of holiness considered a valid reason for observing the dietary laws?

"Holiness" in Hebrew is *kedusha,* from the word *kadosh,* meaning "separated." Whatever was holy was something apart, something set aside. To be holy people, Israel had to be apart, separate from their idol-worshipping neighbors. The dietary laws were instituted as one means of making the Jewish lifestyle different from that of their neighbors.

As the Talmud points out, if Jews are not permitted to eat with their neighbors, they will not socialize with them. And if they do not socialize, there will be less intermarriage, thus guaranteeing the survival of the Jewish people. This may well be the underlying reason for all the dietary laws: to ensure Israel's survival by keeping it holy (that is, separate).

Why is the word "kosher" used to describe articles not related to food consumption?

The word "kosher" (an anglicization of the Hebrew word *kasher*) actually did not originally apply to food. It is first used in the Bible (Esther 8:5 and Ecclesiastes 11:6) to mean "good" and "proper." In later rabbinic literature it referred primarily to ritual objects (*talit, tefilin,* etc.) and meant "fit for ritual use." *Kasher* is also used to describe witnesses who are "fit" and "proper" (competent) to testify.

Why are animals that chew the cud and have split hooves kosher, while others are not?

The Bible gives no reason why only animals with split hooves and that chew the cud are kosher. Nor does it explain why certain fish and certain fowl are kosher, while others are not. All explanations are purely speculative.

Why do many Jews argue that there is no need today for the laws of *kashrut*?

A popular misconception is that the dietary laws were ancient health measures that are no longer applicable. The argument is advanced that since illnesses like trichinosis, definitely linked to pork products, have been eliminated, there is no further need for dietary observances.

Moses Maimonides, the twelfth-century philosopher and doctor, states in his philosophical work *Guide for the Perplexed* that the dietary laws are good for the individual Jew because they train him in self-control and teach him to temper his feelings and curb his appetite. Many argue that self-control can be achieved in other ways.

The response to these arguments has been (as stated above) that the purpose of the dieteray laws was to bring holiness and unity to the Jewish people, not good health.

Why is the word *terayfa* used to describe any food that is not kosher?

The Hebrew word *terayfa* (or, as some mispronounce it, *trayf*) means "torn." The Book of Exodus (22:30) states:

"You shall not eat any flesh that is torn [terayfa] of beasts [beasts killed by other beasts in the open field]." All animals killed in this manner are forbidden. The word terayfa has been extended to include all forbidden foods and all foods not prepared in accordance with the dietary laws.

Why is hunting discouraged in Jewish tradition?

Animals killed by hunters, even kosher animals (those that have split hooves and chew the cud), are considered terayfa as designated in the Book of Exodus (22:30). (See previous question.) If a kosher animal, such as a deer, is trapped but not injured, the flesh may be eaten if the animal is slaughtered by a shochet in the prescribed ritual manner.

Rabbi Akiba, one of the martyrs of Jewish history (killed in the first century at the hands of the Romans), ruled that it is even forbidden to take the life of a wild animal without giving it a fair trial before a court of twenty-three judges, the same as for a human being. Undoubtedly, this was not meant to be taken literally, but it did emphasize the sanctity and importance of all living creatures., The Talmud (Chulin 60b) discourages hunting—especially for sport. It is placed in the category of cruelty to animals, a practice condemned in the Bible.

Why must animals and fowl be ritually slaughtered to be kosher?

The Bible reiterates many times that blood may not be consumed because blood symbolizes the very essence and distinctiveness of man (Leviticus 3:17 and Deuteronomy 13:23-25). Based on this, the Rabbis of the Talmud concluded that when an animal is killed for food, care must be taken that as much blood as possible is drained from the meat before it is eaten.

When an animal is slaughtered in accordance with Jewish ritual law, the jugular vein is severed, the animal dies instantaneously, and the maximum amount of blood leaves the body. In order to draw out even more blood from the meat, additional rules of *kashrut* must be followed. See page 92.

Why must a *shochet* slaughter the animal before it can be considered kosher?

A *shochet* is a trained ritual slaughterer. He is well-versed in the laws of *shechita* (kosher slaughtering) and is able, through the use of a perfectly sharpened knife (called a *challef*), to sever the jugular vein with one stroke.

Why are certain fish not kosher?

According to the Bible (Deuteronomy 14:9-10), all crustaceans are considered nonkosher: "These [fish] you may eat of all that are in the waters: whatsoever has fins and scales may you eat; and whatsoever has no fins or scales, you may not eat; it is unclean to you." The reason is not explained in the Tora.

Some fish have fins and scales, but lose them at some point. Orthodoxy does not permit the use of such fish (swordfish and sturgeon), but some Conservative authorities permit their use.

Why can some foods be used with either meat or dairy meals?

Foods that are neither meat (*fleishig* in Yiddish) nor dairy (*milchig* in Yiddish) products nor derivatives of such products are called *pareve* (or *parev*), a Yiddish word meaning "neutral." They may be used when preparing or serving meat or dairy meals. *Pareve* products include all fish, all foods that grow in the earth, and all food products made from them.

Also included are all nonanimal manufactured food products, such as nondairy creamers and artificial sweetners.

Why may the same glass dishes be used for serving meat and dairy meals?

Since glass dishes are not absorbent, they can be used for both meat and dairy. However, as a common practice most authorities forbid such use and consider it inappropriate to employ the same dishes on a routine basis (although it is generally accepted that the same water glasses may be used for dairy and meat meals).

Why do Jews who observe the dietary laws not eat meat and milk at the same meal?

In the Book of Deuteronomy (14:21) and the Book of Exodus (23:19), the following biblical command is set forth: "Thou shalt not seethe [cook] a kid in its mother's milk." From this commandment, later generations of scholars whose opinions are recorded in the Talmud and other religious literature drew the conclusion that any mixing of meat and milk, whether in cooking or in serving, is a violation of the laws of *kashrut*.

Why do some Jews only drink milk that has been processed under the supervision of Jews?

Out of fear that the milk of a nonkosher animal might have been mixed with the milk of a kosher animal (as a result of carelessness or with intention to improve its taste) many ultra-Orthodox Jews are very careful to ascertain the source of the milk they drink. They will drink the milk of an animal only if a Jew was present at the milking and bottling. This type of milk is called *chalav Yisrael,* meaning "milk of Jews."

Why do Jews who observe the dietary laws wait a set number of hours after having eaten a meat meal before eating a dairy meal?

This law is an outgrowth of the biblical law forbidding cooking a kid in its mother's milk (Exodus 23:19 and Deuteronomy 14:21). The length of the period of waiting between eating meat and dairy has varied from one to six hours, depending on the community and the views of rabbinic authorities. Among Germans and most West European Jews the custom has been to wait three hours between a meat meal and a dairy meal. East European Jews were in the habit of waiting six hours. Among Dutch Jews the prevailing custom has been to wait seventy-two minutes—one hour and twelve minutes.

Why do some Jews wait for a period of time between eating hard cheeses and eating a meat meal?

Normally, a waiting period is not required if one wishes to eat meat after dairy foods. But since hard cheeses adhere to the teeth and take longer to digest, a number of authorites have ruled that a period of time should elapse between eating hard cheeses and meat or meat products. Depending on the rabbinic authority, the waiting requirement extends from one hour and up. In all cases, authorities suggest that after eating dairy foods a person rinse his mouth with water before proceeding to eat meat or meat products.

Why does meat have to be *kashered* (made kosher) before it can be cooked?

Meat has to be *kashered* because according to biblical law (Leviticus 7:26-27) it is forbidden to eat blood. Before cooking (except broiling) the meat of an animal that has been ritually slaughtered, it is necessary to drain the flesh of as much blood as possible.

The *kashering* process involves washing the meat with water. After it is washed, the meat is placed in a large receptacle filled with water and is soaked for a half hour to soften it so that it will absorb salt. The water must cover all surfaces of the meat. After this has been done, the meat is placed on a flat, grooved board, which has been set on an incline so liquids can drain off. The meat is then salted thoroughly on all sides with coarse (kosher) salt; it remains on the board for one hour. Coarse salt is used because of its effectiveness in absorbing a good percentage of the blood from the meat. The meat is rinsed off twice and is now considered *kashered,* in proper condition for all cooking.

Most kosher butchers will kosher meat for their customers if requested.

Why is it forbidden to leave meat in an *unkashered* state for more than three days from the time of slaughtering?

If meat remains unsoaked and unsalted for longer than three days, the blood congeals, and it cannot be *kashered* in the normal manner. Such meat can only be used if it is broiled over an open fire, which releases the blood. However, if within three days the *unkashered* meat has been washed off with water, it can still be *kashered* within three days of the washing. It can then be cooked in the normal fashion.

Why is it not necessary to *kasher* food that is to be used for broiling?

Meat intended for broiling need not be *kashered* because the broiling process itself drains off a maximum amount of blood—at least as much as is drained off when the normal soaking and salting procedure is followed. Nevertheless, some people do sprinkle salt on meat before broiling.

Why can liver not be *kashered*?

Liver is saturated with blood, which no amount of *kashering* will remove. Therefore, the only way in which liver can be made kosher is to broil it under an open fire. After the liver is broiled, it can then be fried, sautéed, or prepared in any other manner.

Why is it not permissible to dip a fowl (chicken, goose, duck, etc.) in hot water for removal of its feathers?

Any meat that has been scalded before *kashering* becomes *terayfa* because the blood will coagulate when it cools. Feathers must be removed by other means. Even the flame used to singe the remaining down after the fowl has been plucked must be a low one, since heat tends to coagulate the blood.

Why should meat not be frozen before it has been *kashered*?

If meat is frozen before being *kashered,* the blood contained within it will congeal, making it impossible to totally remove the blood through soaking and salting—the standard process for *kashering* meat. If meat is intended for broiling, it can be frozen before *kashering*. During broiling, most of the blood, even that which has congealed, will be effectively removed.

Why is it not necesasary to *kasher* fish?

The biblical prohibition regarding the consumption of blood refers explicitly to mammals and fowl (Leviticus 7:26); it does not mention fish. Aside from this, the amount of blood in a fish is minimal.

Why is it claimed that steaks served in kosher restaurants are not as good as steaks served in nonkosher restaurants?

The best steaks come from the hind quarter of the animal. This section of the animal's body is rich in blood because of the many veins attached to the sciatic nerve (*gid ha-nashe* in Hebrew), which runs through this part of the animal.

Jewish dietary law requires that the sciatic nerve and the blood vessels attached to it be completely removed from the meat. This is based on the biblical encounter between the patriarch Jacob and an angel who wrestled with him one night. Jacob's hip socket was wrenched in the encounter, and he became lame. "Therefore, the Children of Israel, to this day, do not eat the sinew of the thigh-vein which is upon the hollow of the thigh" (Genesis 32:33).

Some expert butchers are able to execute the difficult task of cutting out this sinew, and if it is done, the hind quarter of the animal may be eaten. In general, the process is too costly, and kosher butchers do not handle the hind quarter at all. Packing houses sell the hind quarters of kosher slaughtered animals to the general market.

Why are there different dietary laws for Passover?

The principle of fermentation figures into the dietary laws

of Passover but does not apply to the general Jewish dietary laws. Any product that is fermented or can cause fermentation (souring) may not be eaten on Passover but may be eaten during the balance of the year.

Why are some wines considered kosher and others nonkosher?

The Talmud indicates that wine to be used in connection with idolatrous worship, called *ya'yin nesech,* was absolutely forbidden to Jews. Later, this prohibition was extended to include all wine *touched* by Gentiles, even if the wine was made specifically for Jewish use.

Today is it generally presumed that Christians and Muslims are not idolaters, and wine handled by them may be used. Nevertheless, many members of the Orthodox community do not use such wine under any circumstances, while others will use it only if it has been preboiled. (The reason: Since wine that had been boiled was not permitted to be used in pagan worship, the presumption was that wine that had been boiled could not be associated with pagan use.)

The above applies only to wine made from grapes. Wines made from other fruits or grains are permitted even if made by non-Jews.

Why will Orthodox Jews not eat cheeses that are not specifically certified to be kosher?

In cheesemaking, rennet, an extract of the enzyme rennin, found in the lining of mammals' stomachs, is used to help hasten the coagulation of the milk. Even when the rennet used is derived from the stomach of a kosher animal, cheeses made with it are not considered kosher by Orthodox Jews. They believe that in these cheeses meat and dairy have been mixed. Conservative Jews, for the most part, do eat cheese made with rennet. The nature of rennet, they feel, has totally changed since its extraction and can therefore no longer be considered a meat product.

Why is gelatin used by some observant Jews and avoided by others?

Gelatin, a tasteless, odorless, brittle substance extracted by boiling bones, hoofs, and animal tissues is considered nonkosher by some authorities because its source is often a nonkosher animal. Others consider it kosher because, they, feel the nature of the substance has changed sufficiently in the course of its manufacture to make the original matter inert, removing it from the category of a food item.

Why are some foods called *glatt kosher*?

The word *glatt* is Yiddish for smooth. It refers in talmudic law to the lungs of an animal. If a lung of a slaughtered animal is found to be scarred in any manner, hence not smooth, the lung is examined further to see if there is any break or perforation in the skin. If so, the animal is considered nonkosher.

Some very observant Jews, however, consider an animal with even the slightest blemish on its lungs to be nonkosher. This group will consume the meat only of animals whose lungs are perfectly smooth. Meat from such animals has come to be known as *glatt kosher*. The concept has become distorted, however, and all types of kosher foods are now referred to as *glatt*. This is a misnomer since the word *glatt* relates specifically to animal foods. A piece of cake or candy or cheese cannot be *glatt kosher*.

Why do some food packages carry a Ⓤ or K or some other symbol on them?

Generally, the manufacture and/or processing of kosher foods is supervised by various organizations in cooperation with the Orthodox rabbinate. Each vies for the lucrative business involved in certifying a product as kosher. As many as seven organizations offer certification, and each uses it own symbol. The K and the ⓤ are the most popular. The ⓤ is the symbol of the Union of Orthodox Jewish Congregations.

Why do *pareve* ("neutral") products often carry a symbol certifying their *kashrut*?

All nonmeat and nondairy products—such as salt, sugar, and coffee—do not require kosher certification. Nonetheless, many food manufacturers do print a ⓤ or K on the package of their *pareve* products. They do so, in all likelihood, to assure Jews that the product is kosher and to encourage the Jewish population to purchase their products.

Why will some Jews not eat in a restaurant even if there is a kosher sign in the window?

Observant Jews look for two things before eating in a restaurant—even though a kosher sign is displayed. First, they will want to be sure that the owner of the restaurant is a Sabbath observer and hence considered more worthy of trust. Second, they will want to ascertain that the restauranteur has received a certificate of *kashrut* from the local rabbinate.

According to the law in some states (New York, for example), any restaurant advertising itself as kosher must be kosher. If proven otherwise, the violator (the restaurateur) is fined for breach of civil law.

Why are kosher foods so expensive?

The extra cost involved in kosher slaughtering by a *shochet* (ritual slaughterer) and the inspection of products by examiners *(mashgichim)* is added to the retail price of kosher products. Whether the extra cost should be as high as it usually is has been hotly debated.

Why is it permissible to use a single dishwashing machine for cleaning both dairy and meat dishes and utensils?

The water used in the dishwashing machine is so hot that the machine automatically cleans *(kashers)* itself. The machine can be used for both dairy and meat dishes and utensils as long as they are washed separately and separate trays are reserved for each category. (Although this is the majority view, the issue is still controversial.)

Chapter 5

Objects and Garb

INTRODUCTION

Of all the ritual garb associated with Jewish life, none is more important than the *talit* (prayershawl) and the *tefilin* (phylacteries). And of all the objects or ritual symbols that we employ, none is more important than the *mezuza* that is attached to the doorpost. All three are biblical in origin, and all three were established for the same purpose: to remind the Jew of God's Law.

The biblical source for the *talit* is Numbers 15:37-41, where Moses is told to "Speak to the Children of Israel and bid them to affix fringes *(tzitziot)* to the corners of their garments" so that whenever these fringes are seen, they will be reminded of God's commandments. The *talit* was created as a garment to hold the *tzitziot*.

The biblical source for the *tefilin* is Exodus 13:9 and 13:16, and Deuteronomy 6:8 and 11:18. In these verses Jews are mandated to place a symbol "on the hand and between the eyes" as a reminder of God's commandments.

The biblical source for the *mezuza* is Deuteronomy 6:9, which states, "And thou shalt write them [the commandments] upon the doorposts of thy house and upon thy gates."

Here, too, the purpose of the symbol is to serve as a reminder of the need for God's Law in the universe.

Other objects and garb that have become part of Jewish life over the centuries do not carry the same importance as the *talit, tefilin,* or *mezuza.* The *yarmulke* or *kipa* (skullcap) and the Star of David and *chai* charms worn around the neck or applied as ornaments on a variety of objects have lesser status. They serve a more parochial need: to remind the Jew of his Jewishness.

While this chapter covers a variety of important objects and garb, questions relating to objects and garb that are closely identified with specific holidays and occasions can be found in chapters dealing with those holidays and occasions. Consult the Index for easy reference.

Why is a *talit* (prayershawl) worn?

The *talit* (plural *talitot,* not *taleisim*) is worn as a reminder to observe all God's laws and thereby achieve holiness. Kabbalists speak of the *talit* as a special garment that inspires awe and reverence during prayer. Originally, the word meant "gown" or "cloak." In ancient times this cloak, which looked like a blanket, was worn by men and probably resembled the *abbayah* ("blanket") still worn by Bedouins as protection against the weather.

The source of the law requiring the wearing of *talitot* is the Bible. God said to Moses, "Speak to the Children of Israel and bid them to affix fringes to the corners of their garments . . . that ye may look upon it [them] and remember all the commandments of the Lord . . ."(Numbers 15:37-41). The *talit* itself was created to serve as an outergarment on which these fringes (*tzitziot,* plural of *tzitzit*) could be hung.

The *talit* is worn by male worshippers at all weekday morning services (except on Tisha B'Av, when the *talit* and *tefilin* are worn during the *Mincha* [afternoon] service only), on the Sabbath, and on holidays. The leader of the service, the cantor (chazzan), wears a talit whenever he leads the congregation in prayer. At the weekday Maariv (evening) service the baal tefila (the reader) does not wear a talit. However, during Sabbath and holiday evening prayers, the cantor does wear a talit.

Why is the *talit* not worn in the evening?

The talit is worn only during the day, when there is sufficient light for the fringes to be easily noticed. The biblical commandment (Numbers 15:39) requires that the fringes be seen. Only on Yom Kippur eve, because of the holiness of the day, is the talit worn at night, and even then it is donned before nightfall (before the Kol Nidre is recited) so the prayer over the talit can be recited during daylight.

Why do many Jews wear large *talitot*?

Most Orthodox and some Conservative Jews believe that a talit must cover most of one's body if it is to qualify as a "garment" on which fringes may be hung. Most Jews, however, wear the scarf-type talit. This is considered adequate, since the commandment calls for the wearing of tzitziot, not for the wearing of the talit. The Code of Jewish Law states that the minimum size of a talit should be that which is large enough "to cover a small child able to walk."

The benediction recited when draping oneself with a talit concludes with the words le-hitatef b'tzitzit, "to drape oneself with tzitzit."

Why is blue popular as the color for embroidery on a *talit*?

Blue is a reminder of the blue thread that was once added to the fringes (tzitziot). The commandment is explicit in the Book of Numbers (15:38): ". . . Let them attach a cord of blue to each corner [of the garment]." A blue thread is no longer added to each fringe because the source of that dye is no longer known; instead blue has become the color of the *talit* stripes.

The Talmud (Menachot 43b) indicates that blue was a favorite color of Jews because the Mediterranean, the largest body of water near ancient Israel, casts a blue hue. Tradition holds that the color is a reflection of God's throne, which is believed to be decorated with sapphires.

Why do some *talitot* have black stripes rather than blue ones?

Some scholars believe that since the natural source of the original blue *(techelet)* is no longer known, it would be improper to try to duplicate the color by artificial means. By using black instead of blue, attention is drawn to the difference, and it serves as a poignant reminder of God, which was the original intent of the legislation.

Other scholars believe that blue was forbidden in Roman times because the Romans objected to the use of blue (a color reserved for royalty) by common people.

Why do some Jews drape the *talit* over their heads before reciting the prescribed prayer?

Before reciting the prayer over the *talit,* many Jews cover their heads with the *talit* so as to deepen their concentration. This is much like the ritual followed by many worshippers who close their eyes when reciting the *Shema.*

Why do some people, when donning the *talit,* first lay it on their left shoulder?

The action of laying the folded *talit* over the left shoulder with the four *tzitziot* hanging down loosely is called *atifat*

Yishmaelim, meaning "draping the *talit* in the manner of the Arabs." After a pause the *talit* is placed, in a normal manner, over both shoulders. The precise origin of this custom is obscure.

Why do some Jews pray with the *talit* draped over their heads?

The custom is based on the statement in the Tosefta (Tohorot 4:1): "It is customary for scholars and their students not to pray without first wrapping themselves in their prayer-shawls."

Why does a *talit* have an *atara* sewn on it?

The *atara* (literally "diadem") is a band sewn to the top of a *talit.* Since the *talit* is rectangular, with fringes in each corner, without the *atara* one would not know how to drape it over his shoulders. To avoid disrespect to a holy article and to ensure that it not be handled haphazardly, an *atara* is attached to every *talit.* Some are elaborate bands made of silver squares or fancy metallic embroidery. Most often the blessing that is recited over the *talit* is embroidered on the band. The *atara* is removed when the *talit* is used in the burial of the dead.

Why are *talitot* not worn by women?

As mentioned above, the essential part of a *talit* is the fringe on the four corners. Garments with four corners on which fringes are hung were originally considered men's garb, and since the Bible (Deuteronomy 22:5) forbids a woman from wearing as man's clothing, a woman need not wear a *talit.*

A second explanation is offered for women not wearing *talitot.* It is based on talmudic law which exempts females from observing laws that must be performed at a specific time of day. The exemption is made because the woman's primary obligation is considered to be to the home and family. Since the *talit* must be worn at a specific time (that is, during daylight hours), the wearing of the *talit* is not incumbent upon women.

Although women are not obligated to wear a *talit,* we know of some who did in talmudic and later times. The Talmud (Menachot 43a) speaks of Rabbi Judah the Prince as personally having attached fringes *(tzitziot)* to his wife's apron.

Why do many unmarried men not wear *talitot*?

In talmudic times only married men wore *talitot,* and this was an indication of their marital status (Kiddushin 29b). (However, there is a talmudic reference to an unmarried man who did not cover his head with his *talit,* which would indicate that bachelors did, in fact, wear *talitot.*) Today the practice of unmarried men wearing *talitot* varies with the community. In many Orthodox synagogues, especially those that follow the Polish and/or Polish-Sephardic rites, an unmarried man does not wear a *talit.* In most Oriental communities an unmarried man does wear a *talit.* When leading the congregation in prayer and when being honored with an *aliya,* all men wear a *talit.*

Why are the fringes *(tzitziot)* on some *talitot* made of wool while others are made of silk or rayon?

The law in Deuteronomy 22:10 states: "Thou shalt not wear a garment in which wool and linen have been mixed together." The mixture is called *shaatnez* in Hebrew, and its use is forbidden. Wool is the product of an animal, and linen is a vegetable product. The two are not to be mixed. Therefore, a silk or wool *talit* (animal products) must have silk or wool *tzitziot,* not cotton *tzitziot* (a vegetable product). A rayon *talit* may have any type of *tzitziot* since rayon is synthetic, hence a neutral product.

Why is a man buried in a *talit* from which one of the *tzitziot* (fringes) has been cut off?

One of the *tzitziot* is torn off so as to render the *talit* invalid *(pasul)*. The law was enacted to make the symbolic point that the obligations of Jewish law are no longer required of an individual who is deceased. In addition to the *tzitziot*, the neckband *(atara)* is also removed before the *talit* is draped around the deceased.

Why is an undergarment with fringes (a *talit katan*) worn by male Jews?

Originally, fringes *(tzitziot)* were attached to the four corners of the overgarment, as prescribed in Deuteronomy 22:12: "You shall place twisted cords [*gedilim* or *tzitziot*] on the four corners of your garment." When it became too cumbersome and inconvenient to wear such an overgarment all day long, and especially when styles changed and overgarments no longer always had four distinct corners, a lightweight undergarment that could be draped over the neck was used in its place. This undergarment, which had fringes attached to the corners, was like the large *talit*. But since it was smaller, it was called *talit katan* ("small *talit*"). It is also known as *arba kanfot,* "four fringes."

Why do some Jews walk around with the fringes *(tzitziot)* of their undergarment exposed?

Some Jews take the injunction in Numbers 15:39 literally. They assume the words, "And it shall be unto you for a fringe,

that you may look upon it and remember all the commandments of the Lord," mean that the four fringes must be visible
at all times. The fringes, which are part of the undergarment,
are purposely exposed because each fringe is said to represent the 613 commandments (positive and negative) in the
Tora.

The former Sephardic Chief Rabbi of Israel, Ovadya
Yosef, wrote in response to a question *(Yechaveh Daat* 1*)*
that the tradition among Sephardim is not to wear the *talit
katan* as an outergarment and that *tzitziot* should not be
exposed at any time. The commandment in the Book of
Numbers that fringes be "seen" means that they be seen
when one puts them on each morning and pronounces the
appropriate blessing.

Why do adult Jewish males wear *tefilin*?

Tefilin (phylacteries) are leather boxes containing pieces
of parchment on which selections from the Bible are inscribed. Leather straps are attached to the boxes.

The requirement that *tefilin* be worn stems from the Bible, although the word *"tefilin"* itself is not used. There are
four references in the Bible (Exodus 13:9 and 13:16; Deuteronomy 6:8 and 11:18) which emphasize that Jews are to
place a sign (a symbol) "on the hand and between the eyes"
to serve as a reminder to obey God's commandments and,
particularly, as a reminder that He redeemed them from the
bondage of Egypt and led them to the Promised Land.

The *tefilin* are a sign of faith and devotion. The head *tefila* (singular of *tefilin*) is symbolic of intellectual loyalty; the
hand *tefila* reminds the wearer that he must serve God with
all his might and strength.

Why is the word *tefila*, the singular form of *tefi-
lin*, rarely used?

Since *tefilin* are worn only as a pair, there is little occasion to refer to them in the singular. *Tefila,* the singular form, is the same word that is used in Hebrew to designate a "prayer." Its root form also means "to judge" or "to intercede."

Although in talmudic times *tefilin* were worn all day long (Menachot 36b) this practice was later abandoned, and *tefilin* were worn only during *tefila* (prayer). Because the *tefilin* and the act of prayer became so identified with each other, the same word was used for both.

The Bible (Exodus 13:16) uses the word *totafot,* meaning "symbols," for *tefilin.*

Why is the word "phylacteries" used for *tefilin*?

In the New Testament (Matthew 23:5) "phylacteries" is the word used for *tefilin.* The word, derived from the Greek *phylakterion,* means "a safeguard," and implies that *tefilin* are amulets. While in early societies jewelry and other objects were worn on the head, hands, and arms to protect against evil spirits, there is no evidence that this ever applied to the wearing of *tefilin.*

Why can the *tefilin* cubes placed on the head and on the arm not be interchanged?

In the hand or arm cube *(shel yad),* all the passages are written on one parchment. The cube placed on the head *(shel rosh)* contains four compartments, each of which accommodates a separate piece of parchment on which has been written one of the four passages. The reason for the difference in the number of parchments is unknown.

Both cubes contain the same passages from the Bible:
1. Exodus 13:1-10
2. Exodus 13:11-16
3. Deuteronomy 6:4-9
4. Deuteronomy 11:13-21.

Why is the hand *tefila* worn on the left hand by right-handed people?

Right-handed people wear the hand *tefila* on the left hand, while left-handed people wear it on the right hand. According to one interpretation, this practice is based on a reading of the Hebrew word *yadcha,* meaning "your hand," which appears in the verse, "And you shall bind them for a sign upon *your hand.*" If the Hebrew letter *hay* is added to the end of the word *yadcha,* the word can then be pronounced *yad kayheh,* meaning "the weaker hand." According to this interpretation, the hand *tefila* is to be wrapped around the weaker hand—the left hand of a right-handed person and the right hand of a left-handed person.

Another reason for wearing the *tefila* on the weaker hand is that the Book of Deuteronomy, in which the *Shema* is found and which specifies the law pertaining to the *mezuza* and *tefilin,* states, "And thou shalt bind them for a sign upon thy hand" (6:8), followed by "And thou shalt write them upon the doorposts of thy house" (6:9). From the order of these verses, the Rabbis concluded that "the hand that writes must be the same hand that binds." Hence, if one writes with his right hand, he must wind the straps of his *tefila* with his right hand.

Why are straps attached to the *tefilin*?

Leather straps two to three feet long are attached to the boxes which house the parchments. These leather straps are called *retzuot* (singular, *retzua*) in Hebrew. The strap of the head cube hangs loosely, while the strap of the arm cube is wound around the left arm (the arm that was assumed to be closest to the heart) by right-handed people seven times. The primary function of these straps is to hold the cubes in place.

Why are the straps of the hand *tefila* wound around the arm seven times and around the fingers three times?

The hand *tefila* is wound around the arm seven times because there are seven Hebrew words in the verse in Psalms, "Thou openest Thy hand and satisfiest every living creature" (145:16). After being wound around the arm, the end of the strap is wound three times around the hand and three times around the ring finger and middle finger, forming the Hebrew word *Shaddai,* meaning "God." The winding of the strap three times is also done because Hosea (2:21-22) uses the word "betroth" three times to spell out Israel's triple commitment to God:

And I will betroth thee unto Me forever;
Yea, I will betroth thee unto Me in righteousness,
     and in justice,
And in lovingkindness and in compassion.
And I will betroth thee unto Me in faithfulness;
And thou shalt know the Lord.

Jews who follow Sephardic practice wind the *tefilin* around the arm in an overhand (clockwise) fashion, while the Ashkenazic practice uses a counterclockwise motion.

Why are large Hebrew letters embossed on the sides of the *tefila* worn on the head?

On the *tefila shel rosh,* the cube worn on the head, a large Hebrew letter, *shin,* is embossed on each of two sides. Various explanations for embossing this letter have been offered. Most probably the *shin* stands for *Shaddai,* a synonym for God.

It is interesting that the *shin* embossed on the left side of the head cube has one more vertical branch (four rather than the usual three) than the *shin* embossed on the right side. The extra branch was probably added to the *shin* on the left side of the cube to indicate to the maker of the *tefilin* the order in which the four parchments are to be inserted. It has also been noted that the seven vertical strokes of the two *shins* are equal in number to the number of times the *retzua* (strap) is wound around the arm.

The hand cube has no embossing.

Why is the *talit* put on before the *tefilin*?

Even though in Jewish law the *tefilin* are considered more holy and more important, the *talit* is always put on first. The reason for this sequence is that Jewish law states that the more frequently practiced ritual is to be performed first. The *talit* is used every day of the week; *tefilin* are not worn on the Sabbath or on holidays.

In talmudic and geonic (post-talmudic) times *tefilin* were worn by rabbis and scholars all day long. They therefore put on the *tefilin* before the *talit* in accordance with its primary status. Later, when *tefilin* were worn only at morning prayers, the *talit* was put on first and was removed after the *tefilin* had been removed.

Why do some people remove their *tefilin* after concluding the *Amida (Silent Devotion)* and then immediately put on a second pair for the balance of the service?

In France, a difference of opinion developed between the followers of Rashi (1040-1105) and those of his grandson, Jacob ben Meir (1100-1171), popularly known as Rabbenu Tam, over the arrangement of the four parchments which were placed in the cube worn on the head. The question was: Should the parchment on which Deuteronomy 11:13-21 is written be placed before or after the parchment on which Deuteronomy 6:4-9 (the *Shema*) is written?

The majority sided with Rashi, who believed the order of the Tora should be followed, and from left to right the order should be: Exodus 13:1-10; Exodus 13:11-16; Deuteronomy 6:4-9; and Deuteronomy 11:13-21. Rabbenu Tam believed the last two sections should be reversed, so that Exodus 13:11-16 and Deuteronomy 11:13-21 would be next to each other. Both, he argued, begin with the Hebrew word *ve-haya,* "and it shall come to pass."

To satisfy both views, some Jews wear both types of *tefilin* in the course of the morning service. Until after the *Amida* they wear the Rashi-style *tefilin.* For the remainder of the service they wear the Rabbenu Tam version.

Why are *tefilin* not worn on the Sabbath or on holidays?

Tefilin are worn as an *ot,* a sign, a symbol of one's willingness to affirm God's presence and power. Since the Sabbath and holidays in themselves are observed to indicate one's devotion to God, it is unnecessary wear *tefilin* on those days. Furthermore, if *tefilin* had to be worn on the Sabbath, a person might be tempted to carry them to the synagogue, and carrying on the Sabbath is forbidden.

Why do some Jews refrain from wearing *tefilin* on the Intermediate Days of Sukkot and Passover?

Some Jews, particularly *chassidim* and Sephardim, believe that the Intermediate Days of holidays (Chol Ha-moed) are holy and hence must be observed fully. Accordingly, as on other holidays, they do not put on *tefilin* on these days.

In Israel today, the Sephardic practice of not wearing *tefilin* on the Intermediate Days has gained acceptance, and the

Ashkenazic community also does not don *tefilin* on these days.

Why are women not obligated to wear *tefilin*?

According to talmudic law, women are exempt from performing rituals that must be carried out at a specific time of the day. Since *tefilin* are worn during the morning service, women are free from this obligation.

The more probable reason for the exemption of women is that it is considered improper to wear a holy object like *tefilin* when one is in a state of impurity. And women are periodically considered impure, due to the menstrual cycle.

In ancient times women were permitted to wear *tefilin*. The Talmud (Eruvin 96) notes that Michal, daughter of King Saul, donned *tefilin*. But in the sixteenth century Rabbi Moses Isserles, in his commentary on the *Code of Jewish Law,* ruled that this practice was to be banned. His ruling has been generally observed, although there have been women in history who have worn a *talit* and *tefilin* despite the disapproval of the rabbinate. One such case was the Maid (Virgin) of Ladimir, a chassidic woman *rebbe* born in Russia in the early part of the nineteenth century. She wore a *talit* and *tefilin* every morning. Rabbinic authorities tried to stop her from carrying on "in the manner of a man," but she defied them.

She moved to Palestine, where until the very end of her life she could be seen scurrying early in the morning from her home in Mea Shearim to the Wailing Wall, dressed in *talit* and *tefilin,* to recite her morning prayers.

Today, a limited group of women, especially rabbis associated with the Conservative movement, have assumed the obligation of wearing *tefilin*.

Why are *tefilin* not worn from the day one learns of the death of a close relative until after the funeral?

It is considered improper to express joy on a day of sorrow, and accordingly *tefilin* are not worn by mourners until after the funeral. Wearing *tefilin* is an act of joy and pride, not at all compatible with the feelings of an *onen*—a person who has just suffered the loss of a close relative who has not yet been buried.

Why are *mezuzot* (singular, *mezuza*) placed on the doorposts of Jewish homes?

The *mezuza* is a small parchment inscribed with verses from the Bible. It is rolled up, inserted in a case, and attached to the doorpost.

That a *mezuza* be placed on the doorposts of every Jewish home is mandated in the Bible: "And thou shalt write them [the commandments] upon the doorposts of thy house and upon thy gates" (Deuteronomy 6:9) Its function is twofold: to serve as as a reminder of God's laws and to serve as a symbol of a Jew's loyalty to the Jewish people.

The Jewish historian Flavius Josephus, who lived in Palestine in the first century C.E., wrote in his *Antiquities,* "The greatest benefits of God are to be written on the doors. . . in order that His benevolent providence may be made known everywhere." And Rabbi Moses ben Maimon (Maimonides), the outstanding twelfth-century philosopher, wrote in his famous work *Yad Ha-chazaka,* "By the commandment of the *mezuza,* man is reminded of the unity of God, and is aroused to the love of Him. . ."

Why is the parchment and the receptacle that houses it often referred to as *mezuza?*

Mezuza actually means "doorpost." The parchment and the receptacle in which it is placed have become so closely identified with the doorpost that both the parchment and the parchment-receptacle unit have become known by the same name.

Why is the *mezuza* also called the *Shema*?

The passage (Deuteronomy 6:4-9) written on the *mezuza* parchment begins with the word *shema,* "hear." The full verse is, "Hear O Israel [*Shema Yisrael*], the Lord our God, the Lord is One" (Deuteronomy 6:4). Because of the popularity of this verse, which is part of every religious service and is also recited nightly as a bedtime prayer, many people refer to the *mezuza* by the first word of the verse.

Why is the *mezuza* handwritten on parchment?

The laws that apply to the writing of a Tora apply to the writing of a *mezuza.* A scribe, called a *sofer* in Hebrew, uses a quill taken from a kosher fowl—usually a goose or a turkey—and, with indelible black ink specially prepared from vegetable ingredients, writes the twenty-two lines from Deuteronomy (6:4-9) on parchment. The parchment that is used comes from the skin of a kosher animal, usually a lamb or a goat.

Why does the word *Shaddai* appear on the obverse side of the *mezuza* parchment?

In talmudic times it was believed that the *mezuza* possessed protective powers, that it could ward off evil spirits. Later, in the Middle Ages, under the influence of the kabbalists, not only were biblical passages cited to prove the mystical powers of the *mezuza,* but various names of angels were added to the original contents of the *mezuza.* The *Zohar,* the source book of mysticism, indicates that the acronym *Shaddai* is to appear on the *mezuza* parchment because its three letters—*shin, dalet, yad*—are a synonym for God, created from the first letters in the Hebrew phrase *shomer daltot Yisrael,* "protector of the doors of Israel."

Why do three words, *kozu bemuchsaz kozu*, appear on the obverse side of the *mezuza* parchment?

In medieval times mystics added three cryptogrammatic words to the bottom of the obverse side of the *mezuza*, below the word *Shaddai*. These words, *kozu bemuchsaz kozu*, represent three real Hebrew words, *Adonoy Elohaynu Adonoy*, meaning "the Lord our God is the Lord."

The words *kozu bemuchsaz kozu*, believed by the mystics to have a secret magical meaning, were arrived at by substituting for each Hebrew letter in the phrase *Adonoy Elohaynu Adonoy* the letter that follows it in the Hebrew alphabet. Thus the word *Adonoy*, which is spelled *yad, hay, vav, hay*, was spelled *kaf, vav, za-yin, vav*, forming the word *kozu*. The same system of substituting one letter for another was employed to arrive at the next two words.

Jewish intellectuals, including Maimonides, opposed the addition of these cryptograms to the *mezuza* parchment. They condemned such practice as sheer superstition, but the custom continues to this day.

Why is the *mezuza* parchment rolled up and placed in a receptacle?

In order to protect the writing, it became customary to roll up the parchment and insert it in a metal or wooden container with a small opening on the side of the container, near the top. The word *Shaddai* was positioned so that it would be visible through the opening. Today, many modern *mezuza* cases are elaborately designed, and some do not have apertures to reveal the word *Shaddai*.

Why is the *mezuza* placed at an angle on the upper third of the doorpost?

So as to fulfill its purpose to serve as a reminder for Jews to be aware and to reach up towards God, the *mezuza* is always affixed to the upper one-third (eye level) of the right (most people are right-handed) doorpost of the home and of most rooms in it. It is hung in a slanting position (about a 30-degree angle), with the top pointing toward the interior of the home or room. In this position the word *Shaddai* is most visible.

Some scholars believe that the position of the *mezuza* was arrived at during the Middle Ages, when there was a debate as to whether the *mezuza* should be affixed to the doorpost vertically or horizontally. A compromise was reached, and the slanting position became the acceptable manner for affixing a *mezuza*.

Why is the *mezuza* kissed?

It is Jewish tradition to kiss a holy object as a gesture of reverence. Many Jews follow the custom (of talmudic origin) of touching the *mezuza* with the fingertips, kissing them, and reciting, "May God protect my going out and coming in, now and forever."

Why is the *mezuza* not placed on some doorposts?

A *mezuza* must be placed on the doorpost of the entrance to every building that is a residence and on the doorpost of most rooms within that residence. The exceptions are bathrooms, storerooms, closets, and other areas in which people do not actually "live."

Why are *mezuzot* placed on public buildings in Israel?

Although a *mezuza* need be placed only on the doorposts of a domicile (where people eat and sleep), it has become customary in recent years to affix a *mezuza* to the entrances of all public buildings in Israel. Because parties and celebrations are often held in these buildings, they fall in the domicile category.

Why do we find that synagogues today have a *mezuza* affixed to their entrances?

As mentioned above, a *mezuza,* according to the Bible, is required to be placed on the doopost of a home, a dwelling, a place where one eats and sleeps. In past centuries, synagogues were used only for prayer, and they did not require a *mezuza.* However, as synagogues became houses of study and centers of social activity where food is served, it became necessary to affix a *mezuza* to their entrances.

In his *Mishneh Torah (Hilchot Tefilin U'Mezuza* 11), Maimonides points out that "one may, if he chooses, live all his life in a tent or on a ship" and not be required to fulfill the obligation of affixing a *mezuza* to his doorpost, since a person is not obligated to live in a permanent dwelling if he prefers not to."

Why is it not required to affix a *mezuza* to a *sukka* entrance?

A *sukka* is a temporary structure. As indicated above, a *mezuza* need be affixed only to the entrances of permanent dwellings.

Why is a *mezuza* sometimes left on a house that is being vacated?

If one sells or rents his house to another Jew, he must not remove the *mezuzot* so that the new owner, who may not be able to secure his own quickly enough, will not live in the house without *mezuzot* on the doorposts. If one sells his house to a non-Jew, he must remove all *mezuzot,* lest they be profaned. However, if he has reason to believe that the owner would be offended by such action, the *mezuzot* should not be removed.

Why is a *mezuza* often hung on a chain and worn around the neck?

To the modern Jew the *mezuza* has become one of the primary symbols of Jewish identification. In fact, it is probably the Jewish symbol most widely used today. Often, Jews not only place *mezuzot* on the doorposts of their homes, but wear miniature replicas on neckchains, tiebars and cuff links. To many, the *mezuza* has become a lucky charm, while to others it is a symbol of Jewish loyalty or observance.

Why are charms consisting of Hebrew letters worn on a neckchain?

As far back as talmudic times, in Palestine and Babylonia, Jews, like other peoples, wore charms to safeguard against witches, demons, and the evil eye.

Today, the *chai,* meaning "alive, living, life" is a popular charm. It is considered, by those who wear it, an expression of their Jewish identity.

Since the combined numerical value of the two Hebrew letters that spell the word *chai* is eighteen (*chet* equals eight and *yud* equals ten), it has become customary among Jews to make charitable contributions of *chai* (eighteen) dollars or multiples thereof.

Why is the Star of David *(Magen David)* a popular symbol?

The six-pointed star (hexagram) is called *Magen* (or *Mogen*) *David* in Hebrew. The words *Magen David,* generally translated as "Star of David," literally mean "Shield of David."

In early times, the hexagram was used on Roman mosaic pavements as a decorative design without special significance. Its earliest use in a synagogue dates back 1,800 years, when it appeared next to a five-pointed star (pentagram) and a swastika on a frieze in the Synagogue of Capernaum. In sixth-century Italy, the Star of David emblem appeared for the first time on a tombstone.

The origin of the Star of David is clouded, and it probably has no connection whatsoever with King David. We do find that between 1300 and 1700 Jewish mystics (kabbalists) used the terms "Shield of David" and "Shield of Solomon" interchangeably, usually in connection with discussions about magic.

The Star of David occurs as a specifically Jewish emblem in seventeenth-century Prague, where it appeared on the official seal of the community and on printed prayerbooks. In 1897 it was adopted by the First Zionist Congress as its symbol, and in 1948 it became the central figure in the flag of the new State of Israel.

Aside from the wide variety of religious articles on which the Star of David is used as ornamentation, it is popular as an article of jewelry, usually attached to a necklace. To most wearers it is a symbol of identification with the Jewish people.

Why is a quill used for writing religious documents?

A quill from a kosher fowl is used to write religious documents, including a Tora, a *mezuza* parchment, a *tefilin* parchment, and a divorce document *(get)*. The use of a steel pen (or any other metal object, including a printing press) may not be used because iron products and their derivatives are considered symbols of war: they are materials from which swords and guns and other armaments are made.

This tradition dates back to biblical times, when in the construction of the altar stones were not used if they had been shaped with iron tools. This is based on the biblical injunction, "And if you make Me an altar of stone, do not build it of hewn stones, for if you apply your sword [iron tool] to it, you have profaned it" (Exodus 20:25).

Why do some women wear a *shaytl*?

In biblical and talmudic times women covered their heads with scarves or veils as a sign of chastity and modesty. To expose a woman's hair was considered a humiliation (Isaiah 3:17 and Berachot 24a). Some talmudic scholars regarded the wearing of a headcovering as an expression of guilt for the sin of Eve (Genesis 17:8).

Toward the end of the eighteenth century, despite opposition by some Orthodox authorities, the *shaytl* (Yiddish for "wig") was introduced as a headcovering.

Today, only strictly Orthodox married women wear a headcovering at all times, and the reason generally given is so that they should not appear attractive to men. In the synagogue, although it is not mandatory, it has become the practice for women to cover ther heads, particularly in Orthodox and some Conservative congregations. Among the Reform it is optional.

Why do some Orthodox women wear a *tichl*?

A *tichl* is a large kerchief or scarf used by ultra-Orthodox married women to cover their shaven heads. In biblical times, women covered their heads as a sign of modesty and chastity. Today, ultra-Othodox married women cover their heads with a *tichl* rather than a *shaytl* (a wig) to make themselves less appealing to the opposite sex. Paradoxically, wigs often make women more attractive.

Why do ultra-Orthodox women wear long-sleeved dresses?

Tzniut, modesty, is a basic principle that governs the lives of observant Jews. The ultra-Orthodox believe that women ought to be as fully clothed as possible, hence they require the wearing of long sleeves and a headcovering. Signs posted at the gates of the Orthodox Mea Shearim section of Jerusalem put visitors on notice that women who are not modestly dressed may not enter. Even the wearing of slacks is frowned upon, for that also falls into the category of immodest dress.

Why are yarmulkes worn?

A *yarmulke,* called a *kipa* in Hebrew, is a skullcap worn by Jews. Some wear one at all times, others only during prayer and at mealtime.

The earliest biblical reference to a headcovering is in Exodus 28:4, where it is called a *mitznefet.* It was part of the wardrobe of the High Priest. In other biblical references, the covering of the head and face is regarded as a sign of mourning (II Samuel 15:30). The Talmud, however, associates the wearing of a headcovering more with the concept of reverence (to God) and respect (for men of stature).

The word *yarmulke* is Yiddish, but of uncertain meaning. One view is that the word is derived from the headcovering called *armucella,* worn by medieval clergy. A more probable explanation is that the word *yarmulke* is related to the French *arme* (akin to the Latin *arma*), a type of round medieval helmet with a movable visor. Another Yiddish word for *yarmulke* is *koppel (kappel),* a form of the Latin *capitalis,* meaning "of the head."

The more traditional view is that the word *yarmulke* is a distorted form of the Hebrew words *yaray may'Elokim,* "in fear (awe) of God." This idea is based, for the most part, on a statement made by a fifth-century Babylonian talmudic scholar, Huna ben Joshua, who said, "I never walked four cubits with uncovered head because God dwells over my head" (Kiddushin 31a).

The custom of covering the head received wide acceptance, but not by all. Historian Israel Abrahams points out that in the thirteenth century "boys in Germany and adults in France were called to the Tora in the synagogue bareheaded."

In the Middle Ages, French and Spanish rabbinical authorities regarded the practice of covering the head during prayer and when studying Tora to be no more than custom. Some rabbis were known to pray bareheaded.

Today, Orthodox Jews and many Conservative Jews believe that covering the head is an expression of *yirat Shama'yim* ("fear of God" or "reverence for God"). Orthodoxy demands that the head be kept covered at all times, while most Conservative Jews believe the head should be covered during prayer. In most Reform congregations, covering the head during prayer is optional.

Why do many observant Jews wear beards and sidelocks?

Beards are worn in keeping with the biblical injunction (Leviticus 19:27), "Thou shalt not mar the corner of thy beard," which was apparently a practice of the idolatrous nations of biblical times. Although Jewish law permits the use of scissors and clippers, many Jews, particularly members of *chassidic* sects, will not trim the sidelocks even of children. Long, curled sidelocks *(payot)* on the children of *chassidim* is a common sight.

Why do many strictly observant Jews avoid shaving with a razor?

The Rabbis interpreted the words of Leviticus 21:5 (also referred to in Leviticus 19:27), "They shall not make baldness on their head, neither shall they mar the corner of their beard," to mean that one may not shave his beard with a razor blade or knife. Israel was admonished in the Bible not to follow the idolatrous customs of the pagans. However, in modern times, with the introduction of depilatories and the electric razor (considered a scissors rather than a blade), shaving of the beard by strictly observant Jews has become more common.

Why do women visit a *mikva*?

The *mikva* (sometimes pronounced *mikveh*) is a body of natural water (that is, a pool, a river, a pond, a lake, or an ocean) in which a person who has become ritually impure purifies himself or herself by immersion. In biblical times, the *mikva* was used by men and women to cleanse themselves of a variety of impurities, many of which are described in Leviticus (13 and 15) and in Numbers (19 and 31). Today, the *mikva* is mainly used by a woman upon completion of her menstrual period. A woman may not resume marital relations until she has immersed herself on the seventh day after her period has ended.

Some very Orthodox men still follow an old practice of immersing themselves in a *mikva* prior to the Sabbath and holidays. Scribes engaged in writing a Tora scroll immerse themselves before beginning the process, and some do so each day before they begin work.

Why do *chassidim* gird themselves with a *gartl* ("girdle")?

Chassidim, as well as many Orthodox Jews, wear a *gartl* (also spelled *gartel*)—a cloth belt—around the midsection at all times, but especially when praying. For almost all, this is part of their everyday dress, since prayers are recited many times each day.

Wearing a *gartl* dates back to talmudic times (Shabbat 10a), when the practice was introduced to serve as a reminder that one must be cognizant of the distinction between the upper and lower regions of the body just as he is cognizant of the spiritual and the physical aspects of life.

Chapter 6

The Synagogue

INTRODUCTION

Jewish worship was originally part of the Temple service. The offering of sacrifices—the "service of the altar"—was the primary expression of devotion to God, but the "service of the heart," the use of words alone, coexisted with the sacrificial system.

When the First Temple in Jerusalem was destroyed by the Babylonians in the year 586 B.C.E., there was no longer a "center" for the sacrificial service. And for about seventy years, until the Temple was rebuilt, the only form of worship was the service of the heart, the verbal service. It was at this point in Jewish history that synagogues were established in various locations. While many accepted Isaiah's vision of angels with covered faces, crying out, "Holy, holy, holy is the Lord of Hosts, *the whole world* is filled with His glory," they insisted that prayer be recited in an appointed place. And this became the accepted view of the Rabbis in the Talmud (Berachot 6b): a special room should be set aside for prayer.

Over the centuries the function of the synagogue changed. In addition to serving as a House of Prayer, it became a House of Assembly—a community meeting hall—and hence took on

124

the name *Bet Knesset* ("house of assembly"). In time the synagogue became a place for study as well. Thus, the name *Bet Midrash* ("house of study") was applied to it.

Since the synagogue is an outgrowth of the Temple, and since it also existed side by side with the Second Temple for many centuries, it is not strange that many of the physical features of the Temple were transferred to the synagogue. In the Temples of Jerusalem, the Priest offered his daily *Priestly Benediction* from a platform; hence a *bima,* also called a *duchan,* was erected in the center of the synagogue (in modern synagogues it is in the front of the room). Within the Temple compound there was a section known as *Ezrat Nashim* (women's area); hence a women's gallery was established in the synagogue.

The questions in this chapter deal with the physical features and the practices of both the ancient and the modern synagogue.

Why are representations of the Ten Commandments often used as synagogue decorations?

According to the Bible (Exodus 34), the Ten Commandments—the two tablets of the Law—were brought down by Moses from Mount Sinai. These were placed in the ark, which accompanied the Jewish people during the entire post-Exodus period.

The Ten Commandments has become a popular synagogue decorative motif. Sometimes it is made of wood or stone and mounted above the ark or on the outside of the synagogue building. Oftentimes it is embroidered on the ark curtain or Tora mantle.

Why does the *menora* (candelabrum) in many synagogues have six branches with a Star of David in the center while other *menorot* (plural of *menora*) are seven-branched?

The *menora* that was the centerpiece of the Tabernacle in the wilderness and of the First and Second Temples in Jerusalem had seven branches. After the Temples were destroyed, a tradition developed (Menachot 28b) that the appurtenances of the Temple should not be duplicated and that seven-branched *menorot* should therefore not be constructed. The six-branched *menora* became popular, but any number other than seven was permissible. A Star of David was usually affixed to the center arm of the six-branched *menora*.

Those congregations today that have installed seven-branched *menorot* reason that theirs are not copies of the candelabrum of the Temple. Because modern *menorot* are electrified, they are quite unlike the original that was cleaned each day, the wicks of which were changed, and to which fresh oil was added.

Why does an eternal light *(ner tamid)* burn perpetually in a synagogue above the ark?

Today, in most synagogues a perpetual light hangs over the ark. Originally, the light was part of the seven-branched *menora* that was the centerpiece of Solomon's Temple and the Second Temple. Called *ner tamid* (perpetual light) today, this was the westernmost branch of the original seven-branched *menora* and was therefore called *ner ma-aravi*, "western lamp" (Mishna Tamid 6:1). The light was fed constantly with oil and burned continuously, its chief function being to serve (to be a *shamash*) as a source from which the other six branches would be lighted. The other six lights were extinguished daily for cleaning purposes. The eternal light in the modern synagogue represents that *shamash* of the Temple *menora*.

Why is the synagogue ark, which houses the Torot, usually covered with a curtain?

The special curtain that covers the ark in most synagogues is called a *parochet*. Often elaborately embroidered, the first reference to an ark curtain is found in Exodus 40:21, where Moses "brought the ark into the Tabernacle and set up the curtain and screened the ark." In the days of the First and Second Temples the *parochet* separated the Holy of Holies from the rest of the Temple.

It is customary to hang a white *parochet* on the High Holidays, while a variety of colors is used throughout the year.

Why is the Tora parchment attached to rollers?

A Tora is made up of many pieces of parchment sewn together. In order to make it possible to move the parchment to the portion of the Tora to be read on a particular day, it was found most practical to attach the joined pieces of parchment to rollers, which are generally fashioned from wood or ivory.

A Torah roller is sometimes called an *aytz chayyim* (plural, *atzay chayyim*), meaning "tree of life," the name by which the Tora itself is sometimes called.

Why is the Tora referred to by some people as the *Chumash*?

In its orignal sense, the word Tora signified only the Five Books of Moses. In Hebrew the word for "five" is *chamaysh,* from which the word *Chumash* is derived. In later centuries the word Tora took on the meaning of the whole body of Jewish learning, of which the *Chumash* was only one part.

Why is a Tora mantle placed on a Tora?

The function of the mantle is both to protect the Tora and to beautify it. The care with which the Tora is to be written and dressed is described in the Talmud: "Have a beautiful scroll of the law prepared, copied by a talented scribe, written with fine ink and a fine quill, and wrapped in beautiful silk" (Shabbat 133b).

It is customary to cover all *Torot* in the ark with a white mantle on the High Holidays, while a variety of colors is used throughout the year.

Since it is not considered proper to touch the Tora parchment with bare hands, persons receiving an *aliya* (Tora honor) often touch it with the edge of the Tora mantle (and then kiss the mantle) before reciting the first and last blessings.

Why is the Tora tied with a *gartl*?

After the Tora is rolled up and before the mantle is placed over it, it is tied with a long band of material, usually two or three inches wide. The band is called a *gartl,* a Yiddish word meaning "belt." Its purpose is to encircle the two rolls of the Tora and hold them together.

The *gartl* is made of a variety of materials and colors. Sometimes, the swaddling clothes used at a boy's *brit* is saved and fashioned into the *gartl* used for the Tora that is read on his Bar Mitzva.

Why is a breastplate placed on the Tora?

The breastplate, generally made of silver, measures approximately eight by ten inches. It is attached to a chain and is draped over the poles to which the Tora scroll is attached.

Soldered to the plate, one often finds a small box in which are placed smaller plates engraved with the name of each holiday and each special Sabbath. The plate showing the name of the day being celebrated is placed in front to remind the cantor or Tora reader which Tora to remove from the ark first. The sexton, who selects the Tora to be read, tries to give each Tora an equal opportunity to be used at public readings.

Breastplates are usually designed in imitation of the breastplate worn by the High Priest (Exodus 28:13-30; 39:8-21), which was decorated with four rows consisting of a total of twelve precious stones engraved with the name of each of the twelve sons of Jacob.

Why is a crown placed on the Tora?

The Tora is the holiest object in Jewish life. It is therefore natural to "crown" it with the symbol of kingship. Some authorities ascribe the selection of a crown (*keter Tora;* plural, *kitray Tora*) as the main adornment for the Tora to the statement in the *Ethics of the Fathers* (*Pirke Avot*): "There are three crowns: the crown of the Law (Tora), the crown of the Priestly office, and the crown of loyalty, but the crown of a good name is above them all" (4:17). Hai, a tenth-century scholar and community leader, was the first to make reference to the use of a crown as a Tora adornment.

Why is the Tora dressed with *rimmonim*?

Rimmonim are decorative crowns that fit over each of the two finials (poles) of the Tora rollers. The finials are called *rimmonim* in Hebrew.

Rimmonim are also called *atzay chayyim* (singular, *aytz chayyim*), the same name used for the wood rollers and often for the Tora itself.

Rimmonim and *kitray Tora* are used interchangeably.

Why do small bells hang on the Tora crown and on the *rimmonim*?

The robe *(ephod)* worn by the High Priest when he performed his Priestly duties was decorated with golden bells (Exodus 28:33). The small bells that adorn the Tora crown and the *rimmonim* today were probably inspired by the vestment worn by the High Priest.

In the opinion of some modern authorities, the bells were introduced by Jewish communities in the East, where it was believed evil spirits are warded off by the noise of bells.

Another explanation is that one is required to stand when the Tora is removed from the ark even if one cannot see the Tora. Bells are attached to the Tora ornaments so that when one hears the sound of the bells, he will know that the Tora is being carried in a procession and that it is necessary for him to assume a standing position.

Why is a Tora pointer used?

Called a *yad* ("hand") in Hebrew, the Tora pointer is usually made out of silver and is fashioned in the shape of a hand with an outstretched index finger. A piece of tubing, usually six to eight inches long, is attached to the hand.

By means of the pointer, the Tora reader *(baal koray)* can point to the words of the Tora as he reads them, without obstructing the view of the person honored with the *aliya,* who is following the reading.

Some authorities are of the opinion that the original purpose of using a pointer was to avoid touching the Tora while it is read, an action considered in poor taste and not in keeping with the dignity due a holy object.

The first Tora pointer was probably fashioned in Germany in the sixteenth century. Since then pointers have been presented to congregations as gifts by members who wish to honor or memorialize friends or relatives.

When receiving an *aliya,* why is the Tora touched with one's *talit* or with the corner of the Tora mantle?

Before reciting the first and last blessings over the Tora, people once kissed the Tora scroll with their lips, or touched it with the tips of their fingers and then kissed their fingers. Since the Talmud considered it improper to touch a holy object in this manner, it became customary to touch the corner of the Tora with the mantle or with one's *talit* (sometimes with a prayerbook) and then to kiss these religious objects.

Why are the rabbi, cantor, sexton, and all who serve various functions in the synagogue called *klay kodesh*?

Klay kodesh means "holy vessels." The crown, pointer, *rimmonim,* breastplate, and other Tora adornments are called *klay kodesh,* and the same name has been ascribed to the various functionaries who serve the members of the synagogue, as the various adornments serve the Tora itself.

Why is the Tora read aloud to the public?

That the Tora be read aloud to the public was first mandated in Deuteronomy 31:10, which states, "And Moses commanded them the Priests: 'At the end of every seven years . . . shalt thou read this Law before all Israel.'" The practice was popularized by Ezra the Scribe, as indicated in the Book of Nehemiah (8:1-8): He gathered the people and brought out "the scroll of the Law of Moses" and read it to them "from early morning until midday in the presence of the men and women, and of all who could understand; and the ears of all the people were attentive unto the book of the Law."

Why is the Tora read on Mondays and Thursdays but not on other weekdays?

Many explanations have been advanced for the reading of the Tora on Mondays and Thursdays. One opinion is that Moses went up to Mount Sinai to receive the Tora on a Thursday and returned on a Monday. Another relates the practice of reading the Tora on Mondays and Thursdays, as well as on Sabbath afternoons, to Ezra the Scribe (Baba Kama 82a), who explained that since the Children of Israel, when wandering in the desert, went without water for three days (Exodus 15:22), Jews should not allow three days to pass without hearing the Tora read aloud, which sustains the spirit as water sustains the body.

The most authoritative explanation is that Mondays and Thursdays were market days. Jews came to Jerusalem to sell their wares, and since they were assembled on these days in such large numbers, from the days of Ezra the Scribe (sixth century B.C.E.) onward it became customary to read the Tora on market days.

Why do some congregations follow a triennial (three-year) cycle for the Tora reading?

Among the Jews of Babylonia (sixth century B.C.E. and later) one portion of the Tora was read each week, and all Five Books of the Tora were completed in one year (annual cycle). In Palestine the custom was to read shorter portions each week and to complete reading the Five Books in three years (triennial cycle) [Megilla 29b]. Today, some Conservative and Reform congregations follow the triennial cycle, and in many of these congregations Simchat Tora is observed every three years. All Orthodox and most Conservative congregations follow the annual cycle for the Tora reading.

Why is the honor to recite the Tora blessings called an *aliya*?

Originally, the prophet, Priest, or king read the entire weekly and holiday Tora portion. Later, the reading was divided among members of the congregation, and each person read his own portion. Since the reader "ascended" the platform *(bima)* to recite the portion, the honor was called an *aliya,* which means "ascent" in Hebrew.

In later centuries, when it was evident that many Jews were not knowledgeable enough to read their own Tora portion, a professional Tora reader was assigned to recite the entire Tora reading. This professional was called a *baal koray,* meaning "master of the reading," for he had mastered the musical notes and chant that had become traditional. From then on, those who received an *aliya* merely recited a blessing before and after the reading.

Why is the number of *aliyot* given out not the same at all services?

The number of *aliyot* allocated at a religious service depends on the occasion: on Sabbath afternoons (at *Mincha*), on Mondays, and on Thursdays, as well as on Chanuka, Purim, and on fast days, three *aliyot* are awarded. On Rosh Chodesh (the New Moon observance) and on Chol Ha-moed (the Intermediate Days of the Passover and Sukkot holidays), four *aliyot* are allocated. On all major holidays (Rosh Hashana, Pesach, Shavuot, and Sukkot), five are assigned. Six *aliyot* are given out on Yom Kippur, and on Sabbath morning, seven. The more important the holiday, the more *aliyot* are awarded. The degree of importance of the day was determined by the severity of the punishment given for its violation.

For the violation of the Sabbath, according to the Bible, the penalty is death, and therefore on this day the most *aliyot* are awarded. For violating Yom Kippur the penalty is excommunication. Lesser penalties were meted out for the violation of the major festivals and for the violation of Rosh Chodesh, Chol Ha-moed, Chanuka, Purim, and the fast days.

Why are extra *aliyot* awarded at Sabbath services in some synagogues?

According to tradition, it was Ezra the Scribe who instituted the practice of awarding seven *aliyot* on the Sabbath. Some synagogues increased that number so that more people might be honored. This is done today particularly on the occasion of a Bar Mitzva or a Bat Mitzva, when many relatives and guests are present at the synagogue service. From the sixth *aliya* onward, Tora portions read are generally subdivided, with not less than three verses being read for each person honored with an *aliya*. More than three verses are read when the third verse ends on an unsavory note.

Why are only three people called to the Tora on Mondays and Thursdays?

As explained earlier, the reading of the Tora on Mondays and Thursdays was probably instituted because these were market days, when many Jews came to Jerusalem from various parts of Palestine to do business. Ezra the Scribe declared that on these occasions an abbreviated portion be read from the Tora and that only three *aliyot* be assigned so that the service not be unduly extended.

Why is a *Kohayn* given the first *aliya* and a Levite the second *aliya*?

At one point in Jewish history, Tora honors *(aliyot)* were

extended to individuals according to their scholarship: the learned received the choicest honors, the third *aliya (shelishi)* being particularly highly regarded. When it became obvious that this practice put many people to public shame, the system was changed, It was decided that the first *aliya* be assigned to a member of the Priestly Family, the members of which were the primary Temple functionaries.

The high position of the Priest (*Kohayn*) was specified in Deuteronomy 31:9, where the Bible says, "And Moses wrote down the Law and handed it to the Priests. . . ." The assistant to the Priest was the Levite, and he was awarded the second *aliya*. The remaining Jews, the Israelites (*Yisraelim*), were given the balance of the *aliyot*.

Reform Judaism has abolished the distinction between *Kohayn, Layvee,* and *Yisrael.*

Why are some individuals given preference in the awarding of *aliyot?*

Aside from the *Kohayn* and *Layvee,* who are entitled by law to the first and second *aliyot,* the following individuals are given special attention in the awarding of Tora honors: the father at the Bar Mitzva of his son, the bridegroom on the Sabbath before his marriage, and a person who will be observing a *Yahrzeit* in the coming week. Other than these special cases, synagogue officials (*gabaim*) are free to offer *aliyot* to whomever they see fit.

Why are close relatives not given consecutive *aliyot?*

When pronouncing the Tora blessings, one is in effect giving testimony to God and to the Jewish people. In Jewish law, the testimony of two witnesses is required to convict an individual of wrongdoing, but they cannot be blood relatives.

Using this law as a basis, it was decided that blood relatives not be awarded consecutive *aliyot*.

Some authorities believe the ban was declared because of the superstition that if two members of a family were to receive *aliyot* one after the other, the evil eye would cast a spell upon the family.

Why is a *maftir aliya* awarded on Sabbaths and holidays?

This *aliya* was introduced as an addition to the prescribed number so that the person called on to recite the *haftara* (Prophetic portion) would also have the privilege of reciting the blessings over the Tora. The *maftir* selection read on Sabbaths is actually a repetition of the final verses for the preceding *aliya*.

Why is the Tora portion for the last *aliya* (the *maftir*) read from a second Tora on special Sabbaths and holidays?

On special Sabbaths and holidays, two Torot are removed from the ark because the *maftir* reading for these special days is from a different part of the Bible than is the Tora reading up to that point. Since it would be too cumbersome to keep the congregation waiting, a second Tora, rolled in advance to the proper place, is made available.

Why are certain passages in the Tora read by the reader quickly and in a low voice?

Two passages in the Bible (Leviticus 26:14-45 and Deuteronomy 28:15-68) are called in the Mishna "chapters of curses" (*tochaycha* in Hebrew) because they list the curses that will befall those who do not observe the Law. In addition to being read as part of the Tora reading on the Sabbaths *B'chukotai* and *Ki Tavo,* these passages were also selected to be read on fast days. When these passages were recited, the congregation became filled with fear, and it therefore became customary to recite them quickly and in a low voice.

Congregants were reluctant to be called to the Tora for an *aliya* when these passages were to be read, and it became customary to give these honors to the poor, who were not often called to the Tora because they could not afford to pledge the money usually expected of one so honored. It later became the practice for the reader, the sexton, or the rabbi to take this *aliya.* When the *tochaycha* was read, a person called to the Tora was not called by name, as was normal practice.

Why is a selection from the Prophets usually read in addition to the regular Tora reading?

The reading from the Prophets that supplements and follows the Tora portion read on Sabbaths and holidays is called the *haftara.* A *haftara* selection is not read on Sabbath afternoons or on minor holidays.

The meaning of the word *haftara* is uncertain. According to one explanation, it means "to take leave of," referring to taking leave of the scriptural reading. Another view is that the word means "conclusion," referring to the portion from the Prophets with which the biblical reading of the day is concluded.

Some authorities believe that the practice of reading the *haftara* dates to the time of King Antiochus, a second-century B.C.E. Syrian-Greek, who forbade the Jews of Palestine to read the Tora. Reading from the Prophets, in contrast, was not banned because these books were considered secular in nature. During this period, each week a minimum of twenty-one verses were selected from among the Prophets, and each person who was awarded an *aliya* read at least three of the verses.

When the oppressive legislation was no longer enforced, reading from the Tora was resumed. The practice of reading from the Prophets continued, but the selection was assigned to just one person. In time, the special selection from the Prophets was reserved for the Bar Mitzva, and in some congregations, in more recent times, for the Bat Mitzva. Special *haftarot* (plural) are read on the four special Sabbaths preceding Passover as well as on several other occasions.

The earliest reference to the actual reading of a *haftara* is found in the New Testament in the Book of Acts (13:15), where Paul was invited to deliver a sermon "after the reading of the Law and the Prophets." There is also a reference in Luke (4:17) to Jesus reading from the Book of Isaiah during a Sabbath service in Nazareth.

Why are *aliyot* not awarded to women?

Originally, those who received *aliyot* read their own Tora portions. Women were generally not sufficiently educated to read their own portions, and hence they were not awarded *aliyot*. The same was true for uneducated men. In each case, the principle followed was known as *kevod ha-beriot,* preserving the dignity of the individual by not causing him or her undue embarrassment.

In time the custom changed, and an official Tora reader *(baal koray)* was assigned to read the Tora for everyone. But the practice of not assigning *aliyot* to women did not change.

Today, all Reform and many Conservative congregations honor women with *aliyot*. Orthodox congregations do not.

Why in some synagogues is a special section set aside for women worshippers?

The origin of the special area set aside in the synagogue for women worshippers dates back about 3,000 years, to Temple days. The largest court in the Temple was called *Ezrat Nashim,* Women's Court. Despite its name, it was not intended as an area that would separate women from men. Its purpose was to separate the pure from the impure, regardless of gender. Women were considered impure during their menstrual period (Leviticus 15:19-32); men were considered impure if they suffered from certain skin diseases described in the Book of Leviticus (13:15). Since, on the whole, many more women than men were impure at any one time, the Temple area for the impure became known as the Women's Court. The reading of the Tora by the High Priest on Yom Kippur took place in this large area, as did the reading of the Book of Deuteronomy by the king to the population once every seven years.

The Talmud (Sukkah 42b) notes that to celebrate the very important and widely attended ceremony called *Simchat Bet Hasho'ayva,* the Ceremony of Water Libation (on the evening of the first day of Sukkot, when water was poured on the altar to induce the rains to fall in the coming autumn season), a gallery was built in the *Ezrat Nashim* where all the women were to congregate.

The women's gallery was erected not to create a separation for religious reasons, but for moral ones. The *Simchat Bet Hasho'ayva* celebration was a festive, boisterous occasion which often led to immorality. The Mishna (Sukkah 5:1) says that whoever did not witness the Ceremony of Water Libation never saw a real celebration in his life. Jews took part in a torch dance and joined in song. The celebration lasted all night.

The gallery that was erected to restrict contact between the sexes on this occasion was probably the prototype of the women's gallery introduced as a permanent fixture of prenineteenth-century synagogues. The first reference to it is in the work of Philo, the first-century Jewish philosopher of

Alexandria, Egypt. Historical records indicate that by the thirteenth century the establishment of a separate women's section in the synagogue was widespread.

Today, no Reform synagogues and very few Conservative synagogues separate the sexes. Only in Orthodox synagogues are special sections, or galleries, for women built.

Why is a divider (a *mechitza*) used in Orthodox synagogues?

A synagogue, to be truly Orthodox, must not have mixed pews. A separate section (either a raised gallery or a section on the same floor that is absolutely distinct) must be set aside for each sex so that the men and the women will not be able to see each other during prayer. The women's gallery is called *Ezrat Nashim.*

Some authorities believe that the separation of the sexes in the synagogue is related to an episode that occurred at Mount Sinai. Before Moses received the Ten Commandments, the Israelites were ordered to remain in a state of purity by staying away from their womenfolk for three days. However, the most authoritative explanation connects the origin of the custom with the *Ezrat Nashim* of Temple days. (See previous question.)

In some synagogues today, as in the past, a separate gallery extends around the two sides and the back of the room. In others, women are seated on the same floor but in a separate section that is one or two steps higher then the floor on which the male congregation is seated. In either case, a curtain *(mechitza)* is hung around the entire section, presumably to prevent eye contact from being made between the two groups. The curtain is not always high enough to be fully effective.

Why in some synagogues is the elevated platform *(bima)* situated in the middle of the room?

The platform *(bima)* from which the leaders conduct the service is situated in the middle of the synagogue, as was the Temple altar in early times, when sacrifices were brought.

After the destruction of the Second Temple, the synagogue became the spiritual center, and the reading of the Tora replaced the sacrifices as the highlight of the religious service. The *bima,* which replaced the altar, was situated in the center of the synagogue.

Today, in Sephardic synagogues the cantor *(chazzan)* leads the entire service from this *bima.* In most Ashkenazic Orthodox synagogues the cantor leads the *Musaf* (second part of service), but not the *Shacharit,* from the *bima.* In both, the Tora is read from this *bima.*

In Conservative and Reform congregations there is no special *bima* in the center of the room. The entire service is conducted from the pulpit in front of the ark. This pulpit is also called a *bima.*

Why is it required to have ten adult men present to constitute a quorum *(minyan)* for a religious service?

Traditionally, it is required that ten males above Bar Mitzva age be present at a religious service where the holiness of God and His kingship is to be proclaimed. Ten men constitute a religious quorum (a *minyan* in Hebrew).

Many theories have been advanced for the selection of this number. Philo said ten was decided upon because it is the most perfect number. The Rabbis of the Talmud (Megilla 23b and Berachot 21b) explain that because the ten (evil) spies in Numbers 14:26 are referred to as an *ayda,* a "congregation," ten is the number that constitutes a *minyan.*

Why do Orthodox and Conservative congregations sometimes hold a religious service with less than a *minyan* present?

Where conditions are such that it is impossible to gather the ten adult males necessary for a quorum *(minyan),* services may be conducted with a lesser number. The Talmud (Berachot 47b) says, "nine people plus the [Tora in the] ark" suffices. In the geonic period nine adults plus one boy holding a *Chumash* (Pentateuch) was considered acceptable.

Why do some congregations count women as part of a *minyan*?

In many Conservative congregations, women are counted as part of a *minyan.* Conservative Jews believe that women are obligated to pray like men. They point out that when the Talmud speaks of a quorum, it does not specify men.

Orthodox congregations do not count women as part of a *minyan.* Reform Judaism does not require a *minyan* at all.

Why do Jews sometimes remove their shoes upon entering the synagogue?

In the Bible, the removing of shoes is associated with holiness. Moses is commanded when approaching the burning bush (Exodus 3:5): "Remove your shoes, for the place on which you stand is holy ground." From this evolved a law requiring Priests *(Kohanim)* to perform their Temple duties barefooted. Today, when Priests ascend the pulpit to confer the *Priestly Benediction* upon the congregation, they do so without footwear.

On Yom Kippur and Tisha B'Av many Jews remove their shoes during synagogue services. On Tisha B'Av this is a sign of mourning for the loss of the Temples. On Yom Kippur it is an expression of remorse and penance.

Why is instrumental music prohibited at most Jewish religious services?

The performance of instrumental and vocal music was part of the Temple ritual. In the Bible singers and musicians often are referred to as participants in the Temple service.

After the destruction of the two Temples—the first in 586 B.C.E. by the Babylonians, the second in 70 C.E. by the Romans—as an expression of mourning the playing of music was banned at religious services and all public functions. However, this all-embracing ban became difficult to enforce, and music was permitted at weddings.

Today, some Conservative and most Reform congregations allow musical instruments to be played at religious services. In Conservative congregations the organ is usually the only instrument used. In Orthodox congregations instrumental music is totally banned.

Why are the windows in a synagogue always above eye level?

In the Middle Ages, when is was common for windows to be placed at eye level, non-Jews often looked in through the windows and mocked the worshippers, imitating their movements and gestures. It was then decided that the windows of synagogues be placed high enough so that passersby could not see in.

Why must a synagogue have windows?

The requirement that a synagogue have windows is mentioned in the Talmud where it is suggested that the sky inspires reverence (Berachot 34b). Rabbi A. Kook, former Chief Rabbi of Israel, explained that while praying, the individual must be aware of the world-at-large.

In early times, synagogue windows were rarely decorated. In more recent times, however, to add warmth and beauty, artistically-designed stained glass windows have become part of synagogue decor.

Why is the synagogue devoid of all sculptural decorations?

The second of the Ten Commandments mandates that no graven (sculptured) image be made and that "thou shalt not bow down to them nor serve them" (Exodus 20:4-5). This was the practice of idolators, and the ban is followed by all congregations to this day. Only decorations and art that is not three-dimensional are permitted.

Chapter 7

Posture and Prayer

INTRODUCTION

Prayer was not spawned in a vacuum. It grew out of man's need to open his heart and mind to a Divine Power.

Symbols, gestures, and postures of all kinds have long been part of man's religious expression, and often they are as eloquent and meaningful as the words that leave the lips. Jewish literature contains many stories that make this point. Perhaps one of the most poignant tells of a young boy, the son of a *chassid*, who was unable to speak, and whose education suffered as a result. When taken by his father to the synagogue on Rosh Hashana, the boy was unable to respond "Amen" to the prayers like everyone else, so instead he blew a whistle that he carried with him. The boy's father reprimanded him, but the *rebbe* was more kind. He said to the father, "Your boy's whistling is as acceptable to God as our 'Amens'."

Most gestures and posturing associated with prayer have roots in antiquity. And since they date back so far, it is not unusual to find that many—waving, for example—have grown out of superstition. Some Rabbis stated in the Talmud that the purpose of waving is to keep away evil spirits. (See page

150.) And while most modern Jews do not consider them-selves superstitious, they nevertheless retain the practice of waving the *lulav* on Sukkot.

In this chapter we address ourselves to a variety of prayers and postures whose origins and significance are often difficult to explain.

Why is it not necessary for a rabbi to conduct a religious service or even to be present when such a service is held?

In Jewish life the rabbi serves primarily as spiritual leader and teacher. It is not required that he be present for a religious service to be held. Any knowledgeable layman can conduct daily services, and this is usually the practice. On Sabbaths and holidays, congregations with ample financial resources employ the services of a professional cantor *(chazzan)*.

The cantor is also called the *shaliach tzibbur,* "emissary of the congregation," because he is appointed to lead the con-gregation in prayer. As far back as talmudic times he was called the *koray,* "the reader," and also the *baal tefila,* "leader (or master) of prayer."

Why is the weekday prayerbook and the Sabbath prayerbook called a *Siddur* while the holiday prayerbook is called a *Machzor?*

Siddur means order [of prayers]" and *Machzor* means "cycle [of prayers]." At first these words were used inter-changeably to refer to the prayerbook. The *geonim* of the seventh and later centuries used the term *Seder Tefila* ("order of prayers") for their prayerbook, which contained the liturgy for the entire year.

As the centuries passed, more and more prayers and poems *(piyyutim)* were composed for holiday services, and these found their way into the prayerbook. As a result, the prayerbook became rather heavy for worshippers to hold while at prayer, and so in recent centuries individual prayerbooks were printed for each holiday (Rosh Hashana, Yom Kippur, Pesach, Shavuot, and Sukkot). These were called *Machzorim* (singular, *Machzor*). The weekday and the Sabbath prayerbooks were called *Siddurim* (singular, *Siddur*). The name designations are completely arbitrary.

Why are some prayers in the prayerbook in Aramaic?

Throughout Jewish history Hebrew was considered the holy language, the language of prayer. But Aramaic, for many centuries, was the everyday language of the masses. Most Jews of the early centuries were familiar with Aramaic, but few knew Hebrew. Hence, a number of the more common prayers, such as the *Kaddish,* were recited in the Aramaic vernacular. (The *Kaddish* was originally recited at the end of a sermon, and later at the end of a study session. Since the sermon was delivered in Aramaic, the *Kaddish* was recited in Aramaic.)

Why was the prayer *U-mipnay Chata'aynu* introduced into the liturgy?

The Bible mandates that sacrifices be offered only on Mount Moriah, the holy site in Jerusalem. After the Second Temple was destroyed, the sacrificial system could no longer be continued. The prayer *U-mipnay Chata'aynu,* imploring for a speedy restoration of the Temple so that sacrifices might once again be offered, was introduced into the Sabbath and holiday *Musaf* services.

148 • THE JEWISH BOOK OF WHY

Why were three daily periods of prayer established?

According to tradition, the three daily services—*Shacharit, Mincha,* and *Maariv*—were introduced by the Patriarchs. Abraham introduced the morning prayers *(Shacharit);* Isaac introduced the afternoon prayers (*Mincha*); and Jacob introduced the evening prayers (*Maariv*).

Scholars, however, explain that these services were introduced much later, and that the *Shacharit* (literally "morning") service represents the early morning sacrifice brought daily in the Temple in Jerusalem. The *Mincha* (literally "offering") service represents the offering brought in the Temple each afternoon. After the destruction of the Temple in 70 C.E., these two services continued to be recited in the synagogue, and they serve as reminders of the sacrificial system.

The *Maariv* (literally "evening") service has no connection with the sacrificial cult. The Talmud records a second-century difference of opinion between Rabbi Gamliel II, head of the Sanhedrin at Yavneh, and his colleague Rabbi Joshua over the number of prayer services to be held daily. Rabbi Gamliel, mustering proof from the Bible (Psalms 55:18, Daniel 6:11) contended that prayers should be recited three times a day. Rabbi Joshua believed that since the *Maariv* service was not connected with the sacrifical system of the Temple, it should be optional. Rabbi Gamliel's view prevailed.

Why is a *Musaf* service sometimes added to the *Shacharit* service?

The sacrifical system was at the heart of the Temple ritual. Public and private offerings were made daily. A public sacrifice was brought each morning and afternoon; and on the Sabbath, New Moon (Rosh Chodesh), and festivals a *Musaf* ("additional") sacrifice was brought. The *Musaf* service recited in the synagogue today is a reminder of this special Temple sacrifice.

Why are two different types of *Kaddish* recited?

The original form of the *Kaddish,* recited after a sermon or at the conclusion of a study period, contained a paragraph beginning with the words *Al Yisrael,* "for the sake of Israel," which is a prayer for the welfare of scholars. In the early Middle Ages (about the year 1000), this paragraph was omitted and the remaining text became what is known today as the *Mourner's Kaddish.*

Why do Western Jews face east in prayer?

The Temples of Jerusalem were central to Jewish life for about one thousand years, and the synagogue, which replaced them symbolically and functionally after their destruction, still retains many Temple practices in its liturgy. As a token of respect, Jews face Jerusalem (to the east for Western Jews) when they pray. In synagogues in the Western world, the ark is erected on the eastern wall so the congregation will be facing east as it prays.

Why does a worshipper lean his head on his left arm during the recitation of *Tachanun*?

Tachanun (Penitential Prayers) is recited in full at morning prayers on Mondays and Thursdays. The custom of bowing and prostrating oneself when reciting penitential prayers is derived from Deuteronomy 9:18. After smashing the first pair of Ten Commandments, Moses said, "And I fell down before the Lord. . . ." Moses (and later Joshua) begged forgiveness for the sin of the Golden Calf, and since those years *nefilat apayim,* "falling on the face," became a posture assumed by the worshipper when seeking absolution from sin. "Falling on the face" is only performed when a *Sefer Tora* is present.

In talmudic times, the practice of falling to the ground during the recitation of *Tachanun* continued. However, because synagogues were often small and there was inadequate space for prostration, the custom soon changed. Placing one's head on one's left arm became the accepted form. The left arm was designated as a reminder of the Daily Sacrifice brought in the Temple; the animal sacrifice was laid on its left side to be slaughtered.

It might be pointed out that when wearing *tefilin,* a right-handed man leans his head on his right arm when reciting *Tachanun* in order to avoid touching and thus demeaning the *tefilin,* which he wears on the left arm.

Why are objects often held up and waved in Jewish worship?

The first mention of waving in Jewish worship is found in connection with the sacrificial system. In Leviticus 7:34 and 14:12 reference is made to the sacrifice being "waved" before the Lord. The act of waving has been interpreted as an aid in bringing the offerer of the sacrifice closer to God. Some talmudic authorities believed that waving keeps away the evil spirits.

Foremost among the objects waved are the *lulav* (palm branch) and *etrog* (citron) on Sukkot. At Sephardic services, as a man returns to his seat after having received an *aliya* (Tora honor), his fellow congregants hold a corner of their *talitot* (prayershawls) and wave at him while offering him their blessings.

Why does one kiss religious objects?

In the Bible the kiss is more than a simple greeting. It is an expression of affection, devotion, and reverence. There are many examples: Esau and Jacob kiss after not seeing each other for a long time; Aaron kisses his brother, Moses; Samuel kisses King Saul; Orpah kisses Naomi, her mother-in-law.

Since Bible days, holy objects have been saluted with a kiss to indicate affection and loyalty to God. The Tora is kissed by the worshippers when it is carried by in a synagogue procession or by an individual when he recites the blessings over it. (Sephardic Jews wave their hands toward the Tora when they are not close enough to kiss it.) The *mezuza* is touched and kissed by one entering or leaving a house. The fringes of the *talit* are kissed whenever a person dons one. When a holy book (prayerbook or Bible) is dropped, it is kissed after it has been picked up from the ground.

Today, local customs vary. Perhaps among the more interesting customs is that followed by Russian Jews, who use the index finger to kiss the *mezuza* and the little finger to kiss the Tora scroll.

Why do some Jews sway when they pray?

The custom of swaying (in Yiddish, *shuckling*) while praying is an old one. The *Zohar,* a mystic work written by Rabbi Simon bar Yochai, a second-century C.E. scholar, offers an explanation of the custom: Rabbi Jose asks Rabbi Abba, "Why is it that of all peoples Jews alone are in the habit of swaying the body when they study the Law?" Rabbi Abba answers: "It is proof of the excellence of their souls. The spirit of the man is the candle of the Lord referred to in Proverbs 20:27. The light of that candle flickers and wavers in harmony with the light of the Tora."

In his famous book *The Kuzari,* the twelfth-century Spanish poet and philosopher Yehuda Halevi offers this explanation for swaying: "It often happens that a number of people have to read from one book at the same time [since printed books were not yet available], and each of them was compelled to bend down in order to read a passage and then straighten himself up again. This resulted in continual bending forward and moving backward [that is, swaying], the book being on the ground." The habit of swaying continued even when books became plentiful.

A third explanation for the origin of swaying is given by the fourteenth-century German-born scholar who later moved to Spain, Rabbi Jacob ben Asher (also known as Baal Ha-turim). In his commentary on the passage "When the people saw it [Moses receiving the Ten Commandments], they were moved" (Exodus 22:18), he says that this accounts for the swaying of the body during the study of the Tora, which was received with awe, trembling, and shaking. The verse in Psalms (35:10) is interpreted similarly. The verse reads: "All my bones shall [move and] say, 'Who is like unto thee O Lord?'"

Swaying has been explained by some authorities as the body keeping time to the rhythm of a prayer being recited.

Why is the word "Amen" used often during public prayer?

The Talmud (Shabbat 119b) indicates that "Amen" is an acrostic formed from the first letter of the three Hebrew words *El Melech Ne'eman* ("the Lord is a trustworthy King"). The word "Amen" itself appears for the first time in the Book of Numbers (5:22).

As a response by a congregation to a prayer (Psalms 89:53) or as a declamation (Deuteronomy 27) "Amen" means "truly" or "so be it." In Temple times, the response to the blessings of the Priests was "Blessed be His glorious Name forever and ever." After the Temples were destroyed, "Amen" was used in its stead (Taanit 16).

Why is "Amen" said at the conclusion of some prayers?

Because many congregants in early times were unable to read, the leader of the service would read an entire prayer. The congregation would listen, and at the conclusion respond "Amen" (see previous question for meaning). This was true, in particular, of prayers like the *Amida (Silent Devotion)* and the *Kaddish*.

Why is kneeling rarely seen at Jewish religious services?

Bowing and kneeling were an integral part of the ceremonies and rituals of the Temples in Jerusalem.

While the Second Temple was in use, Ezra read the Tora to the great assemblage in Jerusalem:

> And Ezra opened the book in the sight of all the people. . . .
> And Ezra blessed the Lord, the great God. And the people
> answered: "Amen, Amen," with the lifting up of their hands;
> and they bowed their heads, and fell down before the Lord
> with their faces to the ground (Nehemiah 8:5-6).

Many of these postures were later adopted by the synagogue. The Talmud (Berachot 36a) says of Rabbi Akiba that when he prayed privately, he would begin in one corner of the room, and as a result of his kneeling and prostrations he would end up in the opposite corner of the room.

When Christianity adopted kneeling and prostration as postures of prayer, the Rabbis prohibited them in Jewish worship. An exception was made on Yom Kippur, when an account of the ancient Temple service is read. At that time, the cantor and members of the congregation kneel and prostrate themselves, as did the High Priest when he officiated.

Why are some prayers recited while standing?

The formal posture for prayer is the standing position. As the synagogue service grew longer, it became difficult for congregants to stand for prolonged periods, so only the more important prayers were recited while standing. What we today call the *Silent Devotion* or the *Eighteen Benedictions* (known as the *Tefila* in talmudic times) was the longest prayer said while standing. Because it originally consisted of eighteen benedictions, this prayer came to be called the *Shmoneh Esray,* meaning "eighteen." When a nineteenth benediction was added at a later date, it became known as the *Amida,* "the standing prayer." *Amida* is the more accurate designation, since on the Sabbath and holidays "the standing prayer" consists of only seven benedictions.

There are no hard-and-fast rules as to which prayers must be said while standing, although it is generally accepted that the *Barchu,* the *Hallel,* and the *Kedusha* are sufficiently important to warrant this formal posture.

Some authorities maintain that those prayers that are selections from the Bible and thus are studied are to be recited in a sitting position, because sitting is the normal posture for study. This may explain why one does not have to stand while the Tora is read, but it does not explain why similar portions of the daily morning prayerbook—from Nehemiah 9 and from Exodus 14 and 15—recited prior to the *Barchu* are recited in a standing posture.

Why is the *Shema* recited in a standing position in some congregations?

This is a relatively new practice. In some Conservative and Reform congregations the *Shema* is considered so important that congregants rise out of respect when it is recited. In Orthodox congregations one does not rise when the *Shema* is recited because this prayer, which comes from the

Bible, was the subject of study in the classroom, and as explained above, prayers in this category are recited in a sitting position (see previous question).

Why do some worshippers cover their eyes when reciting the *Shema* prayer?

To deepen concentration and to block out distractions while reciting the *Shema,* many worshippers close their eyes and cover them with the palm of one hand. The words "Hear O Israel, the Lord is our God, the Lord is One" (Deuteronomy 6:4) are then pronounced, with the final word, *echad* ("one"), prolonged and uttered with gusto.

Why is the last letter of the first and last word of the first verse of the *Shema* prayer set in larger type?

In the Tora and in many editions of the prayerbook, the *a'yin* (the last letter of the Hebrew word *shema*) and the *dalet* (the last letter of the Hebrew word *echad*) are much larger than the other letters. Together they form the word *ayd,* meaning "witness." Commentators have indicated that the purpose of such treatment of the letters is to remind Jews of their duty to serve as witnesses to God's sovereignty by leading exemplary lives.

Why is the *Amida (Silent Devotion)* repeated by the cantor at some services and not at others?

Beginning with talmudic times, the *Amida* (called the *Tefila* ["prayer"] in the Talmud because it was the most important prayer) was repeated aloud by the leader of the service because many congregants could not read. Their participation consisted of responding "Amen" after each blessing.

Because it was mandatory for the *Amida* to be recited at all daytime services, it was repeated in all such cases. However, because recitation of the *Amida* was not required at the evening service (Berachot 27b), but merely customary, there was no need for the leader of the service to repeat it.

Why are three paces taken by the worshipper at the beginning and end of the *Amida*?

The custom of stepping forward three paces when starting to recite the *Amida (Silent Devotion)* and moving backwards three paces when concluding it derives from the common metaphor which likens God to a king—the King of Kings. A subject approaches a king with reverence and departs reverently; one never turns his back on royalty.

The forward movement of the worshipper at the opening of this important prayer has also been explained as being derived from the life of Abraham who, when he prayed to God to save the inhabitants of Sodom and Gomorrah (Genesis 18:23), "came forward" to pray.

Why do worshippers stand erect, with feet together, during the *Kedusha* segment of the *Silent Devotion*?

The practice of standing with feet together during recitation of the *Kedusha* is indicated in the Talmud (Berachot 10b). It is related to the verse in Ezekiel in which the prophet describes the four creatures that appeared to him in a vision: "And their feet were straight together" (1:7). When the three words "holy, holy, holy" are pronounced, many worshippers step on their tiptoes to reach ever upward.

Why do Jews lift their heels three times when reciting the *Kedusha* prayer?

This custom is based on the repetition of the word *kadosh* ("holy") three times in Isaiah 6:3: "Holy, holy, holy is the Lord of hosts; the whole earth is full of His glory." The kabbalists were the first to suggest that the triple sanctification of God's name is an indication that one must reach towards God with his whole body.

Why do the Priests *(Kohanim)* bless the congregation at various religious services?

In the Bible (Numbers 6:22-27) the Priests were commanded to bless the Children of Israel:

May the Lord bless thee and keep thee.
May the Lord cause his countenance to shine upon thee and
   be gracious unto thee.
May the Lord lift his countenance toward thee and grant
   thee peace.

The *Priestly Benediction* is called *Birkat Kohanim* in Hebrew, and the ceremony in which it is recited is popularly known as *duchening.* The word *duchening* is derived from the Hebrew *duchan,* meaning "a platform." The Temple Priests would mount a platform each day and bless the assembled congregation.

In Jerusalem synagogues today this rite is performed by *Kohanim* each morning. In the Diaspora it is generally performed only on the more important holidays in the Jewish calendar—Rosh Hashana, Yom Kippur, Passover, Sukkot, and Shavuot—when the congregation is usually larger and more spiritually attuned. Sephardic congregations follow a tradition of *duchening* at every Sabbath service.

The *Priestly Benediction* is also pronounced by rabbis— even those who are not *Kohanim*—at weddings, Bar/Bat Mitzvas, and other happy occasions.

Why are the hands and fingers of the Priest (Kohayn) spread apart when he delivers the Priestly Benediction?

While pronouncing the *Priestly Benediction,* the Priest stretches both arms and hands forward, extending the fingers straight ahead and separating the little finger and ring finger of each hand from the other fingers, forming a V shape. Although this custom is not mentioned in the Talmud, it is referred to in Midrash Rabba, which comments on verse 2:9 of the Song of Songs: "My beloved [Israel] is like a gazelle or a young deer who stands behind our wall and looks in through the windows; he peers through the latticework." The Rabbis of the Talmud believed this to be an allusion to the Priest as he blessed the people: the "windows" represent the Priest's shoulders and arms, the "latticework" his fingers.

In a later period, outstretched hands became symbolic of the Priesthood. It is common to find this representation engraved on tombstones of members of the Priestly Family.

Why is it forbidden to look at the hands of Priests (Kohanim) while they are pronouncing the Priestly Benediction?

According to the Talmud (Chagiga 16b), "One's eyes will grow weak if he looks at the hands of the Priests" while they are blessing the congregation. Another reason is that the Priests will be distracted if they sense that they are being scrutinized while pronouncing the blessings.

Why is the Tora raised high after it is read?

In Ashkenazic congregations, since it is not easy for all assembled to see the Tora while it is being read, at the conclusion of the reading it is raised, unrolled so a few leaves can be clearly seen, and held up before the entire congregation. The congregation then recites: "This is the Tora that Moses placed before the Children of Israel. . . ."

In Sephardic congregations, *before* the Tora is read it is held high and displayed. The Tora reader points to the portion that is to be read and the congregation then recites the words mentioned above.

Why does breast-beating often accompany prayer?

Particularly during the High Holidays, but throughout the year as well, when the words "we have sinned" or "we have transgressed" are uttered during prayer, they are accompanied by beating the left breast (over the heart) with the right hand. This breast-beating is not intended to induce pain but to remind one of the words being uttered and to encourage sincere penitence.

Why isn't the Ten Commandments included in the prayerbook?

In Second Temple times, after the Priests offered the morning sacrifice (Sabbath included), they would proceed to the area of the Temple known as the Court of Hewn Stones. There, they participated in a prayer service, a part of which included the reading of the Ten Commandments.

When the Temple prayers were incorporated into the synagogue service (which ultimately replaced the Temple as the central institution of Jewish life), recitation of the Ten Commandments was omitted because certain sects (Samaritans in particular) overemphasized its importance by claiming that the Ten Commandments was given to Moses on Mount Sinai but that the rest of the Tora was not. Not to lend credence to this belief, in talmudic times (Berachot 12a) the Ten Commandments was no longer included in the prayerbook.

Despite this ban, some congregations continued to recite it. In time, however, the Ten Commandments was totally eliminated from the prayerbook.

Why is the Yiddish expression *farmisht di Yoitzres* used?

Farmisht di Yoitzres (In Hebrew, *Yotzros* or *Yotzrot*) means "mixed up the [prayers referred to as] *Yotzrot*."

The *Shacharit* (morning) service officially begins with the *Barchu*, for it is at this point that a *minyan* (quorum of ten) is required. The two prayers recited immediately after the *Barchu* are known as the *Yotzrot* (creation) prayers because they refer to God as Creator. The first refers to God as "Creator of light as well as darkness." The second refers to God as "Creator of the heavenly bodies." When a leader of the service confuses these benedictions, reciting one before the other, people say *"er hawt farmisht di Yoitzres,"* "he confused the *Yotzer* prayers." This became a folksaying, referring to anyone who mixes up things.

Chapter 8

The Sabbath

INTRODUCTION

In an ancient legend, God speaks to the Children of Israel, saying, "My children, if you are willing to accept the Tora and observe its precepts [mitzvot], I will grant you a most precious gift."

"And what is this precious gift to be?" ask the Children of Israel.

"The world-to-come," is the reply.

"Tell us what the world-to-come is like," retort the Children of Israel.

And God responds, "I have already given you the Sabbath. The Sabbath is a taste of the world-to-come."

Throughout history, the Sabbath has been central in Jewish life. From biblical times onward, it has been observed as a day of rest and spiritual rejuvenation. It has added joy to lives that were otherwise drab.

Families were drawn together on the Sabbath. Parents and children dined together. They prayed together. They studied together. They sang together. They were a family.

The essence of the Sabbath is expressed in Exodus

20:8-10: "Remember the Sabbath day and keep it holy. Six days shall you labor and do all your work, but the seventh day is a Sabbath day of the Lord, you shall do no work on it. . . . And God rested on the seventh day. . . ." Honoring the Sabbath, the Rabbis later added, is the road to personal salvation. ("Were Israel to observe but two consecutive Sabbaths, the world would be redeemed"—Shabbat 118a).

But what is work and what is rest? What is work and what is pleasure? Is rest a purely physical phenomenon? Is one man's work another man's pleasure? Is one man's pleasure another man's pleasure?

Among other things, this chapter directs its attention to such questions—questions Jews have been asking since the time of Rabbi Akiba, who was found by his students to be sitting and crying on the Sabbath. "Master, why are you crying on the Sabbath?" they asked. "Isn't the Sabbath supposed to be a day of pleasure?"

Wiping away his tears, Akiba answered, "*This* [crying] is my pleasure."

Why do Jews observe the Sabbath as a day of rest?

The Sabbath as a day of rest has its origin in the Bible. Genesis (2:1-3) tells that after creating the world in six days, God rested on the seventh day.

In the Decalogue (Ten Commandments), which appears in the Book of Exodus (20:2-14) and is repeated in the Book of Deuteronomy (5:12-15), the Sabbath is referred to as a day of rest for servants as well as masters, and as a day commemorating Israel's redemption from Egyptian bondage. And in the Book of Exodus (31:16-17) the same idea is presented:

And the Children of Israel shall keep the Sabbath throughout the generations for a perpetual covenant. . . for in six days the Lord made heaven and earth, and on the seventh He ceased from work and rested.

Why is the penalty for desecrating the Sabbath more severe than the penalty for desecrating Yom Kippur?

The Sabbath is considered the most important day in the Jewish calendar, even moreso than Yom Kippur. The Bible states that the penalty for desecrating Yom Kippur is excommunication (Leviticus 23:30), while the penalty for desecrating the Sabbath is death (Exodus 31:15).

Why are the Sabbath candles lighted before sunset on Friday?

In the Jewish calendar all days begin at nightfall (of the evening before the actual day in question) and extend for twenty-four hours. So as not to desecrate the Sabbath by miscalculating the time night actually falls, it has become customary to light the Sabbath candles early—usually eighteen minutes before sunset and approximately forty minutes before nightfall. The Sabbath ends on Saturday night approximately twenty minutes after nightfall, when a *Havdala* service is held. (See page 178.)

Why does Jewish law classify as "work" many more activities than are mentioned in the Bible?

The Bible categorizes only a few activities as "work," including plowing and harvesting (Exodus 34:21) and the kindling of fire (Exodus 35:3). But the Talmud, elaborating on this concept of work, lists thirty-nine categories (Mishna Shabbat 7:2).

The kind of activity that was called "work" was related to the construction and functioning of the Tabernacle *(Mishkan)* and Temple. From these primary categories a large number of subcategories evolved over the centuries, and according to Jewish law these, too, are prohibited on the Sabbath.

Why may Jews cook on holidays but not on the Sabbath?

The Bible (Exodus 35:3) specifically prohibits the making of a fire on the Sabbath. Therefore, cooking on the Sabbath is prohibited. Because making a fire is permissible on holidays (except Yom Kippur), cooking on these days is permissible as well. Nevertheless, whenever possible, holiday cooking is done in advance.

Why is an *eruv tavshilin* procedure required in order to cook on holidays?

One is permitted to cook on a holiday only food that will be eaten on that holiday. One is not permitted to cook food that will be eaten after the holiday.

When the Sabbath is preceded by a holiday, it is very difficult for the homemaker to prepare Sabbath meals two days in advance for the Sabbath. The law therefore permits the homemaker to cook on the holiday in preparation for the Sabbath through the *eruv tavshilin* (literally, "mixing the foods") procedure. Usually, an egg is roasted before the holiday as a symbol of the *eruv tavshilin*. By this symbolic action, a legal fiction is created whereby the cooking for the Sabbath that will be carried out during the holiday is considered to have actually begun with the cooking of the egg, which was done before the holiday.

Why do some Jews refrain from using electricity on the Sabbath?

Traditional Jews consider electricity to be a form of fire, and making a fire on the Sabbath is prohibited in the Bible. These Jews do not turn on a radio or television or use any electrical appliance on the Sabbath. Some authorities who doubt whether electricity can truly be labeled fire explain the ban on electricity as a protective measure (shevut), to safe-guard against other violations that might stem from permitting the use of electrical appliances.

Why do some Jews engage in leisure-time activities on the Sabbath (dancing, playing ball, swimming) whereas others refrain?

Although the *Code of Jewish Law* forbids such activities as playing ball, swimming, and dancing on the Sabbath, some authorities find them permissible because they add to the joy of the Sabbath Day. However, even liberal authorities feel that some activities should be restricted on the Sabbath so as to set that day apart from the rest of the week.

Interestingly, one Orthodox authority permits swimming in a private pool on the Sabbath only if the sides of the pool are high enough to prevent water from overflowing. If the water were to overflow, it would create a stream, an activity forbidden on the Sabbath.

Why do some observant Jews ride in a car on the Sabbath?

Jews of varying persuasions interpret the words "Sabbath rest" and "Sabbath holiness" differently. In accordance with their interpretations, some Reform and Conservative Jews find it acceptable to ride in a car to a synagogue if the syngaogue is not within walking distance of their homes. Others use a car for social purposes—to visit friends, relations, a hospital patient—but not for work purposes.

It is interesting that a study of religious observance in Israel completed by Dr. Yehuda ben Meir of Bar Ilan University (1980) revealed that 22 percent of Israeli Jews do not ride on the Sabbath.

Why is it permissible to violate the Sabbath to save a life?

In Jewish law, to save a life and to safeguard the health of the individual takes precedence over the laws of the Sabbath. Consequently, activities normally prohibited on the Sabbath may be engaged in when an emergency arises.

Why do observant Jews cover the burners of the stove with a metal sheet on the Sabbath?

Although a fire may not be kindled on the Sabbath to cook food, tradition demands that to be true to the designation "Sabbath, a day of delight" some hot (or warm) food should be served. Because actual cooking is forbidden, in observant homes one or more of the stove burners is kept at a moderate temperature (enough to keep food warm but not to cook it), and over the burner(s) is placed a sheet of tin (called a *blech* in Yiddish) or aluminum. The heat is thus retained and distributed over a larger area than that covered by the burner itself, and pots of precooked food and preboiled water are set on it to be kept warm for use as needed.

Why is the *Shabbes goy* an important part of Jewish life?

Shabbes goy is a Hebrew-Yiddish term for a non-Jewish person who is engaged by a strictly observant family to perform certain activities forbidden to Jews on the Sabbath: to put lights on and off, start a fire, etc. Without him strict compliance with Jewish law would be difficult.

The importance of the *Shabbes goy* to the Jewish community was once quite evident. On the afternoon before Yom Kippur, in the vestibule leading to the synagogue of most Orthodox congregations, long tables covered with white tablecloths were set up with rows of collection plates for a variety of organizations and study groups within the community. One of the plates was for donations to the *Shabbes goy,* an integral part of the Jewish community.

Why do some synagogues permit use of an organ and other musical instruments at Sabbath services?

Instrumental music was an important part of the service in Temple days, but as an expression of mourning for the destruction of the Temple it was not carried over into the synagogue service. However, in recent times many congregations have come to believe that the richness and joy music beings to the service adds to the Sabbath spirit, and that mourning on the Sabbath is contrary to Jewish tradition.

Why is a white tablecloth used to cover the Sabbath table?

The Talmud (Pesachim 100b, Tosefot) describes the custom of *covering* the Sabbath table with a white cloth as a memorial to the manna which *covered* the earth during the sojourn of the Israelites in the desert. Another explanation is that the two rows of showbreads (shewbreads) continuously on display in the Tabernacle were laid out on a "pure table," as the Bible puts it. White is a symbol of purity.

Why are candles kindled on Friday (and holiday) nights?

In early talmudic times candles were kindled in every household every night of the week for the practical purpose of illuminating the home. An average dwelling consisted of two rooms, and usually one lighted candle would be carried from room to room to provide light as needed. But on Friday night two candles were used, one for each room, since the carrying of lighted candles was prohibited.

Before the eighth century a blessing over the candles was not recited. But afterwards, in order to combat the hostility of the Jewish Karaite community, which forbade the use of all light on the Sabbath, it became mandatory to light candles and to recite a blessing, thus making it a holy act.

Another explanation for the candlelighting practice is based on the verse in the Book of Esther (8:16) which describes the victory of Esther and Mordecai over Haman as having been celebrated with "light and joy." For this reason, on all joyous occasions (Sabbath, holidays, weddings) candles are lighted.

Why are two or more candles lighted on the Sabbath (and holidays)?

In addition to the explanation offered above, the lighting of two candles represents the two important references to the Sabbath in the Bible: "*Remember* the Sabbath" (Exodus 20:8) and "*Observe* the Sabbath" (Deuteronomy 5:12).

A variety of customs has emerged over the centuries, differing from community to community and family to family. Some people light seven candles, or a seven-branched candelabrum, to correspond to the seven days of the week or the seven-branch *menora* that was a centerpiece of the Temple in Jerusalem. In some homes the woman will light a candle for each member of the family, including grandchildren. The Talmud (Shabbat 23b) encouraged this custom when it said, "The multiplication of candles [light] is a Sabbath blessing."

Why are women required to light the Sabbath candles?

The primary but not exclusive obligation for lighting Sabbath candles belongs to women. The traditional explanation is found in the Talmud (Shabbat 31b), where Rashi comments that since it was a woman who was the cause of man's downfall (Eve when tempted by the snake), causing the light of the world to be dimmed, it is woman's obligation to light the candles and bring back light. But if for some reason the woman of the house cannot carry out the candlelighting duty (if she is ill, giving birth, etc.), the obligation rests with the man.

Single men and women who run their own households are obligated to light Sabbath candles.

Why does the Sabbath begin for the housewife at candlelighting time, but later for the husband?

Many consider the Sabbath to begin with candlelighting for the woman and with recitation of the *Kiddush* for the man. Although this has been the accepted practice, authorities are not in complete agreement. Some authorities question whether the moment of candlelighting marks the beginning of the Sabbath or whether the Sabbath begins after the evening prayers and the *Kiddush* have been recited.

Why are the Sabbath candles kindled *before* the candlelighting blessing has been recited?

Normally, when a blessing is to be recited, the recitation precedes the activity, before any benefit is derived from the action. However, in the case of Sabbath candlelighting, the activity (the candlelighting itself) is performed *before* the blessing is recited. If a person were to recite the blessing first, he or she would, by that act, in effect have ushered in the Sabbath. To kindle candles afterwards would constitute a violation of Jewish law, which forbids making a fire on the Sabbath.

Why do women, after they have kindled the Sabbath candles, cover their eyes while pronouncing the benediction?

One opinion is that by covering her eyes, the woman is blocking out all extraneous thoughts, thereby giving full concentration to the words she is expressing.

The more legalistic explanation is that one may not enjoy the fruits of a blessing until after a blessing has been recited. Accordingly, immediately after lighting the candles, the eyes are covered and the blessing is recited. By covering her eyes while reciting the blessing, the woman is in effect delaying the enjoyment to be derived from witnessing the light of the Sabbath candles until after the blessing has been recited. (See previous question for a fuller explanation.)

On holidays, the prayer is recited before the lighting of the candles, since it is not a violation of Jewish law to light a fire on such days.

Why is the Sabbath compared to a bride and a queen?

The idea of calling the Sabbath a bride goes back to the time of the talmudic scholars of the third century. On Friday evening, just before nightfall, the scholars would dress themselves in Sabbath clothes and go out into the fields and say "Come, let us go out and meet the Sabbath queen." Or, they would say, "Come, bride; come, bride."

Isaac Luria, the sixteenth-century mystic of Safed, and his

followers were known to be loyal to this tradition. Late Friday afternoon they would march in procession to the outskirts of the town to greet the queen, the Sabbath bride, with song.

Why did the hymn *Lecha Dodi* ("Come My Beloved"), which is part of the Friday evening service, become so popular?

This hymn, composed by Solomon Alkabetz, a sixteenth-century kabbalist living in Safed, was made popular by the mystics of Safed who went out into the fields to greet, in a symbolic ceremony, the coming of the Sabbath—the Sabbath bride. (See the previous answer.)

Why is *Shalom Alaychem* sung on the Sabbath?

From earliest times it was believed that angels accompanied man to and from the synagogue. The Talmud (Shabbat 119b) describes this in detail. And it was also believed that it is proper to welcome these visiting angels. The kabbalists of the sixteenth century therefore introduced the *Shalom Alaychem* ("peace unto you") hymn and other songs *(zemirot)* of welcome to the Sabbath.

Why is the *Kiddush* recited?

Wine was used daily in talmudic times, and a blessing was recited before it was drunk. But since the Sabbath is a holy day, its sanctity was reinforced by reciting an additional prayer known as the *Kiddush* ("Sanctification") before drinking wine on that day. According to the Talmud, the *Kiddush* was introduced between the sixth and fourth centuries B.C.E. by the scholarly body known as the Men of the Great Assembly. It celebrates two events: Creation and the Exodus.

The *Kiddush* is recited in the home before eating Sabbath and holiday meals. It is also chanted in the synagogue so that strangers in town, spending the Sabbath or holiday away from their homes, will have an opportunity to hear the prayer recited in the company of fellow Jews.

Why is the word *challa* used to describe the Sabbath bread?

The Hebrew word *challa,* usually defined as "cake" or "loaf," is mentioned in the Book of Numbers (15:20). The Children of Israel were commanded to set aside, from the bread they bake, a small portion of dough (this ritual is referred to as "taking *challa*") for the sustenance of the Priests. This obligation, according to the Talmud (Mishna Challa 1:4), applied only to dough prepared for the baking of bread, not pastry. Hence, the word *challa* became associated with bread only.

After the destruction of the Second Temple, *challa* continued to be "taken" by those who baked bread. But since Priests no longer carried on their former Temple activities, the piece of dough was burned up.

The word *challa* was first used in the Bible (Leviticus 24:5) to describe the twelve showbreads *(lechem ha-panim)* that were arranged on the altar in the Tabernacle. The twelve loaves or cakes *(challot)* were laid out in two rows of six each. According to most authorities, this is the origin of the use of *challa* on the Sabbath and holidays.

Why are two *challot* placed on the Sabbath (and holiday) table?

According to tradition, the origin of the custom dates back

to the period of the Children of Israel's forty-year trek through the desert, after escaping enslavement in Egypt. When there was no food, God miraculously sent down manna from heaven, which settled on the earth like dew. Enough manna fell each day to meet the needs of one day only.

So that the Israelites would not have to collect the manna on the Sabbath (which would have constituted work), on the sixth day a double portion of manna was sent down, and each person gathered *twice* as much manna as usual (Exodus 16:22). The Hebrew words *lechem mishneh* are used here, meaning "a double allotment." Hence, as a remembrance of that event, two *challot* are served on Sabbaths (and holidays).

A second explanation is that two *challot* serve as a reminder of the loaves of bread *(lechem ha-panim)* permanently displayed first on the Tabernacle table (Exodus 25:30) and later in the Temple in Jerusalem. In each case twelve loaves were laid out in *two* rows; they were displayed all week long. These showbreads were required to be continually displayed in the presence of God. Each Sabbath freshly-baked breads were prepared to replace the old ones, which became the property of the Priests. The Priests were required to eat them in a holy place, since the bread was holy. The two *challot* placed on the Sabbath table today represent the two rows of showbreads displayed in the Tabernacle and Temple of old.

The custom of placing two loaves of bread on the Sabbath table has also been explained as an extension of the old practice of serving a loaf of bread with each cooked dish. In ancient times it was customary on weekdays to eat only one cooked dish, and therefore only one loaf of bread was placed on the table. But the Sabbath was special, and two cooked dishes were served in order to add to the joyous nature of the day—each with its own loaf of bread. Thus, it became traditional to serve two loaves of bread with each Sabbath (and holiday) meal.

Why have Sabbath (and holiday) *challot* been made in a variety of shapes and styles?

In order to venerate and celebrate the Sabbath (and holidays), over the years, in different communities, Sabbath and holiday *challot* have been made in a variety of shapes and styles: rectangular, oblong, flat, braided, round, filled with raisins, sprinkled with seeds (to represent the *manna* of the desert). Jewish law makes no demands as to the size or shape in which a *challa* should be made for any occasion.

Why are the Sabbath *challot* covered with a decorative cloth?

The Sabbath in Jewish tradition has been compared to a bride. Just as the veil of the bride is removed after the blessings under the canopy have been recited, so are the *challot* "unveiled" after the blessing is recited and the bread is about to be cut.

A second explanation advanced is that since the *Kiddush* is recited over the wine *before* the *challa* blessing is recited, the *challa* is kept covered so it should not be slighted. When one does not have wine for *Kiddush,* the *Kiddush* is recited over the *challot.* In such cases the *challot* are not covered.

Why is *challa* dipped in salt before it is eaten?

In Jewish tradition the table is like an altar. The Talmud says: "A man's table is like the altar that brings atonement" (Berachot 55a). Salt was used with all sacrifices brought on the altar in Temple times, and the custom of dipping bread in salt evolved as a memorial to the sacrificial system.

Why was *cholent* such a popular Sabbath food among European Jews?

Since food may not be cooked on the Sabbath but can be

kept warm until served (see page 166), *cholent* proved to be a good dish to prepare for the Sabbath: it could be kept warm overnight in a closed oven.

Many explanations have been advanced for the origin of the name *cholent*. The most popular is that it derives from the Old French word *chald* (now spelled *chaud*), meaning "warm."

The *cholent* dish itself is prepared differently in different communities, but it basically consists of meat, beans, potatoes, and various other local vegetables that are cooked for two to six hours. Late Friday afternoon, after it has been fully cooked, the *cholent* is placed in a closed oven and kept there until it is used at the Sabbath midday meal.

In the ghettos of Eastern Europe the *cholent* dish prepared by many housemakers was often taken before the Sabbath to a baker or to the home of a neighbor who had a good oven. The preparation was left there until it was needed for lunch on the Sabbath.

Among Sephardim, the Sabbath preparation that is prepared before sundown on Friday and kept warm all night is called *hamin* (*dafina* in Morocco). Chickpeas and a variety of spices give this dish its characteristic flavor.

Why is fish eaten on the Sabbath?

Fish, according to the Talmud, should be enjoyed by every family on the Sabbath. The Talmud asks, "When may those who have less than fifty *shekels* [hence, are quite poor] enjoy a vegetable and a fish dish?" And the answer is, "On Friday night; on the Sabbath."

The fish dish of the Sabbath has also been tied to the story of Creation. The Midrash suggests that since fish were created on the fifth day, man on the sixth, and the Sabbath followed on the seventh, this combination should be kept intact by man eating fish to celebrate the Sabbath.

Why do Jews eat *gefilte* fish on the Sabbath (and holidays)?

Since it was expected that all homes serve fish at least once during the Sabbath, and since the cost was often beyond the reach of many families, a preparation called *gefilte* fish was created by the housewives of Eastern European communities. This recipe reduced the cost considerably.

Gefilte fish means "filled" or "stuffed" fish. The dish was so called because originally, after the two or three types of boned fish used in its preparation (usually carp, pike, and whitefish) were ground up and seasoned with onions, salt, pepper, etc., the mixture was stuffed into the skin of the fish. It was then cooked for an hour or more.

Another fish dish that is similar in some ways to *gefilte* fish is *ge-hakte* ("chopped") herring. Because of its lower cost, this was also often served as the Sabbath dinner fish dish. It was prepared by skinning a few herrings and chopping them together with hard-boiled eggs, onions, apples, sugar, pepper, and a bit of vinegar.

Why is an *Oneg Shabbat* celebrated in many homes and synagogues on the Sabbath?

The idea of holding gatherings on Sabbath afternoon, at which time lectures are given, games played, and songs sung, was first suggested and instituted by Russian-born Chaim Nachman Bialik (1873-1934), the poet laureate of the Jewish people. He held the first *Oneg Shabbat* in his home in Tel Aviv after he settled there in 1924.

The name for the celebration was suggested to him by the verse in Isaiah (58:13) "*Ve-karata la-Shabbat oneg,*" "And you shall call the Sabbath a delight [*oneg*]." The name was later applied to the lecture series and/or social hour held in synagogues on Friday nights. The custom became the vogue in a great many synagogues in America and throughout the world.

Why are Sabbath songs *(zemirot)* sung at the Sabbath table?

This custom was introduced by the kabbalists of the sixteenth century, primarily Isaac Luria (the Ari) of Safed. The kabbalists wanted to infuse the Sabbath with joy and spritiual meaning. The custom of singing Sabbath songs spread from Safed to all parts of the world.

Why is the Tora read on Sabbath afternoon at the *Mincha* service?

The reading of the Tora on Sabbath afternoon was introduced by Ezra the Scribe, who also introduced the reading of the Tora publicly on Mondays and Thursdays. Ezra felt that since many tradesmen could not come to Jerusalem to hear the Tora read on Mondays and Thursdays (both market days), the reading of the Tora on Sabbath afternoon would provide an extra opportunity for these Jews to fulfill the obligation of hearing the Tora read. Three *aliyot* are given out during the Sabbath afternoon reading, just as on Mondays and Thursdays. Sometimes a Bar or Bat Mitzva celebration is held at this service.

Why is a third meal *(Se'uda Shelishit)* prescribed for the Sabbath?

Three meals have been prescribed by tradition as the appropriate number to be eaten on the Sabbath. The first is eaten on Friday night; the second on Sabbath at about noontime, after the morning service; and the third late in the afternoon, usually after the *Mincha* service.

The third and final meal of the Sabbath, called by many *Shalashudis* or *Shalosh Se'udos,* is more accurately called *Se'uda Shelishit* (literally, "the third meal").

It became part of the Sabbath tradition to eat three meals because the biblical verse (Exodus 16:25) describing the miracle of the manna in the desert uses the word *ha-yom* ("today") three times: "And Moses said: Eat that [the manna] *today,* for *today* is a Sabbath unto the Lord, *today* you shall not find it in the field."

The *Se'uda Shelishit* is usually a very simple meal. *Challa,* herring or herring salad, simple cakes, and soda are served. It is common for a member of the congregation to sponsor the meal to commemorate a marriage, a *Yahrzeit,* and the like.

Why is a *Havdala* ceremony conducted?

Havdala is a Hebrew word meaning "separation, division." The *Havdala* ritual, during which a blessing is recited over wine, candles, and spices, is a ceremony of separation held on Saturday after nightfall, traditionally when three stars are visible in the sky, approximately twenty minutes after nightfall. It distinguishes the holy from the mundane—the holy Sabbath from the secular workweek. The origin of this ceremony is attributed to members of the fourth and fifth-century B.C.E. Men of the Great Assembly (Berachot 33a).

Why is the *Havdala* cup of wine filled to overflowing?

Filling the cup to overflowing is considered a good omen, an expression of hope that the week to follow will bring with it goodness in abundance. The origin of the custom is rooted in the belief, common in early societies, that the spilling of wine is a safeguard against evil spirits. These spirits, it was believed, could be bribed with a bit of wine to avoid doing harm (Eruvin 65a).

Why is a braided candle with a double wick used for the *Havdala* ceremony?

Originally two lighted candles were held aloft during the

Havdala ceremony because the prayer recited uses the plural form for light: "Blessed art Thou . . . who created the *lights* of fire" (". . . *boray me'oray ha-aysh*"). Today, as a substitute, a single braided candle with a double wick is usually used. It provides a torchlike flame to satisfy the verse in Psalms (19:9), "The commandment of the Lord is pure, *enlightening the eyes.*" Blue-and-white and red-and-white are the most popular color combinations used.

Why do some people dab their eyes with the wine that spills over onto the *Havdala* tray?

After the *Havdala* blessings have been recited, the flame of the candle is doused in the wine that has overflowed from the goblet into the wine tray beneath it. An ancient superstition states that if the eyes are touched with the overflow liquid, weak eyes will be cured. The origin is obscure but is probably associated with the hope that some of the holiness of the Sabbath will last throughout the week.

Why is the child who holds the *Havdala* candle urged to hold the candle high?

When a boy holds the candle, people sometimes say to him, "Hold it high so you will get a tall bride." When a girl holds it, she is told, "Hold the candle high so you will get a tall groom." This bit of fantasy has been offered as the reason for holding the candle high, although the custom was probably originally adopted so that the people witnessing the ceremony would be able to see the dancing flame more easily when the blessing, "Blessed art Thou O God, Lord of the Universe, who created the fiery luminaries in the heavens," was pronounced.

Why does one cup the hands and scan the fingernails when reciting the *Havdala* prayer?

One cups the hands and scans the fingernails while reciting the benediction over the light to signify that the person is making use of and receiving pleasure from the light that emanates from the candle.

A second explanation is that the reflection of the light cast on the fingernails causes a shadow to appear on the palm of the hand, thus the distinction between light and darkness is marked—and the Sabbath Day has finally come to an end.

Why are spices used during the Saturday night *Havdala* ceremony?

Originally, spices were distributed throughout the home after a meal in order to dissipate food odors. This was probably not done after Sabbath meals, and when it was performed on Saturday night for the first time in twenty-four hours, it was given religious significance by appending it to the *Havdala* ceremony and reciting a special prayer over it.

An alternate explanation is that spices are intended to raise spirits and offset the sadness which often sets in at the end of the joyous Sabbath Day, when the problems of everyday life have to be faced once again. Nowadays, instead of spreading spices around the house, they are placed in a spice box, which is passed around for all to sniff after the blessing has been recited.

Why are males the only ones who drink the *Havdala* wine?

There is an old, obscure superstition which says that if a woman drinks from the *Havdala* glass, she will grow a beard, which is good enough reason for her to abstain.

Another explanation is that Adam's wife caused his downfall when she ate of the Tree of Knowledge. In Jewish folklore, the fruit of that "tree" was grapes. Eve squeezed the grapes to make wine, and because of her sin, the story goes, women may not drink the *Havdala* wine.

Why do many people eat a *Melaveh Malka* meal on Saturday night?

Melaveh Malka, which means "accompanying the queen," is the name given to the extra meal served after the Sabbath. Partaking of this meal is an additional way of bidding farewell to the Sabbath queen.

According to legend, the custom originated with King David. David had asked God when he would die, and God told him it would happen on a Saturday. From that time on, when each Sabbath was over, David made a party to celebrate his survival. The nation at large rejoiced with him and adopted the practice of celebrating the *Melaveh Malka* on Saturday night.

Why do some people delay the recitation of the *Maariv* prayers and the *Havdala*?

To hold onto the Sabbath a bit longer so as to enjoy her blessings and thus postpone the "pain" of parting with the Sabbath, some Jews choose to wait an extra period of time after nightfall before reciting the *Maariv* prayers and the *Havdala*.

There is a tradition which states that the souls of the departed are constantly being judged, but the process is halted on the Sabbath. Those in *gehinnom* (hell) enjoy added respite when the Sabbath is extended.

Chapter 9

Passover

INTRODUCTION

Passover, the first of the major Jewish festivals mentioned in the Bible, is observed and celebrated by more Jews than any other holiday in the Jewish calendar. A recent survey shows that 99 percent of the Israeli population observes the holiday in some fashion—by eating *matza,* by abstaining from those foods forbidden on Passover *(chametz),* by cleaning their houses thoroughly, by attending a Seder, or by attending a synagogue service.

Why Jews are attracted to Passover is not difficult to understand, for the festival's roots in Jewish history are deep. Passover celebrates the escape of the Children of Israel from the Egyptian "house of bondage," and it serves to remind us of the importance of continuing the battle for freedom in every generation. Added to this basic spiritual concept, the pageantry and the special foods connected with Passover have made it unique among holidays.

Passover began and remains a family holiday. The Bible (Exodus 12) says, "God said to Moses and Aaron: this month [Nissan] shall be unto you the beginning of months . . . On the tenth day of this month they [the Children of Israel] shall take to them every man a lamb, according to their father's houses, a lamb for a household. . ." This lamb, the Paschal lamb, was to be held until the fourteenth of the month, when it was to be slaughtered, roasted, and shared by members of the family. Today, the array of delicacies associated with family Seder celebrations, as well as the foods prepared for the rest of Passover, continue to attract family members to share in the Passover experience.

This chapter answers many questions asked about Passover foods as well as questions relating to the theme of the holiday. This was beautifully summed up by Morris Joseph in his *Judaism as Creed and Life:* "Passover has a message for the conscience and heart of all mankind. . . . It is Israel's, nay God's, protest against unrighteousness. Wrong, it declares, may triumph for a time, but even though it be perpetrated by the strong on the weak, it will meet with its inevitable retribution at last."

Why is Passover celebrated?

Passover, along with Shavuot and Sukkot, is a major festival ordained in the Bible. Three elements have merged to make Passover a particularly distinctive and meaningful holiday—a holiday that symbolizes in words and deeds the ideal of freedom.

Originally, Passover was two separate holidays. One was an agricultural holiday called "Chag Ha-matzot" (Festival of Unleavened Bread). The other was a pastoral holiday called "Chag Ha-pesach" (Festival of the Paschal Lamb). Both holidays developed independently in the springtime of the year, in the Hebrew month of Nissan (March-April).

Chag Ha-pesach is the older of the two festivals. In ancient times, when most Jews were still nomadic desert shepherds, Jewish families celebrated the advent of spring by offering an animal sacrifice. At one point in the Bible, Moses begged Pharaoh to allow the Children of Israel to go out into the wilderness to observe their feast in honor of God. This episode preceded the actual Exodus of the Jews from Egypt.

The agricultural festival, Chag Ha-matzot, was a separate spring festival during which the Jewish farmers of Palestine celebrated the beginning of the grain harvest. Before cutting the grain, they would discard all sour dough (fermented dough used, instead of yeast, to leaven bread).

In the course of time, these two springtime Festivals came to be associated with another event that occurred in the springtime of the year: the Exodus from Egypt. The Bible presents these springtime celebrations in this fashion:

1. Chag Ha-pesach (Exodus 34:25), the Festival of the Pesach (Paschal lamb), became identified with the happening in Egypt when God "passed over" the houses of the Children of Israel, sparing them the tenth plague, which was visited upon the oldest son in each Egyptian family. Pesach comes from the Hebrew root *pasach* meaning "Paschal lamb" and "pass over."

2. Chag Ha-matzot (Exodus 23:15), the Festival of Unleavened Bread, known long before the Jewish experience in Egypt, was tied to the hasty departure of the Children of Israel from Egypt, when they "took their dough before it was leavened" (Exodus 12:34).

Why is Passover so widely observed?

The excitement of different foods and elaborate family get-togethers has made Passover the most popular Jewish holiday. A survey of the Israeli population, released in 1980 by Dr. Yehuda ben Meir of Bar Ilan University, reveals that 99 percent of Israeli Jews celebrate some kind of Seder and that 82 percent do not eat any prohibited foods during the holiday. By comparison, only 79 percent eat only kosher meat during the year, and only 44 percent observe *kashrut* fully.

In the last years of the Second Temple, the Passover holiday was very popular. The Jewish historian Flavius Josephus and the Roman historian Tacitus estimated that the number of participants who celebrated Passover in Jerusalem in the year 65 C.E. was "not less than three millions." This figure corresponds with the statement in the Talmud (Pesachim 64b) that describes the census taken by King Agrippa. Agrippa ordered the Temple Priests to set aside one kidney from each offering of the Paschal lamb. Since not less than ten people shared in eating the lamb, from the number of kidneys set aside it was estimated that 3,000,000 Jews were in Jerusalem to celebrate Passover that year (five years before the destruction of the Temple).

Why is Passover observed for seven days in Israel but for eight days in other countries?

The Bible commands that Passover be observed for seven days. After the exile from Palestine (in 70 C.E.), when Jews lived in countries throughout the world, an extra day was added.

This additional day was necessitated by uncertainty of the calendar. The Jewish (lunar) calendar was based on the appearance of the New Moon, which was officially announced after witnesses testified to its arrival. Since errors could easily be made, especially in transmission of this information from the source in Jerusalem to distant places in outlying areas, an extra day of observance was added to Passover, Sukkot, and Shavuot in order to avoid possible desecration of the holiday. (See also page 293.)

Most Jews in the Diaspora today observe Passover for eight days, but Reform Jews and some Conservative Jews follow the Israeli practice of observing the holiday for seven days.

Why are special charitable collections, known as *maot chittim,* made immediately before Passover?

The words *maot chittim* mean "money for wheat," wheat needed to bake *matzot* for Passover. Since on Passover Jews may not eat bread or products that ferment, a special fund is established to assist the poor in purchasing Passover necessities. The custom of donating money to the *maot chittim* fund is an ancient one, governed by the talmudic rule that "those who have enough give, and those who don't have enough take."

Why are the firstborn required to fast before Passover?

This custom, of biblical origin, is based on the account presented in Exodus 12:21-28, in which all Egyptian firstborn were slain and the firstborn of Israel were spared. The word "Passover" (*Pesach* in Hebrew) is from the verb *pasach,* meaning "to spare, to pass over."

To commemorate and express gratitude for the sparing of the firstborn of Israel, the day preceding Passover became a fast day for the firstborn male in each family. In time the requirement changed: the fast was excused if the firstborn undertook to study a talmudic tractate over the course of the year and to complete his studies on the day before Passover. In practice (and with exceptions), the studying was and is assumed by the local rabbi, who on the morning before the day of Passover assembles all the firstborn of the community. After morning prayers the group joins the rabbi in studying the last section of the tractate that he has been studying in anticipation of the occasion. This practice is called a *Siyum* or *Siyum Masechta,* meaning "completing a tractate [of the Talmud]."

Why must the Jewish home be scoured clean before the Passover holiday?

To find *chametz* in a home after the holiday has begun is considered a serious breach of Jewish law. From biblical times onward, the law has required that every bit of leavened bread and all materials and products associated with it (that is, *chametz*) be removed from the house before Passover so that it will not even be seen during the holiday.

Why is leaven *(chametz)* removed on Passover?

Matza was used in the sacrificial system of the Temple. Offerings had to be absolutely pure, and anything leavened *(chametz)* was considered impure because it had fermented, or soured. (The word *chametz* literally means "sour.") *Matza*—unleavened bread—on the other hand, was a symbol of purity. The Talmud says, "leaven represents the evil impulse of the heart" (Berachot 17a).

The following five grains, and anything made from them, are considered *chametz:* wheat, barley, spelt (a primitive species of wheat), rye, and oats. Use of these grains is prohibited on Passover, except for the making of *matza*. The exception was made because the eating of *matza* is mandated in the Bible (Exodus 13:7), and to make *matza* grain has to be used. Also, since *matza* is made only from two ingredients, the flour of the grain and water, it can be prepared for baking quickly and will not become fermented. Traditionally, *matza* is made from wheat flour.

Why is it not permissible to make cakes out of ordinary flour on Passover?

Because flour is subject to fermentation *(chametz)*, it may not be used on Passover. Pastries and cakes can only be made out of *matza*-flour (*matza* that has been ground fine). This flour is made from *matza* that has been previously baked and is therefore no longer subject to fermentation.

Why is there a difference of opinion about which foods may be eaten on Passover?

Originally, in the Ashkenazic community only five grains were considered *chametz:* wheat, barley, spelt, rye, oats. Post-talmudic authorities (the *geonim*) added rice and legumes *(kitniot)* to this group. Legumes include beans, peas, and the fruit of any plant of the pea family.

The Sephardic community did not accept this geonic prohibition because the main articles of food in their geographic locations were rice and legumes. Consequently, today Sephardic Jews eat both legumes and rice on Passover, while Ashkenazic Jews do not.

Why do Jews "sell" their *chametz* to non-Jews before Passover?

All *chametz* must be removed from one's home and one's ownership during Passover. This calls for the sale of all such food and articles that one owns and/or of the subleasing of places where one has *chametz* stored. The procedure must be *bona fide,* without conditions attached, if it is to comply with Jewish law.

Because of the hardship often involved, a procedure was created whereby a Jew "sells" his *chametz* to a rabbi, who in turn "sells" it to a non-Jewish person with the understanding that the sale is only symbolic. The non-Jew is considered the owner of all this *chametz* throughout Passover. But once the holiday is over, it is understood that for monetary consideration the transaction is to be nullified and that the *chametz* once again becomes the property of the Jew. Through this legal fiction, the biblical requirement (Exodus 13:7) that a Jew not have *chametz* in his possession during Passover is fulfilled.

Why is a search for *chametz* conducted on the night before Passover Eve?

The search for leaven is called *bedikat chametz*. The Book of Exodus (13:7-8) says:

> Unleavened bread shall be eaten for seven days, and there shall be no leaven seen with you in all your borders. And you shall explain to your son on that day, saying: "It is because of what the Lord did for me when I came out of the land of Egypt."

After the house has been thoroughly cleaned and scoured, the master of the house, on the evening of the fourteenth of Nissan, concludes the process of removing all *chametz,* seen or unseen, by conducting a religious ceremony in which he symbolically searches for the last vestige of leaven in every room of the house.

The procedure usually consists of a family member placing small pieces of bread in key places in the house, usually on one windowsill in each room. It is customary among some to distribute ten pieces, representing the kabbalistic notion of ten *sefirot*—ten manifestations of God. To others, the ten pieces of bread are reminders of the ten wicked sons of Haman. The head of the house, followed by any children present, then proceeds from room to room by candlelight. With a feather, the bread crumbs or pieces are brushed into a wooden spoon. All of this (spoon, bread, and feather) is wrapped together and burned the following morning. Appropriate prayers are recited during the burning.

Single persons, male or female, living in their own house

or apartment are obligated to carry out the ceremony.

Why is it necessary to change dishes on Passover?

It is not necessary to replace all dishes on Passover. Crockery dishes, which are absorbent, have to be replaced for the duration of the holiday. Glass and pyrex dishes and others that are nonabsorbent can be soaked in hot water, thoroughly scoured, and then set aside for twenty-four hours. This process of "making kosher" is called *kashering*. The same holds true for eating utensils: metal spoons, forks and knives can be *kashered;* wooden or porcelain utensils cannot, since not all particles of *chametz* (leaven) can be removed from the latter.

Why is *matza* eaten on Passover?

Matza is eaten to satisfy the biblical commandment commemorating the hasty departure of the Children of Israel from Egypt: "They took up their dough before it had time to leaven" (Exodus 12:34).

The message is further amplified in Deuteronomy 16:3: "For seven days thereafter you shall eat unleavened bread . . . for you departed from the land of Egypt hurriedly—so that you may remember the day of your departure from the land of Egypt as long as you live." The implication of this verse, as interpreted by the Rabbis, is that it is mandatory to eat *matza* on the first night of Passover, and it is optional to eat it for the balance of the week—so long as *chametz* is not eaten.

Why is *matza* called "poor man's bread"?

The Bible (Deuteronomy 16:3) and the Haggada read at the Seder refer to unleavened bread (*matza*) as *lechem oni,* or "poor man's bread," which is also translated as "the bread of affliction." This name is used because *matza* is made simply of flour and water. (See next question concerning "bread of opulence.")

Why is *matza ashira* ("rich *matza*") not used at the Seder?

Matza ashira is so called because it contains "rich" ingredients. Whereas ordinary *matza* (also called "poor man's bread") is made only of flour and water, *matza ashira* is made of flour mixed with wine, oil, honey, or eggs instead of water. It is sometimes called "the bread of opulence."

The Talmud (Pesachim 36a) finds that this type of *matza* does not fit the definition of the *lechem oni* ("bread of affliction") mandated in the Bible for the celebration of Passover. For the Seder, it is not allowed, except for the aged or sick, who may require this softer type of *matza* for health reasons.

Why do some Jews use special water for the baking of *matza*?

According to ancient belief expressed in the Talmud (Pesachim 94b), at night the sun underneath the earth heats up the wells and streams, and their waters become tepid. Rabbi Judah ordered that such water not be used in the preparation of *matza* because the tepid water accelerates the process of fermentation. He required that *matza* be made with *ma-yim she-lanu,* meaning water that has "lodged" or been kept overnight in the home at cool temperatures.

Why are perforations made in *matzot*?

Perforations are made just before the rolled-out dough is

placed in the oven. They allow for the escape of air, thus retarding fermentation. The perforations also prevent the dough from rising and swelling while baking.

In early times artistic designs were often perforated in the *matza*, but this was later banned because it took too long to execute, and the possibility of fermentation increased. By law, the whole process, from kneading to baking, must be executed within eighteen minutes, a period of time in which no fermentation will take place. Today, handmade *matzot* are perforated quickly with a wheel (called a *raydle*). The *matza* machine has an automatic perforator that makes lines about one-quarter to one-half inch apart.

Why was there opposition to the use of machine-made *matzot*?

With the introduction of machine-made *matzot* in the middle of the nineteenth century, a violent controversy began among scholars. The controversy still exists. Many argued that the machine process causes fermentation; that the milling by heavy machinery causes the wheat to give off moisture. They also argued that pieces of dough adhere to the baking surface and thus cause fermentation before the baking process ends.

Why are most *matzot* square?

Originally all *matzot* were shaped round. In 1875, a *matza*-baking machine that made square *matzot* was invented in England. The machine was subsequently introduced into the United States.

There was opposition to the use of the *matza* machine itself, as explained in the preceding question. Some rabbis claimed that to satisfy people accustomed to eating round *matzot* the corners of the square *matzot* were trimmed off. This rounding process, it was argued, prolonged the preparation time and possibly allowed for fermentation to set in. These objections were countered with the argument that the machine process was a speedy one, that it did not allow sufficient time for fermentation to begin. Today many Jews prefer to use only round *matzot,* machine or handmade.

Why is *matza* not eaten all day prior to the Seder?

In the Jerusalem Talmud (Pesachim 10:1), Rabbi Levi was the first to propose the rule that *matza* should not be eaten on the day prior to the first Seder because doing so removes the novelty of eating *matza* for the first time at the Seder itself. He put it as follows: "One who eats *matza* on the eve of Passover is like one who has intimate relations with his bride-to-be in his [future] father-in-law's home." Some Jews do not eat *matza* for an entire month prior to the holiday to further heighten the experience of eating *matza* for the first time at the Seder.

Why are three whole *matzot* placed on the Seder table?

At regular holiday and Sabbath meals two loaves of bread *(challot)* are placed on the table as reminders of the showbreads (shewbreads) displayed in two rows by the Priests in Temple days. On Passover, since bread may not be eaten, two *matzot* are used instead. A third *matza* is added as a reminder of the joyous nature of this holiday of freedom.

Some authorities interpret the use of three *matzot* as representing the three groups in Jewish religious life: Priests, Levites, and Israelites.

A number of talmudic scholars were of the opinion that

when Abraham welcomed the three angels at the door of his tent, it was Passover. And when he asked Sarah to take "three measures of fine meal" and bake cakes, she made three *matzot*. In commemoration of that event, they said, three *matzot* are placed on the Passover table.

According to some authorities, the Gaon of Vilna insisted that only two *matzot* are to be placed on the Seder table.

Why will some Jews eat only *shemura matza* at the Seder?

Shemura matza—also called *matza shemura* or *matza shel mitzva*—means "guarded *matza*."

Unlike ordinary *matza, shemura matza* is guarded from the moment the grain is cut to the moment the *matza* is baked in the oven. To reduce the chances of the *matza* fermenting (fermented food is prohibited on Passover), the *matza* is prepared in moisture-free (or as dry as possible) premises. During the baking process, all activity is carefully supervised so as not to prolong the procedure needlessly, further reducing the possibility of fermentation setting in.

According to the Rabbis of the Talmud (Pesachim 120a), the positive obligation to eat *matza* applies only to the first night of Passover, although it is quite clear that bread and leavened products may not be eaten at any time during the holiday. For this reason, the *matza* selected for consumption at the Seder table is particularly special, and *shemura matza* is the only type very observant Jews use. *Chassidim* eat only *shemura matza* for the duration of the holiday.

Shemura matza is generally made completely by hand in special bakeries not otherwise in operation throughout the year. The cost per pound is, of course, much higher than machine-made *matza*.

Why is a Seder held?

The Seder is a special Passover home service held on the

first night of Passover and repeated on the second night by those who observe the second day of the festival as a full holiday.

The original Passover service (not yet called a Seder) is described in Exodus: a lamb was to be slaughtered and consumed by each family.

For many centuries after the Exodus, until King Josiah of Israel instituted the reforms mentioned in II Kings 23, Passover was not celebrated as prescribed in the Tora. After the establishment of the Second Temple (sixth century B.C.E.), however, the celebration of Passover was revived, and the verse in Exodus (13:8), "And you shall instruct your son [about the meaning of the Exodus]," took on new meaning.

The major celebrations were held in Jerusalem, to which Jews from all over would flock and offer a sacrifice of a Paschal lamb, which they would then eat together with their families. Jews outside of Jerusalem celebrated the holiday by eating a festive meal. In time, ceremonies, symbolic foods, psalms, and songs were added to the celebration, which evolved into the modern Seder.

It is not clear when the first "modern" formal Seder was conducted, but it is believed that Rabbi Gamaliel II, at the end of the first century C.E., may have begun the tradition. It was he who stated, "Anyone who had not said these three words on Passover had not done his duty: *Pesach* [Paschal lamb], *matza* [unleavened bread], *maror* [bitter herbs]." Scholars interpret his statement as meaning that Jews are obligated to eat these three items and to recite the Haggada, in which the symbolism of each is explained.

Why is the family celebration on the first two nights of Passover called a "Seder"?

Seder means "order." The recitation of the Haggada, the

ritual, and the foods that are eaten follow a prescribed order which is outlined in every Passover prayerbook (Haggada).

Why do some Jews hang a piece of *matza* on a wall in their synagogues?

This custom prevails in some Oriental and European communities. The Bible says: "Seven days shalt thou eat unleavened bread . . . to remember the day when thou camest forth out of the land of Egypt *all the days of thy life*" (Deuteronomy 16:3). For the communities mentioned above, the *matza* on the wall is a constant reminder. (See also page 204 about the hanging of *matza* in homes and synagogues.)

Why do Jews in Israel observe only one Seder, while most Jews in the Diaspora observe two?

Since in Israel only the first and last day of Passover are full holidays (the five intervening days are considered half-holidays—*Chol Ha-moed*), a Seder is held only on the first night. However, in the Diaspora most Jews observe the first two days of Passover as full holidays (because of the uncertainty of the calendar) and therefore hold a Seder on each of the first two nights. Reform Jews and some Conservative Jews follow the Israeli practice.

Why does the person leading the Seder tradition-ally recline against a pillow?

The custom of eating in a reclining position, which is of Persian origin, symbolizes freedom and independence. Greek and Roman patricians also followed this practice, and Jews who lived in their midst adopted it as a meaningful expression of their desire to lead a free, unharried existence.

The Mishna (Pesachim 10:1) requires that even the poorest person in Israel must not eat on the first night of Passover unless he reclines.

Why do many Jews who lead a Seder wear a *kittel*?

The long white robe (usually linen) called a *kittel* is the same type of garment traditionally worn at services on Rosh Hashana and Yom Kippur. It is also the same type of garment (a shroud) in which a person is buried and which a groom sometimes wears under the canopy. In the case of Passover it represents release from bondage and the celebration of a life of freedom.

The name for *kittel* in post-talmudic literature is *sarginos*. According to Rashi the word derives from the Latin *serica* or *sericum*, akin to the old French *sarge* and the Middle English *serge,* and refers to a garment of wool or linen.

Why is the Haggada recited at the Seder?

The Haggada as we know it today is a small volume which recounts the dramatic story of the Exodus. It also contains psalms and songs to be recited and sung in celebration of the event. The Haggada was introduced by the Members of the Great Assembly almost 2,500 years ago in order to comply with the biblical verse, "And you shall instruct your son on that day. . ." (Exodus 13:8). The Haggada is basically a book of instruction, particularly for the young.

Why have so many versions of the Haggada been published?

Since the first Haggada appeared in book form in the thirteenth century, more than 3,500 Haggadot (plural) have been published in almost every country where Jews have lived in substantial numbers. Usually, the Hebrew text has been accompanied by a translation into the vernacular of the country, along with notes, comments, and illustrations.

Each new Haggada incorporated alterations in the text, as well as additions and deletions to suit the particular community. The purpose was always to make the message pertinent and meaningful, although at times there were other motivations. The Jews of Yemen, for example, added these words to the *Kiddush:* "He [God] called us a community of saints, a precious vineyard, a pleasant plantation. . . ." Similar passages are found in Haggadot in other countries. Sephardic Jews in Turkey recite in Spanish legends about the Exodus not found in the traditional Haggada. Jews who live in Moslem countries include in their Haggadot legendary comments in Arabic. German and Polish Jews introduced poems into their Haggadot, some of which are now very popular. Two extremely popular songs, "One Only Kid" *(Chad Gadya)* and "Who Knows One?" *(Echad Mi Yodaya),* were adapted in German Haggadot from old, familiar nursery rhymes.

The Haggada as we know it today is the result of centuries of change and development.

Why is a tray of symbolic foods placed at the head of the Seder table?

A Passover tray (Seder tray), which usually has six circular indentations, is placed on the Seder table so that the various symbolic foods can be displayed individually and prominently.

They are pointed to during the reading of the Seder service, and the symbolism of each is explained.

The symbolic foods are:

- *maror* (bitter herbs)
- *karpas* (a vegetable)
- *chazeret* (a second, more bitter vegetable)
- *charoset* (a nut and apple mixture)
- *zeroa* (the shankbone or neck of poultry, roasted)
- *baytza* (a hard-boiled egg, browned in its shell)

Why is *maror* (bitter herbs) set on the Seder tray and served at the Seder meal?

Maror, most often served in the form of horseradish, symbolizes the bitter lot of the Israelites during their enslavement in Egypt. Each Seder participant is offered a small helping of the bitter herbs at two points during the Seder service. First, it is served together with *charoset.* Later, it is served between two pieces of *matza,* in what is referred to as the Hillel's Sandwich.

Why is *karpas* (vegetable) placed on the Seder tray and served during the Seder?

The custom of serving *karpas* dates back to Jerusalem of the first and second centuries, when it was common to begin a formal meal by passing around vegetables as hors d'oeuvres. The vegetable served might be cucumber, lettuce, radish, parsley, potato, or any other type in season. The vegetable is dipped in salt water before being eaten. (See pages 205 and 206 for the significance of the salt water.)

Why is the vegetable called *chazeret* placed on the Seder tray?

Chazeret (also pronounced *chazeres*) carries the same symbolism as the *maror* (bitter herbs) that is placed in one of the six compartments of the Seder tray. The vegetable selected for the *chazeret* is cucumber, watercress, radish, or any other vegetable that tends to become bitter.

The use of *chazeret* has been related to the biblical verse, "They shall eat it [the Paschal lamb] with unleavened bread and bitter herbs" (Numbers 9:11). It has been explained that since the Book of Numbers speaks of herbs in the plural *(merorim)*, this vegetable, *chazeret,* was included on the Seder tray in addition to the *maror* vegetable.

Not all authorities considered it mandatory to use *chazeret* at the Seder meal. We know that Rabbi Isaac Luria, the sixteenth-century mystic (also known as the Ari, which is an acronym for his name, ha-**A**shkenazi **R**abbi **I**saac), did use *chazeret* at his Seder table. But we also know that the equally famous eighteenth-century scholar Rabbi Elijah of Vilna, Lithuania (better known as the Vilna Gaon), did not use *chazeret*. Practically all Seder trays manufactured today have six compartments (indentations), one reserved for *chazeret*.

Why is *charoset* placed on the Seder tray and served at the Seder meal?

Charoset (also pronounced *charoses*) is a mixture of chopped apple, walnuts, and cinnamon, moistened with wine. Ground ginger is sometimes added. *Charoset* is symbolic of the mortar the Children of Israel were compelled to make for their Egyptian taskmaster during their period of enslavement in Egypt. Aside from the token amount placed on the Seder tray, a small amount is served together with the bitter herbs *(maror)* to reduce the bitter taste of the horseradish (Pesachim 10:3).

Not all Jews prepare *charoset* in the same manner. Heinrich Heine, in his early nineteenth-century novelette *The Rabbi of Bacherach,* describes the *charoset* prepared in a German household as consisting of raisins, cinnamon, and nuts. In the Mishna (the first portion of the Talmud) *charoset* is described as consisting of nuts and fruits, pounded together and mixed with vinegar.

Why is a shankbone *(zeroa)* placed on the Seder tray?

The shankbone (*zeroa* in Hebrew) is a reminder of "the mighty arm" of God, as the Bible describes it, which encouraged Pharaoh to release the Children of Israel from bondage, It is also symbolic of the Paschal lamb offered as the Passover sacrifice in Temple days. In some households a meat bone is roasted then placed on the Seder tray. In other households the neck of a chicken or some other fowl is used instead.

Why is a roasted hard-boiled egg *(baytza)* placed on the Seder tray?

The egg is symbolic of the regular festival sacrifice brought in days when the Temple stood in Jerusalem. On Passover, in addition to this regular sacrifice (*Korban Chagiga* in Hebrew), the Paschal lamb was offered as a second sacrifice.

Some authorities have interpreted the roasted egg as being a symbol of mourning for the loss of the two Temples that once stood in Jerusalem. (The first was destroyed by the Babylonians in 586 B.C.E., the second by the Romans in 70 C.E.) With the Temples destroyed, sacrifices could no longer be offered. The egg symbolized this loss and traditionally became the food of mourners.

In some Middle Eastern communities, eggs are very popular on Passover. Kurdish Jews and Libyan Jews, in particular, eat large quantities of eggs at the Seder.

Why are four cups of wine served during the Seder?

Traditionally, at regular Sabbath and festival meals two cups of wine are served. One is drunk after the recital of the *Kiddush* at the beginning of the meal; the other is filled and held aloft while the *Grace After Meals* is recited. Since Passover, the Festival of Freedom, is so joyous and memorable a holiday, two additional cups of wine are served at the Seder. One of these two cups (the second Seder cup) is consumed after the story of the Haggada has been recited, immediately before the meal is served. The second additional cup (the fourth Seder cup) is consumed at the conclusion of the service, just before the closing song and hymns are sung.

Additional explanations have been offered for the custom of drinking four cups of wine at the Seder. The most popular states that the four cups are drunk because the Bible uses four different verbs in describing the drama of Redemption from slavery in Egypt. The four references to the Redemption can be found in the Book of Exodus:

1. I will *bring* you out of Egypt.
2. I will *deliver* you from their bondage.
3. I will *redeem* you with an outstretched arm.
4. I will *take* you to Me for a people.

Why is red rather than white wine served during the Seder meal?

Red wine is traditionally served at the Seder table because the Talmud considers red wine superior to white wine. Beginning in the Middle Ages, when non-Jews noticed that Jews used red wine during Passover, rumors spread that Jews mixed the blood of Christian children into their wine.

These blood-libel accusations, although proven to be unfounded, persisted even into the twentieth century. In 1928, in the Upstate New York town of Messina, such an accusation was filed. The rabbi of the town was questioned when a little Christian girl happened to disappear at Passover time. The girl was found unharmed the next day, and the town mayor apologized publicly. Instances such as this encouraged the use of white wine at the Seder, and several rabbinic authorities even forbade the use of red wine. However, the use of red wine still predominates.

Why is wine spilled from the cup when the Ten Plagues is recited?

Many early societies believed that evil spirits could be bribed with wine. Accordingly, some wine was always spilled from the cup before any of the wine in that cup was drunk.

At the Passover Seder a small amount of wine is traditionally removed from the cup when the name of each of the Ten Plagues is recited. It is explained as an expression of sorrow for the pain suffered by the Egyptians from each plague.

In some households, instead of spilling the wine directly from the goblet into a saucer, the small finger is dipped into the wine, and a drop at a time is tapped into the saucer. The use of the finger is said to be a reminder of the verse in Exodus (8:15) in which Pharaoh's magicians, unable to duplicate the miracles performed by Moses, had to admit that it was the "finger of God" that executed these miracles that in the end made the Exodus possible.

In most households, instead of using one's finger, the end

of a spoon is used to remove a small amount of wine from the goblet.

Why is a piece of *matza*, called the *afikomon*, "stolen" by children and hidden until it is "ransomed"?

During the early part of the Seder service, a piece of the middle *matza* is placed in a napkin or a bag. This *matza,* called the *afikomon,* is distributed to all Seder participants after the meal and is then eaten as a dessert. (*Afikomo*n is a Greek word meaning "dessert.")

The custom of setting aside a piece of *matza* was instituted 700 years ago. To make the Seder more exciting for children, youngsters were allowed to "steal" and hide the *afikomon.* Since the Seder could not continue until a piece of the *afikomon* was eaten by everyone, the leader of the Seder had to search for it. If he could not find it, he would offer a gift to the children, and they would fetch the *afikomon* from its hiding place.

In some families the leader hides the *afikomon,* and the children receive a gift if they find it.

When the *afikomon* is finally returned, the leader of the Seder breaks it into small pieces, which he shares with everyone at the table. The Seder then continues with the recitation of *Grace After Meals.*

In the Middle Ages many superstitious people believed that the *afikomon* had the power to drive off evil spirits. They would, therefore, hang a piece of the leftover *afikomon* in their homes and in their synagogues.

Jews in Kurdistan used to put pieces of the leftover *afikomon* in their rice, flour, and salt canisters. The piece of *matza,* they believed, would bring them luck and would insure that their food containers would not be empty throughout the year.

Why do some Jews, particularly those from North Africa, save a piece of the *afikomon* and carry it with them whenever they make a journal?

To many Jews from North Africa, particularly Morocco, the piece of *matza (afikomon)* served immediately before the recitation of *Grace After Meals* is a safeguard against evil spirits. Because they believe the *afikomon* has the power to calm the sea, they carry a piece with them whenever on a journey. When ocean waters become stormy, they throw the piece of *afikomon* into the water.

Why are hands washed at the Seder table?

According to ancient practice recorded in the Talmud, hands are washed before food is dipped into a liquid or sauce. Since during the Seder each participant dips the *karpas* (vegetable) into salt water, it was customary for each person to first wash his hands. Although this practice has fallen into general disuse, it remains part of the Seder ritual. A pitcher of water is carried around the table by the mistress of the house, and water is poured onto the hands of each participant. In some households the participants leave the table to wash their hands.

Why is salt water placed on the Seder table?

In Jerusalem of the first and second centuries it was customary at mealtime to dip a vegetable (an hors d'oeuvre) in salt water. This was probably done partially for health reasons: salt was known to have antiseptic as well as seasoning value. Salt was used in connection with sacrifices because of its action as a preservative: the meat would stay fresh longer if it had been sprinkled with salt.

A popular explanation for the use of salt water at the Seder table connects the practice with the many tears (salty) which were shed by the Israelites during their years of bondage in Egypt.

At the Seder, salt water is used first as a dip for the *karpas*. Later, immediately before the meal, a hard-boiled egg is dipped in the water by all participants. The egg is a reminder of the holiday sacrifice (*Korban Chagiga*) brought in Temple days.

In some households today a small dish of salt water (or vinegar) is placed on the Seder tray alongside the six other symbolic foods.

Why is the fourth of the Four Questions in the Haggada different today from what it was originally?

The Four Questions asked at the Seder are mentioned in the Talmud (Mishna Pesachim 10:4). Originally, the fourth question did not ask, "Why do we recline tonight?" The fourth question read, "On all other nights we eat meat which has been roasted, stewed, or boiled, but on this night we eat only roasted meat."

After the Temple was destroyed (70 C.E.) and the sacrificial system abandoned, the question referring to roasted meat was eliminated and the question about reclining was substituted. The new question was introduced because reclining symbolizes freedom, the motif of the Passover Seder.

Why is a special goblet, the Cup of Elijah, placed on the Seder table?

After the *Grace After Meals* has been recited, a goblet that has become known as the Cup of Elijah is filled with wine. Elijah was the great prophet of Israel who dominated the Palestinian scene about twenty-eight centuries ago. He was the conscience of Israel in the days of sinful King Ahab and his wicked wife, Queen Jezebel.

In time, the name and person of Elijah became synonymous in Judaism with the Messianic Age. According to tradition, Elijah did not die: he ascended to heaven in a chariot and vanished. His return has been anticipated by generations of Jews ever since.

Elijah's return, some Jews believe, will mark the advent of an age of harmony, peace, and understanding among all peoples and nations. The cup of wine placed on the Seder table symbolizes that Elijah would be a welcome guest.

Why is Elijah called "Elijah the Tishbite"?

Elijah was a wise, courageous, and dedicated prophet, unafraid to defy even royalty—especially King Ahab and Queen Jezebel.

Elijah was known by several names. He was called Elijah the Gileadite because he lived in Transjordanic Gilead. But he was not a citizen of the area. He belonged to the class of tolerated half-citizens called *toshavim,* "dwellers." Hence, the name "Tishbi" or "Tishbite" was applied to him.

Why is the front door opened for Elijah during the Seder?

The opening of the front door expresses the willingness and readiness of the Seder participants to bring the Messianic Age into their lives. It reflects their belief that the Messianic Age might come at any time.

Why is the *Omer* counted?

The counting of the *Omer* seems to have been introduced to establish a connection between Passover and Shavuot—holidays separated by seven full weeks. Passover marked the beginning of the grain harvest. The first crop (barley) was cut on Passover, and a small amount (an *omer*) was brought to the Temple as a sacrifice on the second day of the holiday. For the next forty-nine days, each day was marked off (counted), and this period became known as *Sefira* ("the counting"). The Bible (Leviticus 23:15-16) describes it in this way:

> And from the day on which you bring the sheaf offering—the day after the Sabbath ["the Sabbath" meaning the holiday of Passover, and "the day after" meaning the second day of the holiday]—you shall count off seven weeks until the day after the seventh week [Shavuot].

The fiftieth day was Shavuot, on which the next crop (wheat) was harvested and brought to the Temple as a sacrifice.

According to the twelfth-century philosopher Moses Maimonides, the importance of counting the days between the exodus from Egypt and the anniversary of the receiving of the Law at Mount Sinai is to indicate that release from bondage is not an end in itself, that liberty without law is a doubtful blessing.

Why are weddings banned during the *Sefira* period (between Passover and Shavuot)?

According to tradition, students of Rabbi Akiba—who supported (and probably fought with) Bar Kochba, the leader of the rebellion against Rome in 135 C.E.—suffered the effects of a plague. Details are not known, but it is presumed that the plague lasted for thirty-three days. On the thirty-third day (Lag B'Omer) relief came.

The tradition is confused, and there are varying practices as to which thirty-three days during the forty-nine day counting period *(Sefira)* between Passover and Shavuot should be considered days of semimourning, days on which weddings should not be held. (See pages 32, 33, and 208 for days on which weddings are permitted and prohibited.)

Why is a Paschal lamb no longer offered on Passover, as prescribed in the Bible?

The practice of sacrificing animals was in vogue only while the Temple in Jerusalem was in existence. With its destruction by the Romans in 70 C.E., the sacrificial system came to an end, and prayer services (which had been conducted even while the Temple still existed) replaced it completely.

Why is *Chad Gadya* such a popular Seder song?

Aside from the beautiful melodies created for this popular song with which the Seder concludes, the message it carries is extremely significant.

Composed in Aramaic in nursery-rhyme style, *Chad Gadya* was adapted from a popular German ballad and was introduced into the Haggada by German Jews. In fanciful form and with great simplicity it tells the story of the Jewish people: a father bought a little goat for two *zuzim,* two small coins. And then a cat came along and devoured the goat; a dog came along and bit the cat; a stick came along and beat the dog; etc.

So it was with the Jewish people. One nation after another tried to conquer it, but unsuccessfully. The message is: evil designs may be planned and even carried out, but in the end God conquers all, and justice prevails.

Why do the *challot* served on the first Sabbath after Passover sometimes have a key-shaped decoration on top?

The custom probably began in Volhynia, in the Russian Ukraine, where dough in the shape of a key was placed on the first *challot* served after Passover. The key represented the key to the "gate of release" from the bondage of Egypt. According to tradition, the "gate of release" can be opened for one month after the festival.

Why is Pesach Sheni observed?

The Bible (Numbers 9:9-14) makes provision for those who were unable to offer the Paschal lamb on the fourteenth of Nissan by allowing them to do so one month later, on the fourteenth of Iyyar. Some people could not observe the holiday in the month of Nissan because they were in a state of ritual impurity (having been in contact with the dead), others because they were too far from the sanctuary to arrive in time for the holiday. In either case, they could not offer the Paschal lamb at the appointed time, and they fulfilled their obligation on Pesach Sheni ("Second Passover"), sometimes referred to as "Minor Passover."

Most of the ritualistic restrictions of the first Passover do not apply to Pesach Sheni. According to the Mishna (Pesachim 9:3) a person observing Pesach Sheni is required to eat *matza* but is not obligated to rid his house of all *chametz*.

Some Jews today still commemorate Pesach Sheni by eating *matza* on the fourteenth of Iyyar as a reminder of the Exodus. The only change in the liturgy is the omission of *Tachanun*.

Because more than one Passover is mentioned in the Bible, the tractate of the Talmud that deals with Passover laws is called Pesachim (plural), not Pesach (singular).

Chapter 10

Shavuot

INTRODUCTION

Shavuot (also pronounced Shavuos) is one of the three Pilgrim Festivals, the others being Passover and Sukkot. In Temple times, the Pilgrim Festivals were celebrated in Jerusalem, to which Jews from all parts of Palestine and from nearby countries journeyed specifically to commemorate the holidays.

Shavuot is known by many names, including the Feast of Weeks (Chag Ha-shavuot), the Festival of First Fruits (Chag Ha-bikurim), and the Harvest Festival (Chag Ha-katzir). Each of these names reflects the agricultural nature of the holiday, which was celebrated in late spring, when the new wheat crop was harvested, by offering a special sacrifice of thanksgiving in the Temple.

Shavuot falls on the sixth of Sivan, seven weeks and one day after the second day of Passover. Thus, it has become closely linked to Passover. The Talmud considers Shavuot a concluding holiday to Passover and even refers to it by the name Atzeret, meaning "conclusion."

The Bible in no way associates the holiday of Shavuot with God's Revelation on Mount Sinai. The Talmud, however, does make an association between the two. Apparently, the connection was established when scholars, following the biblical account, calculated that the dates of the agricultural festival of Shavuot and the events at Mount Sinai coincided.

When the association was established between Shavuot and the Revelation on Mount Sinai, the original agricultural holiday became a time for celebrating the Tora. Tora study sessions were held all through the night of the holiday, and the holiday was highlighted as a time for Jewish affirmation.

At Shavuot synagogue services today, the Book of Ruth is recited. (Ruth is the Moabite woman whose loyalty to Judaism has become proverbial.) At the end of the nineteenth century, Reform Judaism introduced the Confirmation ceremony into the Shavuot service. Today, in Reform, Conservative, and even some Orthodox congregations, this is a time when girls and boys, generally thirteen to sixteen years of age, confirm their allegiance to the Jewish way of life.

Why is Shavuot celebrated?

In the Bible there are several references to the holiday we call Shavuot or Pentecost, which is celebrated on the sixth day of the Hebrew month of Sivan (May-June).

In Exodus 23:16, the Israelites are commanded to observe the "Feast of the Harvest, the first fruits of your labors which thou sowest in the field." This festival is referred to again, in Exodus 34:22, as the Feast of Weeks, the time when the first "fruits" of the wheat crop were harvested. In the Book of Numbers (28:26), it is mentioned as the Feast of Weeks and the Festival of First Fruits (Chag Ha-bikurim). And Deuteronomy 16:12 gives as the reason for its observance, "You shall remember that you were once slaves in Egypt."

According to the description of the holiday in the Mishna

(Bikurim 3), the village people of Palestine would first assemble in the largest town of their district, bringing with them the first ripe fruits of their fields. They would then proceed on foot to the Temple in Jerusalem, where they would leave their offering and be welcomed with song by the Levites. The Bible does not connect Shavuot with the giving of the Tora on Mount Sinai.

Why is Shavuot called "Chag Ha-bikurim"?

"Chag Ha-bikurim" (Festival of First Fruits) is the name by which the Shavuot holiday is called in Numbers 28:26. The new wheat crop was harvested at this time of year, and the flour made from the first cuttings (the first fruits) was brought to the Priest as a meal offering.

Why is Shavuot called "Chag Ha-katzir"?

Shavuot, the festival observed when the first fruits of the wheat harvest were brought as a sacrifice, is referred to in the Bible (Exodus 23:16) as "Chag Ha-katzir." "Chag Ha-katzir" literally means "harvest festival." A special sacrifice of two loaves of bread baked from the new crop was offered in the Temple.

Why is Shavuot associated with the Revelation at Mount Sinai?

The earliest reference to Shavuot as "the time of the giving of the Tora [Zeman Mattan Toratenu]" is in the Talmud. The third-century C.E. scholar Rabbi Eleazar said that all authorities agree on the necessity of rejoicing with good food and wine on Atzeret (the talmudic name for Shavuot) because on that day the Tora was given to Israel (Pesachim 68b).

Shavuot became increasingly associated with the Revelation at Mount Sinai because as a purely agricultural holiday it had lost its significance. The Jews of Palestine had become an urban people, and to keep the holiday alive it became necessary to associate the Shavuot holiday with an historical event. The event chosen was the Revelation because it occurred about the same time of year that the agricultural festival of Shavuot was celebrated.

Why is Shavuot closely associated with Passover?

The word *shavuot* is the plural form of the Hebrew word *shavua,* meaning "week." The Shavuot holiday, also called the Feast of Weeks, falls seven weeks after the first day of Passover.

The counting *(Sefira)* of seven full weeks—day by day for 49 days—begins on the second night of Passover, at the second Seder. On the fiftieth day—on the sixth of Sivan—Shavuot is celebrated. So, in actuality, Shavuot is the end of the Passover season. For this reason, Shavuot is also called "Atzeret Shel Pesach," meaning "the closing season of the Passover festival" (Pesachim 42b).

Why are the three days before Shavuot special days in the Jewish calendar?

The three days preceding Shavuot are called "Shloshet Yemay Hagbala," meaning "the three days of bounds." These days, mentioned in the Bible (Exodus 19:10-13), commemorate the three days of preparation before Moses received the Ten Commandments on Mount Sinai. Boundaries were delineated, and the people were not permitted to ascend the mountain or even approach its borders.

Today, Shloshet Yemay Hagbala is observed only in communities where weddings are banned during *Sefira.* In these communities, weddings are permitted during the three days preceding Shavuot.

Why is the day after Rosh Chodesh Sivan called "Yom Ha-meyuchas"?

Rosh Chodesh Sivan, like the first day of every Jewish month, is a semiholiday. Shavuot begins on the sixth of the month, and the days in between were also designated as semiholidays. Three of these days—the third, fourth, and fifth—were special days known as "Shloshet Yemay Hagbala" (see previous question), which left only the second day of Sivan unaccounted for. This day was therefore also declared to be a semiholiday, and it became known as "Yom Ha-meyuchas," meaning "the choice day," because it was discovered that Yom Kippur always falls on the same day of the week as this second day of the month of Sivan.

No special observance is connected with this day.

Why does the Talmud call Shavuot only by the name "Atzeret"?

The word *atzeret* means "assembly," and in the Talmud Atzeret is the only name by which the Shavuot holiday is called. The Rabbis of the Talmud considered Shavuot the concluding day of the Passover holiday, which was to be celebrated as a day of "solemn assembly" and "holy convocation." They considered the relationship of Shavuot to Passover to be the same as that of Shemini Atzeret to Sukkot. Shemini Atzeret was considered the conclusion of Sukkot; Shavuot was considered the conclusion of Passover.

Why is Shavuot called "Pentecost"?

Pentecost is a Greek word meaning "the holiday of fifty days." Shavuot occurs on the fiftieth day after the first day of Passover.

Why do some people stay up all night long on the night before Shavuot?

The kabbalists were first to introduce the practice of spending the night before Shavuot in prayer and study so as to be prepared spiritually for the holiday commemorating the giving of the Tora to the Jewish people. The practice is based on an old legend stating that thunder and lightning kept the Children of Israel awake during the time Moses was on Mount Sinai waiting to receive the Tora.

The custom of staying awake is called *Tikkun Shavuot,* meaning "preparing [perfecting oneself] for Shavuot." Among the material studied during the night are selections from the Bible, Talmud, and *Zohar,* in addition to various prayers and *piyyutim* (religious poetry).

Why was there objection to the reading of the Ten Commandments on Shavuot?

The Tora reading for the first day of Shavuot includes the verses in the Book of Exodus (20:2-14) which enumerate the Ten Commandments. This selection was read daily in the Temple, but after the Temple was destroyed, the Rabbis discouraged its recitation in the synagogue lest some people claim that only these commandments, not the whole Tora, were given to Moses on Mount Sinai (Berachot 12a).

Although the custom today is to rise when the Ten Commandments are read from the Tora, during the Middle Ages there were some protests against this practice by those who feared that undue importance would be given the commandments.

Why is the Ten Commandments called "the Decalogue"?

Decalogue is a Greek word meaning "ten words." The

Ten Commandments, in Exodus 20:1, opens with "And God spoke these words [Ten Commandments], saying. ... ."

Why is Shavuot observed in Israel for one day, and in the Diaspora for two?

The Bible (Leviticus 23:15-16) describes Shavuot as a one-day holiday. As with other holidays, because of the uncertainty of the calendar communities outside of Israel traditionally observe the holiday for one extra day. (See page 185.) However, Reform congregations and some Conservative ones follow the Israeli practice.

There is an opinion that Shavuot was always observed as a two-day holiday. This is based on the difference of opinion expressed in the Talmud (Shabbat 86b) as to whether the Tora was given to Israel on the sixth or seventh day of Sivan. Proof is adduced from the fact that the holiday is referred to as *Zeman Mattan Toratenu*, the "time of the giving of our Tora," and not as the "day" of the giving of the Tora.

Why is the Book of Ruth read in the synagogue on Shavuot?

Several reasons are given for the custom of reading the Book of Ruth on Shavuot:

1. The story of Ruth and Boaz takes place in the spring, at harvest time, which is when Shavuot falls.

2. Ruth was the ancestor of King David, and according to a tradition mentioned in the Talmud, David was born and died on Shavuot.

3. Since Ruth expressed her loyalty to the Tora by aligning herself with Judaism, it is proper to the read the story of her life on Shavuot, the holiday of the Tora.

Why is *Akdamut* recited on Shavuot?

Akdamut is the name of an Aramaic hymn read in the synagogue on Shavuot. Composed by Meir ben Isaac Nehorai of Orléans, France, in the eleventh century, it found a place in the liturgy of the day because, in keeping with the spirit of the holiday, it speaks, among other things, of God's love for Israel and of Israel's faithfulness to the Tora.

Why was Shavuot selected as the holiday on which the Confirmation ceremony is to be held?

The Shavuot holiday has long been associated with Tora study and the confirmation of one's loyalty to Judaism. In many Eastern European communities it was customary to introduce very young children (three to five years of age) to a Hebrew school or *yeshiva* on Shavuot. The children were then given cakes, honey, and sweets "that the Tora might be sweet on his lips."

The Reform movement introduced Confirmation for older children (thirteen to sixteen years of age). Most Conservative and some Orthodox congregations have adopted the ceremony. At the Shavuot service these boys and girls confirm their loyalty to Judaism.

Why does the *challa* served on Shavuot have a ladder design on top?

The Shavuot *challa* is shaped round in some communities and is elongated in others. A ladder design is placed on top of the bread to commemorate the giving of the Tora on Mount Sinai. The ladder design was chosen because the numerical value of the Hebrew word for "Sinai" is the same (130) as that of the Hebrew word for "ladder" *(sulam)*. The ladder symbolizes the ascent of Moses to heaven to receive the Ten Commandments.

Why are triangular-shaped dumplings *(kreplach)* served on Shavuot?

Three is a prominent number in Jewish tradition. There are three patriarchs (Abraham, Isaac, Jacob), three parts to the Bible (Tora, Prophets, Holy Writings), and three types of Jews *(Kohanim,* Levites, Israelites). Also, the Tora was given to the Israelites in the third month (Sivan) through Moses, the third child of his parents. Finding so many associations between the number three and the personalities and events connected with the giving of the Tora, some communities follow the custom of eating three-sided (triangular) cheese-filled or meat-filled *kreplach* on Shavuot.

Why are cheese products eaten on Shavuot?

The eating of cheese products on Shavuot has been variously explained. One explanation is that dairy foods (and honey) should be eaten on the day the Tora was received on Mount Sinai because the words in the Song of Songs, "honey and milk under thy lips" (4:11), imply that, like milk products and honey, the words of the Tora are pleasant and good for our spirits.

Another explanation suggests that the basis for this custom is to be found in Exodus 23:19: "The choicest first-fruits shalt thou bring to the House of the Lord. Thou shalt not seethe [cook] a kid in its mother's milk." The "first-fruits" in the first part of the verse refers to the Shavuot holiday. The second part of the verse, which mentions meat (a kid) and milk, is taken to mean that the two main dishes to be served at the holiday meal are to be first a dairy dish, followed later by a meat dish.

A third explanation for the tradition of eating dairy foods on Shavuot is based on a legend which maintains that when the Israelites reached their homes after receiving the Tora at Mount Sinai, they had little time to prepare a meat meal (since a good deal of time is needed for the kosher slaughtering of an animal). Instead, they hastily put together a dairy meal, which could be more quickly prepared.

Why are two cheese *blintzes* traditionally served on Shavuot?

The two *blintzes* represent the two tablets of the Ten Commandments. Cheese is traditionally eaten on Shavuot, as explained above.

Why is the synagogue decorated with greenery on Shavuot?

According to an ancient tradition, Mount Sinai was once a green mountain with trees and shrubs. This tradition led to the custom of decorating the synagogue with greenery, a practice disapproved of by some early authorities who considered it an imitation of certain Church rites and Christian home rites (Christmas trees, wreaths, etc.).

Despite this initial dissapproval, on Shavuot synagogues and homes are decorated with plants, flowers, and branches of trees, thus emphasizing the agricultural beginnings of the holiday.

Chapter 11

The High Holidays

INTRODUCTION

Unlike the other major Jewish holidays, the High Holidays—Rosh Hashana and Yom Kippur—are not related to historical events. Nor are they joyous holidays. The Days of Awe, as they have come to be called, are purely religious holidays which celebrate God's role as Master of the universe. They emphasize morality, self-examination, spirituality, and holiness.

Actually, the Days of Awe are much more than the ten-day period from Rosh Hashana to Yom Kippur. They commence a full month before Rosh Hashana with the beginning of the month of Elul.

In the synagogue, every Sabbath before the coming of the New Moon is a special Sabbath. But the Sabbath before the New Moon of Elul is very special, for from that day on, at every weekday morning service, the blasts of the *shofar* reverberate in the synagogue, reminding Jews that the most awesome holidays in the Jewish calendar are approaching.

Rosh Hashana (the New Year) is celebrated the world over for two days, on the first and second day of the month of Tishri (generally during September). (An exception: most Reform congregations celebrate the holiday for only one day, on the first of Tishri.) Yom Kippur (the Day of Atonement) falls on the tenth day of Tishri and is observed by everyone from sundown to sundown as a day of fasting and prayer.

Rosh Hashana, in its lengthy morning services (from two to seven hours, depending on the congregation), stresses the concept of "return to God," who in His mercy is willing to receive the penitent, forgive his sins, and offer him an opportunity to begin the New Year with a clean slate. According to Jewish tradition, God's decision is not made in haste.

The gates of repentance remain open until the Day of Atonement, at which time the final decree is established: "Who will live and who will die; who will be serene and who will be disturbed; who will be poor and who will be rich; who will be humbled and who will be exalted."

The solemnity of Yom Kippur and its message of renewal through repentance has affected the lives of many people. Perhaps most notable are the Catholic Aimé Palli`ere, who turned to Judaism after attending a Yom Kippur afternoon service, and the brilliant young Jew Franz Rosenzweig, who was about to abandon Judaism but had a change of heart after spending one Yom Kippur day in a small Orthodox synagogue in Berlin.

Yom Kippur is popularly considered the most sacred day in the Jewish calendar, although in the Jewish legal system the Sabbath surpasses it in importance. Its five services, beginning with the *Kol Nidre* service and ending twenty-four hours later with the *Neila* service, bring to an end the Days of Awe. After the *Neila* ("the closing of the gate") service, the *shofar* is sounded and the congregation leaves to face another year.

Why is there more than one New Year in the Jewish calendar?

Although Rosh Hashana literally means "head of the year" or "beginning of the year," the *civil* calendar year for the early Jewish nation actually began with the month of Nissan (March-April), when the first crops were harvested, that is, at Passover time. The month of Tishri, when the High Holidays fall, was the beginning of the Jewish *religious* year, although the Bible refers to it as the seventh month of the year.

There are other New Years in Jewish tradition listed in the Talmud (Rosh Hashana 1:1). The Rabbis acknowledged four beginnings of the year relating to different events:

1. the first of Nissan for royalty (dating of royal events)
2. the first of Tishri for agriculture (the beginning of the harvest season) and in commemoration of Creation
3. the first of Elul for the tithing of cattle
4. the first (but according to Bet Hillel, the fifteenth) of Shevat as the New Year for Trees

Why is Rosh Hashana observed for more days than the Bible calls for?

The Bible prescribes that Rosh Hashana be observed for one day, on the first of Tishri. (Rosh Hashana is the only holiday that is celebrated on the New Moon—that is, the first of the month.)

In early centuries, the testimony of witnesses was used to determine the official date of arrival of the New Moon, and then messengers were sent forth to notify outlying communities. If the witnesses were to arrive too late for the messengers to be sent out to notify the distant communities on time, those living far from Jerusalem would miss the correct day of observance of the holiday. In order to protect against this, Rosh Hashana was made a two-day holiday, and the two days were considered one long day (*yoma arichta*).

Why are the High Holidays called "Days of Awe" (*Yamim Nora'im*)?

According to the Talmud (Rosh Hashana 16a), all man's actions of the past year are judged by God on Rosh Hashana, and on Yom Kippur judgment is rendered. For religious Jews these became awesome days, *Yamim Nora'im.*

Why are special midnight services *(Selichot)* held on the Saturday before Rosh Hashana?

The *Selichot* are pentitential prayers (*Selicha* is the singular form) that are recited on many occasions during and before the High Holidays. Midnight was one of the times selected for recitation of such prayers because the psalmist wrote: "At midnight I will rise to give thanks unto Thee" (Psalms 119:62).

The midnight *Selichot* service is generally held on the Saturday night preceding Rosh Hashana, unless Rosh Hashana falls on the Monday or Tuesday following the Saturday night. In that case, the midnight *Selichot* service is held one week earlier on Saturday night.

Why is the *shofar* blown during the month of Elul?

Originally, the blowing of the *shofar* was a Temple ritual. It later became a synagogue ritual. The custom of blowing the *shofar* during the month of Elul began in the Middle Ages.

According to one tradition, on the first day of Elul, a month before Rosh Hashana, Moses climbed to the top of Mount Sinai to receive the Ten Commandments for the second time. He blew the *shofar* as a reminder to his fellow Jews not to sin, not to build another Golden Calf (as they had when Moses received the first set of Ten Commandments on the mountaintop). From that time on, the *shofar,* which until then had been blown only on the first day of Elul, was blown each day for the entire month of Elul to remind everyone that the Days of Awe are approaching and that they must take stock of their lives and improve their conduct.

Why is the *shofar* blown on Rosh Hashana?

The *shofar* is a natural wind instrument, one of the oldest known to the world. In earliest times the *shofar* was used by Jews as a musical instrument. Its most important uses, as described in the Bible, were to intimidate the enemy, to declare war, and to call the populace to assembly.

Originally the *shofar* was blown to herald the beginning of each month (the New Moon). On those occasions short blasts were sounded. But on the New Moon of the seventh month (Tishri) long alarm blasts were sounded. The Bible (Leviticus 23:14) states the reason for the long blasts by explaining that the New Moon of the seventh month marked the beginning of a special period—a period of holy convocation. During that month major Jewish holidays (Rosh Hashana, Yom Kippur, Sukkot) were celebrated.

In later times other reasons were advanced for the blowing of the *shofar*. To Philo, the prominent first-century Jewish philosopher, the *shofar* was a reminder of the giving of the Tora, as well as the instrument used in wartime to signal when the army should advance or retreat.

The Talmud advances a more mystical interpretation. It states that the *shofar* is blown in order to confuse Satan and thus prevent him from bringing any charges against Jews before God on the Day of Judgment. When Satan hears the *shofar* blown so loud and so often (according to tradition it is blown every morning during the month preceding the holiday, to be followed by 100 blasts on Rosh Hashana proper), he will believe that the Messiah has arrived and that his influence and power over God will have come to an end.

In recent times the *shofar* was blown when Israeli troops restored Jewish sovereignty over ancient Jerusalem after the Six-Day War of 1967.

Why are Rosh Hashana and Yom Kippur celebrated?

Rosh Hashana, the Jewish New Year, and Yom Kippur, the Day of Atonement, are purely religious holidays. Both are called "holy convocations." They emphasize spirituality, morality, and holiness, and unlike other holidays are not tied to national historic events. They celebrate God's role as King of the universe and Judge of all man's actions.

The Talmud (Rosh Hashana 16b) quotes Rabbi Jochanan's summary of this period in these words:

> Three books are opened on Rosh Hashana:
>
> • The Book of Life of the Wicked
> • The Book of Life of the Righteous
> • The Book of Life of Those In Between

The righteous are immediately promised a good life in the future. The wicked are immediately condemned to death. Judgment of those in between is deferred until Yom Kippur, when a final decision is made as to which category they are to be assigned.

Why is Tishri, the month in which Rosh Hashana is celebrated, not considered the first month of the year in the Bible?

Tishri was the beginning of the New Year in ancient Palestine because it came at a time when all crops of the previous year had been harvested. But it was not the first or most important month of the year. It is called "the seventh month" in the Bible, and Nissan, the month in which Passover—the Festival of Freedom—occurs is the first month. (See also page 222.)

Why is Rosh Hashana celebrated by some Jews for one day and by others for two?

Although in the Bible (Leviticus 23:24) Rosh Hashana is a one-day holiday to be celebrated on the first day of the Hebrew month of Tishri, Orthodox and Conservative Jews everywhere (including Israel) celebrate it for two days, while many Reform congregations observe it for one day.

The change from a one-day to a two-day holiday occurred when it became evident that the precise hour of the appearance of the New Moon for the month of Tishri might not always be ascertained. If clouds filled the sky, there might be no witnesses to the arrival of the New Moon. Therefore, to be certain that Rosh Hashana could be celebrated on the correct day, the holiday was extended from a one-day holiday to a two-day holiday for Jews in Palestine and elsewhere, and the chance for error was decreased. (Yom Kippur was always a one-day holiday because it would be a terrible imposition to expect people to fast for two days.)

Reform Jews believe that doubts about the certainty of the calendar no longer exist today, and by and large they have retained the biblical practice of observing Rosh Hashana as a one-day holiday.

Why does the first day of Rosh Hashana never fall on a Wednesday, Friday, or Sunday?

When the calendar was finally issued by Hillel II in 359 C.E. (see Introduction), it was arranged so that the holidays would not interfere with the observance of the Sabbath and so that the Sabbath would not interfere with holiday observances.

If Rosh Hashana (1 Tishri) were to fall on a Wednesday, Yom Kippur (10 Tishri) would fall on a Friday. If Yom Kippur were to fall on a Friday, that would make it impossible for Jews to prepare for the Sabbath.

If Rosh Hashana were to fall on a Friday, Yom Kippur would fall on a Sunday, which would allow no time for Jews observing the Sabbath to prepare for Yom Kippur, which would begin immediately after the Sabbath.

Rosh Hashana never falls on a Sunday because that would mean that Hoshana Rabba (the last day of Sukkot, would always falls on 21 Tishri) would fall on a Saturday which would not be desirable.

In talmudic times Hoshana Rabba was regarded as a day much like Yom Kippur. It brought to an end the long holiday period beginning with Rosh Hashana, and was considered to be the one final opportunity to reverse an unfavorable decree issued against the individual on the High Holidays. If Hoshana Rabba were to fall on the Sabbath, this would interfere with the ceremony of beating a bunch of *hoshanot* (willows) during the synagogue services, an action forbidden on the Sabbath. Beating the willows was a way of expressing guilt and remorse, similar to the *malkot* ceremony practiced on Yom Kippur. (See also page 255.)

Why is a ram's horn, rather than a cow's horn or that of another animal, used as a *shofar*?

The ram's horn is used in commemoration of the sacrifice of Isaac. The last moment before Abraham was to sacrifice Isaac, a ram caught in a thicket was used as a substitute sacrifice. To honor the ram Jews use a ram's horn at religious services. Horns of cows were rejected because these animals were associated with the worship of the Golden Calf by the Children of Israel in the desert, a sin vigorously condemned by Moses.

Why is the *shofar* not blown when Rosh Hashana falls on the Sabbath?

In Temple days the *shofar* was blown on the Sabbath in

the Temple area by the Priests *(Kohanim)*. However, it was not blown on that day elsewhere in the country.

After the Second Temple was destroyed, Rabbi Jochanan ben Zakkai, head of the academy in Yavneh, permitted the *shofar* to be blown on the Sabbath wherever there existed a central *Bet Din* (court of law). Generally, however, the practice of *not* blowing the *shofar* on the Sabbath was followed until the eleventh century, when the renowned scholar Isaac ben Jacob Alfasi, born near Fez in Morocco, declared it permissible.

The Alfasi was of the opinion that the blowing of the *shofar* was not "work" *(melacha)* in the sense of the word as applied to Temple activity. (After the Second Temple was destroyed, there was a ban on all activity [work] that duplicated the work of the Temple.) The Alfasi (and others) considered the blowing of the *shofar* an "art" *(chochma),* not work. A few communities accepted this view for a short while, but the restriction of not blowing the *shofar* on the Sabbath was restored before long.

Most authorities did not accept Alfasi's view because, they argued, if the *shofar* were to be blown on the Sabbath, it might lead to an infraction of Sabbath law. The person delegated to blow the *shofar* might wish last-minute instruction and would carry the *shofar,* in violation of the Sabbath law, to the home of his teacher.

Why have three different sound patterns been established for the blowing of the *shofar*?

Two of the three *shofar* sound patterns are mentioned in the Bible: the *tekia* and the *terua* (Numbers 10:5-8). In the Mishna (Rosh Hashana 4:9), the *tekia* is described as a long blast and the *terua* as three *yevavot* or wavering (undulating) sounds.

Actually, the exact nature of these sounds was never firmly established. In the third century, talmudic scholars debated the exact nature of the *terua,* and they finally agreed that the *tekia* was to be one single, long blast. Some thought the *terua* was to be a moaning sound, while others felt it should consist of nine staccato blasts.

A compromise was reached: the *terua* would consist of nine staccato notes, and the *shevarim* would be introduced (Rosh Hashana 33b). The *shevarim* was to fall in between the single straight blast of the *tekia* and the nine staccato notes of the *terua,* and its pattern became three undulating notes.

Why is the *shofar* sounded more times in some congregations than in others?

Over the centuries, scholars have differed with regard to the number of *shofar* blasts to be sounded and the proper pattern to be followed.

One established sequence for the blowing of the *shofar* is as follows:

> *tekia, shevarim-terua, tekia*
> *tekia, shevarim, tekia*
> *tekia, terua, tekia*

On Rosh Hashana, this sequence of ten blasts is sounded three times after the Tora reading, immediately before the *Musaf* service. The sequence, with variations depending on local custom, is again sounded at three points during the *Musaf* service:

1. After *Malchuyot,* in which God's kingship is affirmed.
2. After *Zichronot,* in which God's Covenant with Israel is affirmed.
3. After *Shofrot,* in which the belief in the coming of the Messiah is affirmed.

Finally, a series of blasts (from ten to forty) is sounded at the end of the Rosh Hashana service in those congregations that follow the tradition that demands that the total number of blasts heard on Rosh Hashana be one hundred. (See next question.)

Why are one hundred *shofar* blasts sounded in some congregations?

At one point in history (the exact time is uncertain), the idea took hold that the total number of *shofar* blasts to be sounded on Rosh Hashana is one hundred. This tradition is probably based on Rabbi Meir's comment that a Jew must recite one hundred blessings every day (Menachot 43b). Since hearing the *shofar* blown is considered a blessing ("Blessed is the people who knows [appreciates] the sound of the *shofar*"—Psalms 89:16), over the years many congregations have insisted that on Rosh Hashana the *shofar* be sounded one hundred times. (See previous question.)

Why is a white robe (a *kittel*) worn by some worshippers on Rosh Hashana and Yom Kippur?

In Jewish tradition white garments are symbolic of humility and purity of thought. When the High Priest entered the Holy of Holies on the Day of Atonement, rather than dressing in his usual golden vestments he wore simple white linen garments.

Wearing a white *kittel* on Rosh Hashana and Yom Kippur, not only by rabbis and cantors but by members of the congregation, was encouraged by the statement of Isaiah, whose words are read in the *haftara* reading on Rosh Hashana: "Though your sin be as scarlet [hence real and uncontestable], they shall be as white as snow [after repentance]" (Isaiah 1:18). The custom of dressing in white spread, and it has become traditional for men and women to dress in white on the High Holidays as well as to replace the colored ark curtain (parochet), the Tora mantles, and the cover on the reader's table with white ones. It has also become customary to decorate the synagogue with white flowers.

Why is *Hallel* not recited on Rosh Hashana?

The *Hallel* prayer is recited on all Jewish holidays except Rosh Hashana, Yom Kippur, and Purim.

According to a legend in the Talmud (Rosh Hashana 32b), the angels appeared before God and asked why His children were not reciting *Hallel* (psalms of praise) on Rosh Hashana and Yom Kippur. God replied: "How can they recite *Hallel* at such an awesome time, when the Book of Life and the Book of Death are open before Me and no one knows what his fate will be?" For this reason, *Hallel* is not recited on Rosh Hashana or Yom Kippur, holidays which are devoted to self-examination and are not considered joyous in the same sense as Passover, Sukkot, or Shavuot.

The reason why *Hallel* is omitted on Purim is not clear, but it is probably associated with the death of so many innocent people, which, like the drowning of the Egyptians after the exodus from Egypt, was said to have not been pleasing to God.

Why does the cantor kneel and prostrate himself during the High Holiday services?

During the *Musaf* service of Rosh Hashana and Yom Kippur, when the cantor chants "We bend the knee and prostrate ourselves before the King of Kings," he kneels and touches his forehead to the ground. In some congregations many worshippers do likewise.

This custom was practiced in the Temple by the Priests. And although the words "we kneel and worship" are part of the *Alenu* prayer recited daily today, kneeling and prostration have been abandoned for the most part because the Christian Church has adopted these postures. (See also page 153.)

Why are the special prayers recited on Rosh Hashana and Yom Kippur called *piyyutim*?

A *piyyut* (the plural is *piyyutim*) is the Hebraic form of the Greek root word that gave us the English word "poet." The *piyyut,* which constitutes a significant portion of the High Holiday prayerbook, is Jewish religious poetry that has been written since the destruction of the Second Temple.

Why are the words *le-shana tova tikatevu* used so frequently on Rosh Hashana?

These three Hebrew words mean "may you be inscribed for a good year." Used as a spoken greeting on the holiday and also appearing on greeting cards, these words reflect the belief that on Rosh Hashana God records in each person's Book of Life his fate for the coming year.

Why do Jews visit a body of water on Rosh Hashana afternoon to empty their pockets of crumbs?

This ceremony, called *Tashlich,* which means "cast off," is symbolic of self-purification. On the afternoon of the first day of Rosh Hashana (or on the second day if the first day falls on a Sabbath) Jews gather at a body of water to empty their pockets and recite penitential prayers, including the verse from the Book of Micah (7:19), "And Thou wilt cast [ve-tashlich] all their sins into the depths of the sea."

Scholars are not certain about the origin of this custom. Some claim it was inspired by the verse in Micah; others believe the passage was quoted only *after* the custom had been established. Since most of the prominent scholars of the Middle Ages did not approve of the *Tashlich* ceremony, it is reasonable to assume that these scholars believed it was of pagan origin and that emptying crumbs from one's pockets was associated with the primitive idea of giving the devil a gift so he would not cause harm. Primitive man believed that evil spirits lived in streams and wells and could be placated with gifts, hence the expression, "giving the devil its due."

The prevailing attitude of those who go to *Tashlich* today was best expressed by Rabbi Isaiah Hurwitz, a renowned kabbalist who lived at the end of the eighteenth century and wrote in his *Two Tablets of the Covenant* that it is foolish for Jews to assume that they can shake off their sins by shaking their pockets into a stream. Although he opposed the practice of emptying pockets, Hurwitz did accept the concept of ridding oneself of sins. He believed that Jews should go to a stream known to carry fish as a reminder that in many ways man is like a fish; that he must be on guard lest he be trapped in his life as easily as a fish can be trapped in its environment.

Why are round *challot* served on Rosh Hashana?

The round shape, symbolic of the cyclical and eternal nature of life, expresses the hope that the coming year will be complete, unbroken by tragedy.

Over the centuries, in various communities, other *challa* shapes and forms have been served on Rosh Hashana. In Volhynia, in the Russian Ukraine, *challot* were made in the form of a bird. This was based on a verse in Isaiah (31:5): "As hovering birds, so will the Lord protect Jerusalem." A bird-shaped or bird-trimmed *challa* reflects the hope that man's prayers will be carried heavenward.

In various communities *challot* in the form of a ladder were made to symbolize the theme of the popular *Nesaneh (Netaneh) Tokef* prayer, in which the destiny of man is decreed: "Who will live and who will die; who will be rich and who poor. . . ." Man will either ascend the ladder of life and find success in the year to follow, or he will descend and suffer an unfortunate fate.

Before World War II the round, braided *challa* was intro-

duced in Eastern Europe, where it was also common to super-
impose a round ring of dough (in the shape of a bagel) on top
of the round *challa*.

Why do many Jews place new fruit of the season on the Rosh Hashana table?

Observant Jews often deny themselves certain fruits all
summer long so that they may eat them for the first time on
the second night of Rosh Hashana. The special blessing that
is recited when performing an action for the first time (or for
the first time in a season) is the *Shehecheyanu,* which expresses thanks for having reached this important moment in
life in good health and peace.

Generally, the fruits served on Rosh Hashana for the *Shehecheyanu* are grapes, pomegranates, and apples. The
pomegranate is particularly popular because it has many
seeds, which symbolize the hope that the year ahead will be
one in which man will be privileged to perform many worthy
deeds.

Why are *Shehecheyanu* fruits served on the *second* night of Rosh Hashana?

The *Shehecheyanu* fruits (described above) are served on
the second night of Rosh Hashana rather than the first
because the Rabbis were uncertain about the nature of Rosh
Hashana. Was it a two-day holiday or was it a one-day holiday
that extended for two days?

The Talmud considers the two days of Rosh Hashana as
yoma arichta—one long day. If this is the case, it does not
make sense to recite the *Shehecheyanu* prayer during the
Kiddush of the second day (since it was already recited on the
first day), for this would constitute a "wasted blessing"
(beracha l'vatala). But since the *Shehecheyanu* was already

an established part of the *Kiddush* for the second night, a bowl of new fruits was placed on the table, and the recitation of the *Shehecheyanu* was applied to these fruits of the season.

Why is honey served on Rosh Hashana?

The custom of eating sweets on Rosh Hashana is more than 1,500 years old. It expresses the hope that sweetness will enter the lives of all Jews in the coming year. The practice spread quickly, and today on almost every Rosh Hashana table can be found a dish of honey or syrup.

Whereas during most of the year bread is dipped in salt when the blessing over bread is recited, on Rosh Hashana the first piece of *challa* eaten at the meal is dipped in honey. Apple is also dipped in honey to express the hope for "a good sweet year."

It is common practice not to serve sour foods during Rosh Hashana.

Why is honey cake served on Rosh Hashana?

Honey cake, called *lekach* (also pronounced *laykach*), is a traditional Eastern European holiday food. *Lekach* is a Hebrew word meaning "portion." Honey cake is served with the hope and prayer that those who observe Jewish traditions will be blessed with "a goodly portion," a concept expressed in the Book of Proverbs (4:2): "For I give you good doctrine *(lekach),* do not forsake my teaching."

Why is carrot *tzimmes* served on Rosh Hashana?

Carrot *tzimmes* is a honey-sweetened carrot preparation

served on Rosh Hashana to express the hope for a sweet year. One reason for the selection of carrots is that the Yiddish word for carrot is *meiren,* which also means "to multiply," expressing the hope for a productive year in which man's blessings may be multiplied.

Another explanation for the tradition of serving carrot *tzimmes* is that when the carrots are sliced they become coin-shaped, and since they are also golden-colored, they are a symbol of prosperity.

Why is the head of a fish served on Rosh Hashana?

Many primitive cultures believed that whatever is eaten at the beginning of a year will influence the entire year. In Jewish tradition fish was a popular dish because it was associated with productivity. The head of the fish is served on Rosh Hashana with the hope that greatness and leadership may be one's lot in the coming year.

When the fish is first tasted, the *Shulchan Aruch (Code of Jewish Law)* suggests that these words be recited: "May the coming year help us achieve leadership among our fellow man; may we be the head and not the tail."

The Jews of Switzerland introduced fish dishes sweetened with raisins and honey, which are called *lebkuchen* or *leibkuchen.*

The Jews of Iraq do not eat fish at all because the Hebrew word for fish is *dag* which sounds like *daagah,* a Hebrew word meaning "worry, anxiety."

Why do *chassidim* serve beet roots on Rosh Hashana?

The basis for this practice is to be found in the Talmud (Horayot 12a) where the scholar Abaye says that at the beginning of the year a person should eat pumpkins, leeks, beets, dates, etc., for these grow in abundance and are good omens.

Chassidim serve beet roots or beet leaves on Rosh Hashana because the Hebrew word for beet, *selek*, is similar in sound to the Hebrew word *she-yistalku* in the term *shey-istalku oivaynu* ("May we rid ourselves of our enemies"), an expression used on Rosh Hashana.

Why do some Jews avoid eating nuts on Rosh Hashana?

Some Jews will not eat nuts on Rosh Hashana because *egoz*, the Hebrew word for "nut," has the same numerical value as *chet*, the Hebrew word for "sin." *Egoz* has a value of seventeen, and *chet*, if spelled deficient, without the *alef*, also has a value of seventeen.

Why are the ten days between Rosh Hashana and Yom Kippur—the Ten Days of Repentance — especially significant?

The penitential period in the Jewish calendar actually starts at the beginning of Elul (one month before Rosh Hashana). However, the ten days between Rosh Hashana and Yom Kippur have special significance because in Jewish tradition, as the liturgy of the High Holidays states, during this period God passes judgment over every individual, but reserves final judgment until Yom Kippur.

The Ten Days of Penitence are regarded as man's last chance, through his actions, to influence God to reconsider an unfavorable decision (Rosh Hashana 16b). For this reason, the holiday greeting which until Yom Kippur was *le-shana tova tikatevu*, "May you be inscribed in the Book of Life for good," is changed, as Yom Kippur approaches, to *g'mar chatima tova*, "May you be *sealed* in the Book of Life for good."

Why do most people consider Yom Kippur the most sacred day in the Jewish calendar?

Contrary to popular belief, the Sabbath is the most sacred day in the Jewish calendar. But because of the fasting requirement, Yom Kippur is generally thought to be more sacred. In biblical law the penalty for violating the Sabbath (death) is much more severe than the penalty for violating Yom Kippur (excommunication).

Why do Jews observe the *Kaparot* ceremony on the day before Yom Kippur?

The ceremony known in Hebrew as *Kaparot* (also pronounced *Kapores*) evolved from the early belief that it was possible to transfer illness, pain, guilt, and sin to another object, living or dead.

During the *Kaparot* ceremony, still observed by some Jews today, a fowl is waved over the head three times and the following words are pronounced: "This is my substitute, my vicarious offering, my atonement. This cock or hen shall meet death, but I shall enjoy a long, pleasant life of peace." This is accompanied by reading selections from the Book of Psalms and the Book of Job. The fowl is then slaughtered and eaten by the owner and his family or is given to the poor.

The primary reason for the use of cocks and hens was that after the destruction of the Temple no animal used in its sacrificial atonement rites could serve a similar purpose in Jewish life. If a cock or a hen was not obtainable, other animals including geese or fish were used.

The custom of *Kaparot,* which is not mentioned in the Talmud, seems to have begun among the Jews of Babylonia. It is referred to in the writings of the *geonim* of the ninth century and became widespread by the tenth. Although most leading scholars condemned the practice as barbaric, Rabbi Moses Isserles (coauthor of the *Code of Jewish Law*), approved it, and it continued to be observed by German and Polish Jews. However, because many considered the procedure barbaric, the custom of using coins in place of fowl developed. The money was later given to charity.

Why do some Jews allow themselves to be flogged on the day before Yom Kippur?

The custom of having oneself flogged before Yom Kippur is an ancient one, dating back to the days of Rashi (the eleventh century). Today it is rarely practiced.

The flogging ritual dates back to biblical times (Deuteronomy 25:3), when a condemned person was subjected to *not more than* forty lashes. The Rabbis of the Talmud (Mishna Makkot 3:10) therefore set the number at thirty-nine strikes across one's back with a leather strap. As the flogging (*makkot* in Hebrew) is administered, the person confesses his sins. Self-flagellation is prevalent in the Muslim world today.

Why are the *challot* served at the Yom Kippur pre-fast meal sometimes decorated with birds?

On Yom Kippur man is compared to angels (with wings). This custom of decorating *challot* with birds expresses the hope that just as winged creatures fly heavenward with ease, so will man's prayers rise quickly and be answered favorably. Similar type *challot* are made for Rosh Hashana.

Why are *kreplach* served at the pre-fast Yom Kippur meal?

Kreplach are triangular-shaped dumplings usually filled with chopped meat, chopped onion, and seasonings. The chopped ingredients are reminiscent of the flogging (chopping) to which many Jews once subjected themselves before the fast day in order to punish themselves for the sins committed during the preceding year. *Kreplach* are also traditionally served on Purim, Hoshana Rabba, and Shavuot.

Why do Jews fast on Yom Kippur?

The requirement of fasting on Yom Kippur is biblical in origin. The Book of Numbers (29:7) states, "And on the tenth day of this seventh month [Tishri] ye shall have a holy convocation and ye shall afflict your souls. . ." In Jewish tradition to "afflict" the soul means to abstain from food.

Why does Yom Kippur never fall on a Friday, a Sunday, or a Tuesday?

While all other fast days that fall on the Sabbath in a particular year are postponed to Sunday, Yom Kippur must be observed on its appointed day: the tenth day of Tishri, as prescribed in the Bible. The calendar was designed so that the tenth of Tishri should not fall on a Friday, Sunday, or Tuesday.

If Yom Kippur were to fall on a Friday, it would be impossible to prepare food for the Sabbath. If it were to fall on a Sunday, it would be impossible to do on the Sabbath all that is necessary to prepare for the fast. If it were to fall on a Tuesday, Hoshana Rabba would fall on the Sabbath and the requirement that *aravot* (willows) be beaten would not be able to be observed, for this would be a violation of the Sabbath. (See also page 285.)

Why are boys under age thirteen and girls under age twelve not required to fast?

In Jewish law boys reach religious maturity at age thirteen, and girls at twelve. Before that age they are not subject to any of the commandments that apply to adults, although it is customary to train children to observe adult rites at an early age. Thus, boys and girls will begin fasting all or part of the day on Yom Kippur several years before they are actually obligated to do so.

Why do some Jews wear sneakers on Yom Kippur?

Among the pleasurable activities banned on the solemn day of Yom Kippur is the wearing of leather shoes. (Bathing, eating, and sexual intercourse are also banned.) The wearing of leather apparel was luxury in ancient times, and it became customary to wear rubber or canvas shoes (sneakers) on Yom Kippur to symbolize "the day of affliction" (Leviticus 23:27). Many people, forgetting that it is the leather that is banned, mistakenly wear sneakers with leather sides.

Why are sick people often not required to fast on Yom Kippur?

Any religious requirement that might endanger the health of an individual is suspended, even on Yom Kippur. The commandments in Jewish tradition are intended to support life, not endanger it. If a doctor recommends that one eat on Yom Kippur, he or she is permitted to do so.

Why are prayershawls worn at the *Kol Nidre* service but at no other service held after dark?

Kol Nidre is a very special night in the Jewish calendar. A prayershawl is worn to emphasize its holiness. The *talit,* however, is actually donned before nightfall, so one can recite the blessing over it while it is still light. The *Kol Nidre* itself is recited before sunset. (See page 101.)

Why is the *Kol Nidre* prayer chanted three times?

Kol Nidre ("All Vows"), the prayer for nullification of vows made innocently or under duress, is repeated three times so that latecomers will have an opportunity to hear it. A second reason is that in Jewish law, when a person is released from a vow, the court declares three times "you are released."

Why is the *Kol Nidre* chanted before sunset?

The *Kol Nidre* prayer is a legal formula whereby a person is released from a vow. Since this is a legal procedure, it would be a violation to perform it on a Sabbath or festival. It was therefore arranged for the *Kol Nidre* service to begin before the Sabbath or holiday sets in. (See above questions.)

Why have attempts to eliminate the *Kol Nidre* prayer from the Yom Kippur service failed?

Attempts to eliminate the *Kol Nidre* from the service have failed because of the profound emotional pull of the *Kol Nidre* melody. Although the words themselves are legalistic, representing an old formula for the absolution of vows that the individual Jew may have made innocently or under duress, and which hardly apply to modern life, the warm and tender melody has kept the prayer alive.

Why do Jews beat their breasts during certain prayers on Yom Kippur?

The "Confession of Sins" is a long list of sins more generally referred to as *Al Chet* ("For the Sin"). It has become common practice to beat the left breast (over the heart) with the right hand when uttering the word "sinned" or "transgressed." The action is designed to create a mood of penitence within the individual. The breast is also beaten when the *Ashamnu* ("We Have Sinned") prayer is recited.

Why are six *aliyot* awarded at the Yom Kippur service?

Generally, the more important the holiday, the greater the number of *aliyot* (Tora honors) given out. The importance of the holiday is determined by the severity of the punishment for its violation. The Sabbath is the most important day in the Jewish calendar; the penalty for its desecration is death. On the Sabbath seven *aliyot* are allocated. Yom Kippur is the second most important day in the Jewish calendar; the penalty for its desecration is excommunication. On Yom Kippur six *aliyot* are allocated. (See also pages 133 and 134.)

Why is *Yizkor* included in the Yom Kippur service?

The Yom Kippur *Yizkor* service, memorializing close relatives, dates back to the fifth century. Its origin is uncertain, but it was probably first introduced as a prayer for Yom Kippur to stir the people to repent by recalling the lives of their dear departed. Recitation of the *Yizkor* became mandatory during the period of the Crusades (eleventh to thirteenth century), when thousands of Jews were violently slain by the fanatical armies that marched through Europe en route to Palestine. The service provided an opportunity for the individual and the community as a whole to express its common loss.

Why is the Book of Jonah read on Yom Kippur?

The Book of Jonah was selected for the *haftara* reading for the *Mincha* service on Yom Kippur because God is represented there as the God of all nations. The concept of the universality of God is emphasized throughout the High Holiday liturgy. The Book of Jonah also addresses itself to another High Holiday theme: that man can abandon his evil ways, accept responsibility for his actions, and return to God.

Why is the *shofar* blown at the end of the Yom Kippur service?

At the end of the *Neila* service (the fifth and final service of Yom Kippur), one long blast of the *shofar* is blown to end the day of fasting. The extended blast expresses the feeling of the worshippers that they have extended themselves spiritually during the long day of prayer and are now resolved to reach out during the coming year towards new insights and more meaningful living.

Why is herring often served at the Yom Kippur break-the-fast meal?

Since water is not drunk during the twenty-four hour Yom Kippur fast, at the holiday's conclusion salty herring is served to induce thirst and thus encourage the individual to restore the fluids needed by the body.

Why do some Jews arise very early on the morning *after* Yom Kippur to attend a morning service?

In Jewish folklore the belief was prevalent that Satan will make one final effort to entrap Jews and cause them to sin. Convinced that now that Yom Kippur is over Jews will become lax and will not carry out all their religious resolutions, Satan believes he may yet succeed. To prove Satan wrong, many Jews attend the earliest morning service on the day after Yom Kippur.

Chapter 12

Sukkot, Shemini Atzeret, and Simchat Tora

INTRODUCTION

Although Sukkot, like Passover and Shavuot, was originally an agricultural holiday, the Bible also ascribes to it very definite historical roots: "You shall live in booths seven days in order that future generations may know that I made the Israelite people live in booths when I brought them out of the land of Egypt" (Leviticus 23:42-43). The holiday thus commemorates the forty-year trek of the Israelites through the desert to the Promised Land.

Sukkot, Shemini Atzeret, and Simchat Tora are often assumed to be a single holiday. Actually, they are individual holidays that follow one upon the other. Sukkot is a seven-day holiday, the last day of which is called Hoshana Rabba. Shemini Atzeret is observed as a one-day holiday in Israel today, and as a two-day holiday in the Diaspora. In Israel, Simchat Tora is observed as part of their one-day Shemini Atzeret festival. In the Diaspora, Simchat Tora is the second day of the two-day Shemini Atzeret celebration.

The primary symbol of Sukkot is the *sukka* (the hut which simulates the hastily constructed quarters of the Jews as they crossed the desert). Observant families eat, and sometimes even sleep, in their *sukka*. The other major holiday symbols are the four species: the *etrog* (citron), the *lulav* (palm), the *hadas* (myrtle), and the *arava* (willow). The blessing over the four species is recited on each day of the holiday excluding the Sabbath. In Temple times, as Psalms were recited, the people waved their palm branches in unison.

The last day of Sukkot, Hoshana Rabba, is associated with a supplication for rain and is traditionally considered to be the last day on which the decrees of Yom Kippur can be reversed. Hoshana Rabba is celebrated with a ceremonial beating of bunches of willows in the synagogue.

The observance of Shemini Atzeret is expressly mentioned in Leviticus (23:26): "On the eighth day you shall hold a holy convocation; you shall do no work on it."

Simchat Tora (the Rejoicing of the Law or Rejoicing with the Tora) celebrates the conclusion of the reading of the entire Five Books of Moses. An informal service is held and everyone in the congregation (with restrictions in some cases) receives an *aliya*. The Torot are joyfully paraded around the synagogue amidst singing and dancing.

Why is Sukkot celebrated?

Sukkot, the Festival of Booths, is a major festival in the Jewish calendar. It is observed on the fifteenth day of Tishri, two weeks after Rosh Hashana, and usually falls in late September or in October.

Although Sukkot was originally an agricultural holiday like Passover and Shavuot, the Bible (Leviticus 23:42-43) ascribes historical significance to it by stating its purpose: "You shall live in booths seven days in order that future generations may know that I made the Israelite people live in booths when I brought them out of the land of Egypt, I am the Lord your God." The *sukkot* (booths) that Jews build today are reminders of that forty-year sojourn in the desert on the way to the Promised Land.

Why is Sukkot called "Chag Ha-asif" in the Bible?

The Bible (Exodus 23:16) refers to Sukkot as "Chag Ha-asif [the Festival of Ingathering] . . . when you gather in all the yield of your field." As explained in the previous answer, originally, before Sukkot became associated with the Children of Israel's forty-year sojourn in the desert, it was solely an agricultural holiday.

In all probability, the *sukka* (booth) used on the holiday had its origin in the temporary shelters erected by vintners during the vintage season. When these booths were no longer in common use, they survived as a religious symbol dramatizing God's special concern for the Children of Israel.

Why is Sukkot called "Tabernacles"?

"Tabernacles" is derived from the Latin word *tabernaculum,* meaning "a hut, a temporary shelter." The word *sukka* (the plural is *sukkot*) is the Hebrew equivalent.

Why does the Talmud call Sukkot by the simple name "Chag"?

Although the Hebrew word *chag* means "holiday," it is used in the Bible several times to refer specifically to the Sukkot holiday. In the Talmud, Sukkot quite often is referred to as "Chag". This usage came about because Sukkot, the last holiday in the religious calendar, was celebrated with unusual pomp and ceremony.

The *Simchat Bet Hasho'ayva* (the Celebration of Water Libation) was particularly special. On the second evening of the Sukkot holiday, water was brought in a golden flask from the Pool of Siloam to the Temple. The water was poured on the altar as a supplication for a rainy season. The celebrants sang, danced, and carried torches as they marched in processions through the night. The Talmud (Mishna Sukkot 5:1) says: "He who has not witnessed the Celebration of the Libation of Water has never seen merriment in his life."

Why is Sukkot referred to as a "Pilgrim Festival"?

In the Jewish calendar Pesach, Shavuot, and Sukkot are referred to as "Pilgrim Festivals" because on these holidays all men were required to make a pilgrimage to the Temple in Jerusalem (Exodus 23:17). All three were originally agricultural holidays, and in celebration of them the Jews of Palestine brought the first crops of the season to the Temple, where a portion was offered as a sacrifice and the balance used by the Priestly families. Only after this obligation was fulfilled were the new season's crops permitted to be used as food.

Why is a *sukka* covered with branches?

To simulate the type of construction of the original booths used by the Israelites in the desert, the top of a *sukka* is covered with products of the earth—easy to gather. These include branches, shrubs, straw, even slats of wood. Fruits, vegetables, and other food products are not used. The *sukka* covering is called *s'chach,* from the Hebrew verb-root *sachoch,* meaning "to cover" or "to protect." The density of the covering must be such that there is more shade than sunlight in the room.

Why is a *sukka* usually flimsily constructed?

The *sukkot* built by the Israelites were hastily constructed, temporary abodes. To serve as a reminder of those structures, today's *sukkot* are made of loosely assembled walls and have overhead coverings sufficiently sparse to permit the stars to be visible from within. Dwelling in these huts brings man closer to the feeling of insecurity experienced by the Israelites in the desert.

Why do some Jews eat and sleep in the *sukka*?

Some Jews take the words in Leviticus 23, "You shall live in booths," literally. They interpret the word "live" to mean that one should eat and sleep in the *sukka*. No blessing is recited when building a *sukka* so as not to detract from the fundamental obligation, which is to "live" in the *sukka*, rather than just build it. A blessing is recited immediately before eating or sleeping in the *sukka*.

Why are the *etrog* and *lulav*, together with willow and myrtle branches, used as religious symbols on Sukkot?

The use of four species of plants is prescribed in Leviticus 23:40: "And you shall take on the first day [of the holiday] the fruit of goodly trees, branches of palm trees, and boughs of thick trees [myrtle branches], and willows of the brook, and you shall rejoice before your God seven days." The Bible does not specify precisely which trees and fruits are to be taken.

Jewish authorities have interpreted the "fruit of goodly trees" to mean the *etrog* (the citron), and the "branches of [date] palms" to mean the *lulav*. The "boughs of thick trees" refers to the myrtle (called *hadasim* in Hebrew), and "willows of the brook" are the familiar willow trees (called *aravot* in Hebrew). These four species were to be held in the hand and blessed each day of the Sukkot holiday.

Why is the *etrog* (citron) considered the most important of the four plant symbols used on Sukkot?

Unlike the other three symbols, the *etrog* has both fragrance and taste. The palm branch *(lulav),* from the tree of the same name, bears a delicious fruit but has no fragrance. The myrtle branch has an aroma, but it does not bear edible fruit. The willow has no fragrance, and it does not bear fruit. When the blessing over the four is recited, the *etrog,* because of its distinction, is held separately in the left hand while the *lulav* is tied together with the myrtles and willows and held in the right hand.

Why is the *etrog* held in the left hand when the blessing over the four species is recited?

The *etrog,* the most important of the four species, is held in the left hand and is pressed to the body so that it will be closest to the heart, the most important organ in the body.

Why do some Jews prefer to use the variety of *etrog* that has a protuberance—a *pittom*—while others prefer one that does not have a *pittom*?

The *pittom* is the nipple-like protuberance found on one variety of *etrog.* In Aramaic it is called *shoshanta,* meaning "a blossom." To most Jews the *pittom* is the distinguishing mark of the citron fruit, and they therefore prefer to use this variety on the Sukkot holiday. Others believe the variety of citron with the *pittom* is not the original form of the fruit prescribed in the Bible. It is, they say, a hybrid form of citron that should not be used on the holiday.

The *etrogim* (plural) grown in Israel do have a *pittom.* Those grown in North Africa and in some Mediterranean countries do not but are kosher nonetheless.

Not all Jews agree what constitutes a "choice" *etrog* (called in Hebrew *muvchar*). Oriental Jews prefer round, fat ones. Hungarians like oval ones with smooth surfaces. Jews of Galician extraction find an *etrog* with a furrowed surface to be most desirable. And some Jews consider an *etrog* to be *muvchar* only if its protuberance *(pittom)* falls in a straight line with its stem *(ikutz)*.

Why is an *etrog* no longer considered kosher if the *pittom* has broken off?

An *etrog* from which the *pittom* has broken off is no longer complete and cannot be categorized as beautiful. When the Bible says that the fruit of "goodly trees" is to be used on Sukkot, tradition has always indicated that this should be the most beautiful *etrog* that can be obtained, not a defective one.

Why does the blessing recited when the four species are used mention only the *lulav*?

It would seem logical that if only *one* of the four species were to be singled out in a blessing, that one would be the *etrog,* which has been compared to the heart in Jewish tradition and is considered the most beautiful of the four. However, because the *lulav* towers over the others and is hence the most prominent, the blessing mentions it in particular.

Why are two willow and three myrtle branches used when reciting the *lulav* prayer?

The tradition of using more than one willow branch evolved because the Bible speaks of willows in the plural *(aravot)*. This is taken to mean two. When the Tora speaks of the myrtle *(hadas;* plural, *hadasim)*, it describes it in three words: *anaf, aytz,* and *avot* (which means "the thick bough of a tree"). Because three words are used, it has become traditional to use three myrtle branches.

Why are the three myrtle branches placed higher in the holder attached to the *lulav* than are the two willows?

Tradition calls for this arrangement because it considers the myrtles superior to the willows. Myrtles, unlike willows, have a fragrant odor.

Why are willows *(aravot)* with smooth-edged leaves preferred over those with serrated edges?

The *Code of Jewish Law* recommends that the leaves of the willow used as part of the four species be the smooth type because they are considered more attractive than leaves with serrated, saw-like edges. In Yiddish the term *un zaiglach* ("without teeth") is used for the preferred type.

Why is the *lulav* waved in various directions during the recitation of *Hallel*?

Sukkot falls in the autumn of the year. It marks the beginning of the rainy season, and in ancient Palestine farmers were quite anxious about having sufficient rainfall to irrigate their fields. The waving ritual was a way of beseeching God to bless them with rain. To indicate that the presence of God is everywhere, the *lulav* is waved three times each to the east, north, west, and south, then upwards towards heaven, and downwards towards earth.

Why is the *etrog* wrapped in brown cotton?

Israeli growers of *etrogim* discovered that the unbleached brown cotton that is grown in Bangladesh (formerly East Pakistan) is well suited for wrapping *etrogim* which require a long shelf life. Most are picked many weeks before Sukkot for shipment to destinations far from Israel. The brown cotton keeps the *etrog* at a stable temperature and helps it retain its distinctive aroma.

Why is there a procession around the synagogue during the Sukkot service?

The procession is a carry-over of a tradition that began in Temple times. Upon completion of the sacrificial offerings, the *etrog* and *lulav* were carried joyously around the altar, while the people sang words from the Book of Psalms (118:25) with loud, firm voices:

> We beseech Thee, O Lord, save now!
> We beseech Thee, O Lord, make us
> now to prosper!

Today, a similar procession is held after the *Musaf* service in Ashkenazic synagogues and after *Hallel* in Sephardic synagogues. All congregants who have an *etrog* and *lulav* join the cantor and rabbi in circling the synagogue and singing the words of Psalm 118.

Why is there a misunderstanding about the relationship between Sukkot, Shemini Atzeret, and Simchat Tora?

Shemini Atzeret and Simchat Tora are holidays totally independent of the Sukkot holiday.

In Israel, as dictated by the Bible, Sukkot is observed for seven days. The first day only is a full holiday, on which one abstains from work. The next five days are Chol Ha-moed, Intermediate Days, which are considered half-holidays. The seventh and last day of Sukkot is Hoshana Rabba, also a half-holiday. The day after Hoshana Rabba is a separate holiday called Shemini Atzeret. Simchat Tora is not observed as a separate holiday. It is observed as part of Shemini Atzeret.

In the Diaspora, Orthodox and most Conservative congregations observe the first two days of Sukkot as full holidays. Reform congregations follow the Israeli practice.

Why is Hoshana Rabba celebrated?

The seventh and last day of Sukkot was endowed with special sanctity by the last of the Prophets: Haggai, Zechariah, and Malachi. Coming at the beginning of the rainy season, it became known as a Day of Judgment for Rain. (A special service for rain became part of the Shemini Atzeret service held on the next day.)

In addition to the four species (*arba minim*) used on each day of Sukkot during the Temple service, on Hoshana Rabba an extra willow branch was carried. It was held high as the procession made its way around the altar seven times, and verses beginning with *hosha-na,* "please save us," were chanted. The ceremony became known as *Hoshanot* (from the word *hosha-na*). In post-Temple days, the ceremony became part of the synagogue ritual. At a later date it was modified. Instead of using a single willow branch, a bunch of willows (five or six) were tied together.

Why are willows *(hoshanot)* beaten during the synagogue service on Hoshana Rabba?

The practice of beating a bunch of willows on the floor or against the seats of the synagogue on Hoshana Rabba (the last day of Sukkot) began when the final day of Sukkot became associated with the final day of the High Holidays. Yom Kippur was regarded as the day that concluded the Season of Divine Judgment, and Hoshana Rabba the day which brought to a close the long holiday period beginning with Rosh Hashana. Yom Kippur was the day on which the Heavenly Court decided the fate of man, and Hoshana Rabba represented one final opportunity for the evil decree to be reversed. Hoshana Rabba was also considered the Day of Judgment for Rain. Consequently, the beating of one's self on Yom Kippur was carried over to Hoshana Rabba and the beating of willows. (See also page 228.)

Why are *kreplach* eaten on Hoshana Rabba?

Kreplach are dumplings filled with "beaten" (chopped) ingredients—usually onions and meat. Because of the practice of beating *hoshanot* on Hoshana Rabba (See above), it is customary to eat *kreplach* at that time. (See also page 240.)

Why does the top of the *challa* prepared for Hoshana Rabba have a hand on it?

Tradition has it that on Hoshana Rabba (the seventh day of Sukkot) the judgment of God, passed on Yom Kippur, is sealed by a written verdict. The extended hand represents the acceptance of the *kvitel* (the receipt or document) on which the verdict is recorded. The tradition of preparing a *challa* with a hand fashioned of dough on top probably developed in Volhynia, in the Russian Ukraine.

Why is Shemini Atzeret celebrated?

Shemini Atzeret, the Eighth Day of Solemn Assembly, is often thought of as the eighth day of Sukkot. Actually, it is an independent holiday. The Rabbis referred to it as *regel bifnay atzmo,* a separate holiday, and required that the *Shehecheyanu* prayer be recited when the candles are lighted and when the *Kiddush* is recited. (This would not be required if Shemini Atzeret were not an independent holiday.)

Shemini Atzeret is a one-day holiday marking the conclusion of the festivities and observances of Sukkot, and none of the Sukkot ceremonials apply to it. It is prescribed in the Book of Leviticus (23:36) with these few words: "On the eighth day you shall hold a holy convocation; you shall do no work on it." At a later date the communities in the Diaspora added a second day to Shemini Atzeret, which became known as Simchat Tora, the Festival of Rejoicing in the Tora.

In Israel, Simchat Tora is celebrated on the same day as Shemini Atzeret.

Why is *Yizkor* recited on Shemini Atzeret?

Yizkor, the memorial prayer for the dead, is recited on four holidays: Yom Kippur, the eighth day of Passover, the second day of Shavuot, and Shemini Atzeret. The custom of remembering the souls of the departed on these occasions is first mentioned in the Midrash (Pesikta 20), where reference is made to the salvation of souls through prayer and charity.

Shemini Atzeret rather than Sukkot was selected for the recitation of *Yizkor* because the last day of each of the major festivals was thought to be the appropriate time for the recitation of the prayer. Since the Rabbis of the Talmud considered Shemini Atzeret, which was actually an independent holiday, to be the conclusion of Sukkot (see above), this holiday rather than the actual final day of Sukkot was selected for the *Yizkor* recitation.

The recitation of *Yizkor* in general did not become widespread until sometime after the First Crusade (1096), when the names of martyred dead were read from the record books of the Jewish community. Originally, it was recited only on Yom Kippur, but was later added to the liturgy of the major holidays. In the Reform ritual *Yizkor* is recited only on Yom Kippur and on the last day of Passover. Historically, *Yizkor* is not observed in Sephardic congregations, primarily because Sephardim were not affected by the ravages of the Crusaders.

Why is the Book of Ecclesiastes (Kohelet) read on Shemini Atzeret?

According to tradition, Ecclesiastes (one of the Five Scrolls) was composed by King Solomon in his old age when he was frustrated and despondent. Its content, often pessimistic and depressing, was found to be an accurate expression of the mood of the masses who had just experienced a long holiday period, from Rosh Hashana through Sukkot, during which much soul-searching was demanded. Some are of the opinion that with the joyous holiday of Sukkot about to end, it was important, by reading Ecclesiastes, to strike a note of seriousness to balance the gaiety of Sukkot.

If one of the intermediate days of Sukkot falls on a Sabbath, *Kohelet* is read on that day rather than on Shemini Atzeret.

Why is Simchat Tora celebrated?

Simchat Tora, meaning "rejoicing over the Tora," was first celebrated in talmudic times, when the Babylonian custom of completing the reading of the Tora in one year was in vogue. The Talmud, however, does not refer to the holiday by that name. It is referred to as "the second day of Shemini Atzeret" (Megilla 31a).

Simchat Tora is celebrated as a full holiday only in the Diaspora. In Israel, it is observed as part of Shemini Atzeret. This is the practice in most Reform congregations.

The Simchat Tora holiday is celebrated with much merriment. The concluding portion of the Tora is read repeatedly until all have received an *aliya,* and this is followed immediately by reading from *Bereshit,* the first chapter of Genesis. Jewish tradition did not want to leave the slightest impression that once the entire Tora was read, the people would consider abandoning it. And so the cycle of Tora reading for the coming year was begun immediately.

On Simchat Tora, children are called to the Tora as a group. In some Conservative congregations women are also honored with *aliyot.* The Tora reading is followed by a Tora procession *(Hakafot)* in the synagogue. Dancing, singing and handclapping is the order of this day, and the usual formality of the synagogue is temporarily abandoned.

Chapter 13

Chanuka

INTRODUCTION

Beginning on the twenty-fifth day of Kislev—usually during the second half of December—Chanuka celebrates the victory of Judah the Maccabee and his four brothers—all members of the Hasmonean family—over the Syrian-Greeks in 165 B.C.E. The Syrian-Greeks, under Antiochus IV, king of Syria, had forbidden Jews from performing their basic religious functions. They sought to impose on Jews the paganism of the Hellenistic world.

Although Chanuka is celebrated in commemoration of one of the great victories in Jewish history, surprisingly little fuss was made over it until recent times. It is not considered a religious holiday in that work may be performed and children may attend school. Aside from some additions to the liturgy and the lighting of the Chanuka menora each night for the eight days of the holiday, very few changes are made in the normal routine.

In recent years, to counteract the strong influence of the Christmas season and its festivities on the lives of Jewish children, who might otherwise feel "left out," Jewish parents have begun to celebrate Chanuka in a more elaborate way.

Gift-giving on each of the nights of Chanuka has become commonplace, and community celebrations are more in evidence.

Why is Chanuka celebrated?

Chanuka marks the deliverance of the Jews of Palestine from the oppression of the Syrian-Greeks in the second century B.C.E. The Greeks attempted to impose heathen practices upon the Jewish population, but Judah and his four brothers, sons of Mattathias the Priest, all members of the Hasmonean family, led a rebellion against them.

The revolt reached its climax when King Antiochus IV of Syria prohibited the observance of sacred Jewish practices, including circumcision, Temple ritual, Sabbath observance, and the study of Tora. The decisive insult was the conversion of the Temple into a pagan shrine.

In the year 165 B.C.E. the rebels succeeded in defeating the Syrian armies, after which the Temple was cleansed and rededicated. *Chanuka* means "rededication."

Chanuka is celebrated for eight days beginning on the twenty-fifth day of Kislev.

Why were the Greeks who dominated Palestine in the second century B.C.E. called Syrian-Greeks?

Alexander the Great, the Greek king who ruled Palestine, Syria, Egypt, and many nearby countries, died in the year 320 B.C.E. He left no sons to succeed him, and as a result his two leading generals, Ptolemy and Seleucus, began a struggle for power that lasted twenty years. Ptolemy ruled Egypt, and Seleucus controlled Syria. Both vied for control of Palestine, the crossroads of the ancient world. Seleucus was the victor.

In the second century B.C.E. Seleucus and his Syrian-Greek army dominated Palestine, and it was against their domination that the Hasmoneans battled.

Why are the heroes of the Chanuka story called "Maccabees"?

The word *maccabee* is an acrostic created by joining the first letter of the Hebrew words *Mi kamocha ba'elim Adonai,* which means "Who among the mighty is like Thee, O God?" According to one theory, "maccabee" was the battle cry of the Jewish patriots who warred against the Syrian-Greeks in 165 B.C.E.

According to a second theory, *maccabee* is the Hebrew word for "hammer," derived from the root *makav.* Judah, the leader of the revolt against the Syrian-Greeks, was given the name Maccabee because of his great strength.

Why is no reference made in the Talmud to the miraculous military victories of Judah the Maccabee and the Hasmoneans?

By this purposeful omission the Rabbis expressed dissatisfaction over the action of the Hasmoneans, who reestablished the monarchy after their victory over the Syrian-Greeks. Jewish tradition maintained that the right to be royalty belonged only to the House of David, descendants of the tribe of Judah, and the Hasmoneans were not members of the tribe of Judah.

Why isn't the Book of Maccabees part of the Bible?

The Book of Maccabees is part of the Apocrypha, a group of fourteen books of the Septuagint (Greek translation of the Bible), which Judaism did not consider worthy of inclusion in the Bible (Canon). Protestants do not consider the Apocrypha part of the Bible, but Catholics accept eleven of the books.

Why is Chanuka observed for eight days?

In 165 B.C.E. the Hasmoneans recaptured the Temple from the Syrian-Greek army and rebuilt the altar. According to tradition this task took eight days and, therefore, Chanuka is observed for eight days.

The Talmud (Shabbat 21b) also explains that when the Syrian-Greeks captured the Temple, they desecrated all the jugs of oil that the High Priest had prepared for lighting the Temple *menora* (candelabrum). After much searching, only one small undefiled jug still bearing the unbroken seal of the High Priest could be found. This cruse contained only enough oil to burn in the *menora* one day, Nevertheless, the High Priest kindled the *menora* and a miracle happened: the *menora* flame continued to burn for eight days. To commemorate the event, it was decided that thenceforth the holiday would be observed annually by kindling lights for eight days, and Chanuka became known as the Feast (or Festival) of Lights.

Why are eight lights kindled on Chanuka?

Aside from the explanation (above) that a cruse of oil burned for eight days instead of only one day, the Midrash explains that after the sons of Mattathias defeated the Syrian-Greeks and entered the Temple, they found eight iron spears. They pushed these spears into the earth and kindled a light in each one.

Why is one candle kindled on the first night of Chanuka, two on the second, etc., until eight have been kindled on the last night of the holiday?

The Talmud discusses whether one candle should be lighted the first night, two the second, etc. (which was the view of Hillel), or whether eight should be lighted the first night, seven the second, etc. (which was the view of Shammai). The decision was made to follow the view of Hillel, which was based on the principle that in matters of holiness one should add to (increase) rather than diminish (decrease).

Why are the candles of the *menora* lighted from left to right?

Over the centuries various candlelighting practices have evolved. The practice generally accepted today follows the tradition of giving equal importance to the right and left side of the *menora,* indicating that God's presence is everywhere. The candles are therefore inserted from right to left (the newest addition to be on the left), but they are kindled from left to right (the newest addition to be kindled first).

Why is the light of the Chanuka *menora* not permitted to be used for practical purposes?

Unlike the light cast by Sabbath and holiday candles, which was originally used for illuminating the house so one would be able to see, the light of the Chanuka *menora* was intended exclusively to help celebrate the holiday. For this reason the *menora* has traditionally been placed in a window in front of the house so its light becomes visible to passersby, thus publicizing the miracle of Chanuka.

In early times the *menora* was placed outside the entrance of the house, on the left aside, so that as one entered he would walk between the door *mezuza,* which hung on the right doorpost and the lighted *menora,* which stood on the left—that is, between two religious articles involved in the performance of two commandments *(mitzvot).*

Why is a ninth candle, called a *shamash,* used to light the other candles in the *menora*?

This is a continuation of the practice followed when the seven-branched candelabrum of the Tabernacle and Temple was lit. The seventh branch in each of these *menorot* was called *shamash,* meaning "servant." Used to light the others, it was not counted as one of the lights.

A ninth candle is also used because the eight primary candles of the Chanuka *menora* may not be used for practical purposes. By having a ninth candle to light the others, one will not be tempted to use any of the eight primary candles for such purposes.

Why do some people use oil rather than candles in their *menorot*?

Some Jews use *menorot* containing small cups which hold oil—preferably olive oil—a product closely identified with the Land of Israel. A wick is placed in each cup to absorb the oil. The wick is lighted. Those who follow this custom feel closer to the original celebration, at which oil was used.

Why are three blessings recited over the Chanuka candles on the first night of the holiday only?

The first two blessings recited over the candles on the first night of Chanuka refer specifically to the kindling of the lights and the miracle of Chanuka. The third blessing, called *Shehecheyanu,* is recited on the first night of all holidays. It expresses personal gratitude for being alive and well and having reached this day.

Why is it permissible to perform work on Chanuka but not on other holidays?

Chanuka is a post-biblical holiday. With the exception of Purim, only those holidays mentioned specifically in the Bible became full holidays, with restrictions on secular activities. Special synagogue services similar to those held on Pesach, Sukkot, and Shavuot are not held to celebrate Chanuka, although the liturgy has been supplemented by the recitation of *Al Hanisim* and *Hallel,* plus the reading of the Tora every morning of the festival.

Why is *Maoz Tzur* ("Rock of Ages") sung after the Chanuka candles have been kindled?

The *Maoz Tzur,* written by an unknown author between the eleventh century and thirteenth century, extols God as Israel's deliverer, which is the precise theme of the holiday. The author's first name was undoubtedly Mordecai, for he uses the Hebrew letters that spell out Mordecai as an acrostic signature. The melody popular today, adopted from a popular German folksong, has been in use since the middle of the fifteenth century.

Why is *Al Hanisim* recited on Chanuka?

The special *Al Hanisim* ("For the Miracles") prayer was added to the *Amida* prayer and to the *Grace After Meals* some time before the eighth century to mark the great victory of Chanuka, which to Jews throughout the centuries was considered nothing less than a miracle. *Al Hanisim* is also included in the Purim liturgy.

Why were the letters on the *draydel* changed after the State of Israel was established?

A *draydel* is a four-sided top with a different Hebrew letter on each side. A *draydel* game is played, in which each player spins the *draydel* in turn and receives points according to the assigned value of the letter that appears face upward when the *draydel* falls.

Draydel is a Yiddish word derived from the German *drehen,* which means "to turn." The Hebrew name for *draydel* is *sevivone,* from the root *savov,* meaning "to turn."

Draydels used before the State of Israel was established (1948) had the following Hebrew letters on them: *nun, gimmel, hay, shin.* These letters stood for the Hebrew words *nes gadol haya sham,* meaning "a great miracle happened there." After the State was established, the *shin* of *sham* was changed to the letter *pay* for *po,* meaning "here." And so the four letters found on many *draydels* today are *nun, gimmel, hay, pay,* meaning, "a great miracle happened here [in Israel]."

Why is gift-giving so important an aspect of Chanuka?

Gift-giving was a part of the early Purim tradition, but not of the Chanuka tradition. In Eastern Europe, on the fifth night of Chanuka families gathered for a special family night during which children were given Chanuka *gelt* (Chanuka money). Later, when Christians and Jews mingled more freely, Jews were influenced by the Christian tradition of giving gifts to children at Christmastime. Soon, Jewish parents began the practice of giving gifts other than Chanuka *gelt* to their children.

Why do Jews play cards on Chanuka?

This custom began five or six hundred years ago, in the Middle Ages, when *yeshiva* students abandoned their studies to celebrate the holiday. One way in which the students expressed the joy and festive spirit of the holiday was to involve themselves in a game of chance. Rabbis have protested this practice, but it continues to this day.

Rabbi Levi Yitzhak, the famous chassidic rabbi of Berditchev, defended the practice by explaining that Jews played cards on Chanuka nights to train themselves to stay up late, which would enable them to study Tora for longer hours throughout the year. This is not to say that Rabbi Levi Yitzhak condoned gambling throughout the year.

Why do Jews eat potato *latkes* on Chanuka?

Potato *latkes* are eaten because they are fried in oil, and oil symbolizes the miracle of the cruse of oil which lasted for eight days instead of one. *Latkes* are called *fasputshes* or *pontshkes* by some Ashkenazim. In Israel these fried potato pancakes are called *levivot*.

Why do Israeli Jews eat doughnuts on Chanuka?

Israelis eat doughnuts *(sufganiyot)* on Chanuka because, like *latkes* (potato pancakes), they are fried in oil, and oil is symbolic of the miracle of the holiday.

Why do Jews eat cheese pancakes and cheese delicacies on Chanuka?

Although cheese dishes are generally associated with Shavuot, longstanding tradition dictates that cheese delicacies be eaten on Chanuka as well. Although its origin can be traced to the story of Judith, one of the heroines in the Book of Judith of the Apocrypha (about the sixth century B.C.E.), the custom of eating cheese and cheese preparations did not gain popularity until the Middle Ages.

Judith, according to legend, was a daughter of one of the Hasmoneans who fed cheese to Holofernes, the general of Nebuchadnezzar's army, an archenemy of the Jewish people. As a result, the general became very thirsty, consumed large amounts of wine, became drunk, and was beheaded by Judith, leading to a Jewish victory. To commemorate this event, it is said, Jews eat cheese on Chanuka.

Why is goose popular as a Chanuka dish?

Chicken fat and the fat of other fowl was needed to prepare some of the favorite Chanuka delicacies. Being a fatty fowl, it became traditional to serve goose on Chanuka and to render its fat, which was then set aside and saved until Passover. Some of the fat was used to prepare *grivn* (*gribenes*)—the crisp, fried fat of a fowl served with *latkes* on Chanuka.

Chapter 14

Purim

INTRODUCTION

Like Chanuka, Purim is a minor holiday connected to a historical event. One complete book of the Bible—the Book of Esther, often referred to as Megillat Esther or the Scroll of Esther—is devoted to recounting the events that led to the holiday. The dramatic story is read at the synagogue service on the night of Purim and again at the service the following morning.

The name *Purim,* we are told in the Book of Esther, derives from the word *pur* (plural, *purim*), meaning "lots," which were used by Haman, Prime Minister of King Ahasueros of Persia, to choose the date on which he would slaughter the Jews of the country.

Haman's plans were foiled by beautiful Queen Esther and her cousin, Mordecai. Risking her own life, Esther pleaded before the king for her people, and Haman's order was rescinded. Instead of the Jews of Persia being slaughtered, Haman and his family were hung on the gallows prepared for Mordecai. Thus, those days of doom were turned "from sorrow to gladness" and were to be commemorated by "sending gifts to one another and to the poor (Esther 9:22).

The Book of Esther proclaims the fourteenth day of Adar (usually during the month of March) a day of celebration. However, in Shushan, the capital of Persia, the Jews did not completely rid themselves of their enemy until the following day, and so they celebrated Purim on the fifteenth of Adar. Because Shushan was a walled city, it became customary for other cities fortified with outer walls to celebrate the holiday on the fifteenth as well. Jerusalem, a walled city since early times, observes Purim on the fifteenth to this day. (In other parts of Israel the holiday is celebrated on the fourteenth.)

During the reading of the Megilla at the synagogue service, whenever Haman's name is mentioned, it is booed in one form or another: by the stamping of feet or the rattling of noisemakers *(groggers)*. Before the day is over, friends and relatives exchange gifts and join in a festive meal called the Purim *Seuda* (party).

Why do Jews observe the holiday of Purim?

Purim, the Feast of Lots, commemorates the deliverance of the Jews of Persia in the fifth century B.C.E. by Esther and her cousin (the son of her father's brother) Mordecai. Haman, second in command to King Ahasueros, planned to exterminate the Jews of Persia. He ordered that lots be drawn to determine on which day the massacre should take place, and it fell on the thirteenth day of the Hebrew month of Adar.

The plan was frustrated when Queen Esther made a successful appeal to the king to have the decree nullified. Thereupon, the Jews of the country turned on their enemies and avenged themselves on the fourteenth day of the month; and in Shushan, the capital, the rampage continued for one more day. To commemorate the victory, the Book of Esther (called the Megilla, *i.e.,* the "scroll") is read in the synagogue annually on the fourteenth of Adar (usually in the month of March).

Why is the holiday called "Purim"?

To determine the day on which the Jewish massacre was to take place, Haman cast a *pur,* which has been explained as a Persian word meaning "lot." Some authorities believe the origin of the word is Aramaic and means "a small smooth object" used to determine the winner of a lottery. It has a similar meaning in Arabic.

Why do many people think Mordecai was Esther's uncle?

Mordecai was Esther's cousin. The confusion arose over the translation of the Hebrew word *dode,* meaning "an uncle." In the Book of Esther (2:7), Esther is referred to as *bat-dodo,* the "daughter of his [Mordecai's] uncle," whom Mordecai was raising since she was an orphan. It was thought that Mordecai must have been much older than Esther if he was raising her, and this probably led to the erroneous conclusion that they were uncle and niece rather than cousins.

Why do Jews fast on the day before Purim?

The day before Purim, the thirteenth day of the Hebrew month Adar, is called "Taanit Esther," the Fast of Esther. It is the day on which the Jews of Persia fasted to lend support to Queen Esther, who proposed to enter King Ahasueros' presence without prior permission, an act punishable by death. She dared do this only because the fate of her people was at stake.

Haman, second in command to the king, had proclaimed, with the king's consent, that the Jews of the kingdom were disloyal and were to be massacred on the thirteenth day of the month of Adar. Queen Esther managed successfully to be received by the king and to convince him of the inadvisability of allowing Haman to carry out his plan.

When the day of the Fast of Esther falls on a Sabbath, the day of fasting is moved back to Thursday since fasting is not permitted on the Sabbath, a day of joy. Fasting is also not permitted on Friday since that day is needed to prepare for the Sabbath.

Why do the Jews who live in Jerusalem celebrate Purim on a different day from the Jews who live outside of Israel?

In the Book of Esther, a distinction is made between Jews who live in walled cities and those live in unwalled cities. The rule in the Mishna (Megilla 1:1) is that since Shushan, the capital of Persia, was a walled city, all cities known to be walled cities since the days of Joshua were to celebrate Purim on the fifteenth day of the month of Adar, the same date on which it was observed in Shushan (Esther 9:18). (For this reason, the day after Purim became known as Shushan Purim.) All other cities were to celebrate the holiday on the fourteenth of Adar. Jerusalem is a walled city; therefore in that city Purim is celebrated on the fifteenth.

In leap years, when there is an extra month of Adar (Adar I and Adar II), Purim is always celebrated during the second Adar.

Why do the usual holiday prohibitions, such as riding and working, not apply to Purim?

Since Purim is not mentioned in the Five Books of Moses (the Tora), it is considered, like Chanuka, to be a minor festival. The Purim Megilla (Scroll of Esther) is read in the synagogue, and a Purim *Se'uda* is held in the home. Since Purim is a joyous occasion, mourners do not observe *Shiva* in the traditional, formal manner. The only change in the liturgy is that the *Al Hanisim* prayer is added to the *Amida* and the *Grace After Meals*.

Why do Jews read the Megilla on Purim?

Megilla (meaning "scroll") is the name by which the Book of Esther is called. To this day, when it is read in the synagogue on Purim night and again the following morning, the Megilla is unrolled as it is read. Many readers unroll part of the scroll and fold it in sections to resemble a "letter," since the Book of Esther was originally sent out as a letter (in scroll form) to all parts of the kingdom (Esther 9:26). The Megilla tells the story of Esther, Mordecai, Haman, and Ahasueros in detail.

The word *megilla* has become part of the English language and has come to mean "a story repeated in its every detail." In the second century C.E. an entire tractate of the Mishna, called Megilla, was written. The tractate devotes itself to all details of the Purim holiday and its observance, and especially to specific rules concerning the reading of the Scroll of Esther.

Although five books of the Bible are called *megillot* or scrolls (Esther, Lamentations, Song of Songs, Ruth, and Ecclesiastes), when the word *megilla* is used without specification, it refers to the Scroll of Esther. This is so because in early talmudic times (up until 250 C.E.), the Book of Esther was the only scroll read in the synagogue.

Why is the name of God not mentioned in the entire Book of Esther?

Since the Book of Esther was written in the form of a scroll and was sent out as a letter to all the outlying districts of Persia, the name of God was omitted lest the letter be desecrated or otherwise improperly handled. This is the only book or scroll in the Bible in which the name of God does not appear.

Why are noisemakers such as *groggers* used when the Megilla (Book of Esther) is read in the synagogue?

Since Haman was the archenemy of the Jews of Persia, and since he also epitomizes all enemies of the Jewish people throughout the ages, noisemakers of various kinds are sounded whenever his name is mentioned during the reading of the Megilla. This is a method of "erasing" his name. The verse in Exodus 17:14 is often quoted in connection with this tradition: "For I will utterly erase the remembrance of Amalek from under the heavens." Haman's ancestors were considered to be Amalekites.

Among the variety of ancient methods used to "erase" Haman's name, the most literal was to write the name of Haman on two smooth stones or slates and to then rub them and knock them together whenever Haman's name was mentioned during the Megilla reading. Stamping on the floor, turning *groggers,* and blowing horns and whistles are some of the methods employed today.

Why are gifts and goodies sent to friends and neighbors on the day preceding the holiday of Purim?

This custom, known by its Hebrew name *mishloach manot* or, in the vernacular, *shalachmones* or *shelachmones,* means "sending gifts" (literally "portions"), as indicated in the Book of Esther (9:22). This is an expression of joy over the victory of Esther, who frustrated the plot of Haman to annihilate the Jewish community of Persia in the fifth century B.C.E. The custom consists of sending money, food, and delicacies to friends, neighbors, and relatives.

The custom of marking a happy occasion by sending gifts *(manot)* is quite old. It is mentioned in the Book of Nehemiah 8:10, where Ezra instructs the Jews to celebrate the joyous occasion of the resumption of the public reading of the Tora (after a lapse of several centuries) by sending gifts to the needy. Since the word *manot* ("gifts" or "portion") is used in its plural form, it became traditional to send at least *two* eatables to friends as well as charity to the poor.

Why is a Purim feast (*se'uda*) held?

Although Purim is a minor holiday, it has been treasured highly in Jewish tradition, and a holiday meal was therefore instituted. The meal *(se'uda)* was to be eaten on the afternoon of the holiday, rather than on the night before when holiday meals are traditionally eaten.

Why are *hamantaschen* served on Purim?

An interesting variety of delicacies is eaten on Purim. One authority, Kalonymos ben Kalonymos, in his fourteenth-century book *Masechet Purim,* lists twenty-seven different meat dishes.

Most popular of all delicacies eaten on Purim are *hamantaschen* (a German word meaning "Haman's pockets"), triangular-shaped pastries filled with fruit, cheese, or poppy seeds. One explanation for the name is that Haman stuffed his pockets with bribe money.

Originally, *hamantaschen* were called *mohn taschen,*

"poppy seed pockets." A seed filling was used because the Hebrew word for "seed" (poppy seed) is *mohn* (manna); *mohn* sounds like the Hebrew pronunciation of the second syllable of the name Haman. It was popularly held that these three-cornered pastries are eaten as a reminder of the type of hat worn by Haman when he was second in command to the king of Persia.

Why do *hamantaschen* have three corners?

As noted above, the popular explanation is that these pastries are three-cornered to remind us of the type of hat worn by Haman. There is no evidence for this claim, and many believe the shape was introduced in the early nineteenth century to copy the Napoleonic triangular-shaped hat. The more traditional explanation is that the strength of Queen Esther was derived from her antecedents, and the three-cornered *hamantasch* represents the three patriarchs, the founders of the Jewish way of life: Abraham, Isaac, and Jacob.

Why are *hamantaschen* also called *oznay Haman* ("Haman's ears")?

It was once the practice to cut off the ears of criminals before hanging. Since Haman (the criminal) was hanged, a special holiday pastry called "ears of Haman" (*oznay Haman*) was introduced. In Holland the pastry is called *Hamansoren,* and in Italy *orrechi d'Aman.* It is a favorite food in Germany, Switzerland, Austria, Turkey, and Greece.

Why is a Purim *challa* made with long braids?

The Purim *challa,* called *keylitsh* in Russian, is giant-sized and braided. It is designed to represent the long ropes used to hang Haman.

Why are *kreplach* served on Purim?

It is customary to greet the name of Haman during the reading of the Megilla by clapping hands, stamping feet, turning *groggers* (noisemakers), and slapping or beating whatever object happens to be handy. From this, the idea of eating food that had been chopped or beaten evolved in Eastern Europe.

Kreplach, a German word probably derived from the French *crêpe,* was just such a dish. *Kreplach* were (and still are) made by chopping meat and onions, seasoning it, and then using the mixture as a filling in triangular pieces of dough. The triangular shape was used, according to some scholars, to represent the three patriarchs: Abraham, Isaac, and Jacob. (See page 276.)

Kreplach are also eaten at the pre-fast meal of Yom Kippur and on Hoshana Rabba because the same practice of beating and chopping applies to these holidays: on Yom Kippur submitting oneself to flogging—being beaten 39 times *(malkot)* with leather thongs—and on Hoshana Rabba (the seventh day of Sukkot) when willows are beaten against the floor or a chair. (See page 240.)

Why are sweet-and-sour dishes served on Purim in some communities?

Among kabbalists and *chassidic* groups, sweet-and-sour dishes are prepared to express the unusual dual nature of Purim: a holiday that shifts from a day of mourning and fasting (on the thirteenth of Adar) to a day of joy and celebration (on the fourteenth of Adar).

Why are salted, cooked beans and peas eaten on Purim?

According to one tradition, Esther did not want to eat nonkosher food and, therefore, only ate beans and peas, as did Daniel and his friends in the Court of Nebuchadnezzar (Daniel 1:12). Another explanation is that this custom has primitive roots, that the eating of legumes served as a charm against the spirits.

Why was the imbibing of alcohol generally encouraged on Purim?

Being a joyous holiday, the drinking of wine on Purim was taken for granted. The victory achieved by Esther began at a "banquet of wine" (Esther 5:6). Because of the great and unexpected victory over Haman, letting oneself go and getting drunk was looked upon kindly and even encouraged. Rava, the renowned Babylonian talmudic scholar, said (Megilla 7b) that a man is obliged to drink so much wine on Purim that he is no longer capable of distinguishing (*ad delo yada*) between the words "blessed is Mordecai" and "cursed is Haman."

This tradition has been explained as referring to a song sung on Purim in talmudic times. The stanzas of the song ended with the alternate refrain "blessed is Mordecai" and "cursed is Haman." Often, participants in a celebration were so inebriated they would mix up the refrains. They would also mix up other refrains, such as "blessed is Esther" and "cursed is Zeresh [wife of Haman]." The possibility of a mixup, it has been explained homiletically, can also come from the fact that the numerical value of the Hebrew letters of each of the phrases—*baruch Mordecai* ("blessed is Mordecai") and *arur Haman* ("cursed is Haman")—totals 502.

The spirit of joviality led to the institution of a Purim

"rabbi" who created and expounded outlandish lessons by manipulating the meaning of an otherwise sacred text. The frivolity also led to masquerading on Purim and to otherwise forbidden activity.

Why is masquerading permitted on Purim?

In Jewish tradition, masquerading was always banned because it often involved men and women interchanging garments. The prohibition is based on biblical law: "Neither shall a man wear the garments of a woman" (Deuteronomy 22:5). However, because Purim was such a great and joyous festival, the Rabbis permitted this breach of biblical law.

Under the influence of the Roman carnival, Italian Jews at the close of the fifteenth century were the first to add masquerading to the celebration of Purim, and from Italy the custom spread to many other Jewish communities. Today, masquerading is a prominent feature of the Adloyada Purim Carnival held annually in Tel Aviv. Purim masquerade parties are popular in all parts of the world.

Chapter 15

Minor Observances

INTRODUCTION

The minor Jewish holidays are not as demanding as the major ones in terms of religious observance. Unlike the major observances, few of the minor ones are of biblical origin. The General Introduction indicates the dates on which each of the holidays falls.

Among the observances categorized as minor are Chanuka, Hoshana Rabba, Rosh Chodesh, Lag B'Omer, Purim, Chol Ha-moed, Shushan Purim, Pesach Sheni (Second Passover), and Israel Independence Day. On each of these days, specials prayers are added to the liturgy, although the prayers added differ from holiday to holiday. *Hallel,* for example, is part of the liturgy of many of the minor holidays, including Israel Independence Day, but it is not recited on Purim.

Generally, work may be performed on minor holidays, but there are exceptions.

Why is the beginning of each month of the Jewish year celebrated as a semiholiday?

The celebration of the New Moon (Rosh Chodesh) as a

semifestival has deep roots in Jewish tradition. In talmudic times, whenever witnesses testified that they had observed the crescent of the New Moon, the Sanhedrin (highest court), after verifying the testimony, declared the New Moon's arrival official, and that became an occasion for celebration. Special sacrifices were offered in the Temple, the *shofar* was blown, and the population carried on in a festive manner. To the prophets, particularly Isaiah (1:13), the New Moon celebration was equated in importance with the Sabbath.

Why are the special New Moon prayers sometimes delayed or omitted?

Since the destruction of the Temple, the arrival of the New Moon has been a lesser holiday. However, it continues to be commemorated through special prayers. Any time between the third day after the crescent of the New Moon appears and the fifteenth day after its appearance the Hebrew prayer known as *Kiddush Levana* ("Sanctification of the Moon") or *Birkat Levana* ("Blessing of the Moon") is recited. Some postpone the recitation of the blessing during the months of Av, Tishri, and Tevet until after the fast days in those months (Tisha B'Av, Yom Kippur, and Asara B'Tevet). Usually a group assembles outside the synagogue at the end of the *Maariv* service that ends the Sabbath and recites the *Kiddush Levana* prayer.

In the synagogue proper, on the Sabbath before Rosh Chodesh, the new month is commemorated with its own special prayer. This prayer is not recited before Rosh Chodesh Tishri since that month is already blessed with an abundance of holidays.

Why is the New Moon (Rosh Chodesh) celebrated for two days in some months?

In the Jewish calendar there are twenty-nine days in some

months and thirty days in others. Since the moon makes one revolution around the earth every twenty-nine and one-half days, the New Moon actually appears every thirtieth day. When a month has twenty-nine days, the first day of the next month is considered Rosh Chodesh (literally, "head of the month"). However, when a month has thirty days, the New Moon actually appears on the thirtieth day of that month, not on the first day of the next month. Therefore, the arrival of the New Moon at the end of a thirty-day month is celebrated not only on the first day of the new month but also on the preceding day, the thirtieth day of the preceding month. In such cases, the counting of the new month (the first day) starts with the second day of the New Moon celebration.

Two days of Rosh Chodesh are celebrated in months with thirty days, probably in imitation of the procedure followed for Rosh Hashana. The first day of Tishri is the only day mandated by the Tora (Leviticus 23:24) as Rosh Hashana. When the law was changed in talmudic times and two days became mandatory for the observance of Rosh Hashana, the same was done for Rosh Chodesh. Both days were treated as one, and were referred to as "a long day" (yoma arichta).

Why is Israel Independence Day (Yom Ha-atzmaut) observed as a holiday?

Israel Independence Day is celebrated on the fifth day of the Hebrew month Iyyar. It was on this day in 1948 (May 14) that Israel achieved statehood. Not since the year 70 C.E., when the Second Temple was destroyed by the Romans, had Israel been an independent nation.

Yom Ha-atzmaut is celebrated in Israel by holding spectacular parades and lavish festivities in all major cities. It is becoming an increasingly important Diaspora holiday.

Why is Jerusalem Day (Yom Yerushalayim) observed as a holiday?

On the twenty-eighth day of Iyyar in 1967, as a result of the Israeli victory over the Arab armies during the Six-Day War, the two divided sections of Jerusalem were united. For the first time since the year 70 C.E. the Temple Mount and the Western (Wailing) Wall were under Jewish control, and the day has been observed as a holiday, particularly in Jerusalem, ever since.

Jerusalem Day begins with a thanksgiving service at the Western Wall. Torches are lighted in memory of Israeli soldiers who died in the battle for Jerusalem. Since this minor holiday is a festive day that falls during the *Sefira* period, in some Orthodox circles the ban on weddings is waived, as on other semiholidays such as Lag B'Omer and Rosh Chodesh.

Why is Lag B'Omer observed?

The seven weeks between Passover and Shavuot are counted off day by day, and a blessing is recited each night at the conclusion of the evening service. Because of the counting, this period became known as the *Sefira* ("counting") period.

Lag B'Omer occurs on the thirty-third day after the second day of Passover. The word *lag* is an acronym made up of two Hebrew letters, *lamed* and *gimmel,* which have a combined numerical value of thirty-three. (See pages 207 and 208 for a discussion of the *Omer*.)

Special attention is paid to Lag B'Omer because, according to the Talmud (Yevamot 62b), a plague that had struck down many thousands of the students of Rabbi Akiba ended on Lag B'Omer. Because of this event, Lag B'Omer has also been called Scholar's Day.

According to kabbalists, Lag B'Omer marks the day of death of Rabbi Simeon bar Yochai, who is the alleged author of the *Zohar*, the basic book of kabbalism. On the day of his death he is said to have revealed many secrets to his pupils. The day was, therefore, called "Hillula de-Rabbi Simeon bar Yochai," *hillula* being the Aramaic word for "wedding." To mystics, it is a day which marks the harmonious union (marriage) of heaven and earth. Celebrations include merrymaking at the grave of Rabbi Simeon on the mountain of Meron. This is in keeping with the expressed wish of the Master, who requested that the day of his death be celebrated, not mourned.

Why do children celebrate Lag B'Omer by going on field trips?

There is a legend that during the lifetime of Rabbi Simeon bar Yochai (second century C.E.), he hid from the Romans for thirteen years in a cave in the Galilee. There he lived with his son, subsisting on the fruit of the carob tree. Each year, on Lag B'Omer, his students would visit him, disguised as hunters carrying bows and arrows. In the evening they carried on in festive fashion, lighting a huge bonfire at midnight and then singing and dancing until dawn. On the anniversary of the day of Rabbi Simeon's death, this tradition is still carried on at his gravesite at Meron.

Throughout Israel, on Lag B'Omer children are free from school. They spend the day going on field trips and playing outdoor games. In many of the villages of Israel bonfires are lighted, people sit around campfires, sing, roast potatoes, and retell the story of the early Roman occupation of Palestine.

Why are minor fasts not observed on the Sabbath?

Only the fast of Yom Kippur (on the tenth of Tishri) is fixed by date in the Bible, and it must be observed on the date specified. According to most authorities, when other fast days fall on the Sabbath, they are postponed until Sunday so as not to intrude on the joy of the Sabbath Day. The sole exception is Taanit Esther, the Fast of Esther, which, if it falls on a Saturday, is moved back to Thursday. This is in accordance with the view of Maimonides, who said that "fasting must precede the celebration [Purim]" (*Mishneh Torah,* Taanit 5:5). To observe the fast on Friday would interfere with preparing for the Sabbath.

Why are three weeks each summer observed as a period of mourning?

On Tisha B'Av (the ninth day of Av) in the year 586 B.C.E., the First Temple in Jerusalem was destroyed. This was preceded by the breaching of the walls of Jerusalem three weeks earlier, on the seventeenth day of Tammuz (Shiva Asar B'Tammuz). This three-week period became a time of national mourning observed by fasting on both Shiva Asar B'Tammuz and Tisha B'Av. During these three weeks strict observance demands that music not be played, weddings not be held, personal grooming be curbed (no haircuts), and new clothing not be worn.

When the Second Temple was built, these observances lost their importance, but after the Second Temple was destroyed in 70 C.E., they were revived.

Why is Shiva Asar B'Tammuz observed as a fast day?

Shiva Asar B'Tammuz, the seventeenth day of Tammuz (three weeks before Tisha B'Av), is observed as a minor fast day in the Jewish calendar to commemorate a catastrophic event in Jewish history. On that day in the sixth century B.C.E., during the reign of Nebuchadnezzar of Babylonia, the walls of Jerusalem were breached, eventually leading to the destruction of the First Temple.

As on other *minor* fast days, fasting is from dawn until stars appear in the evening.

Why do Jews fast on Tisha B'Av?

Tisha B'Av, the ninth day of the Hebrew month of Av, is a day of mourning for the destruction of the First Temple in the year 586 B.C.E. by the Babylonians, and of the Second Temple in the year 70 C.E. by the Romans. (According to tradition, both Temples were destroyed on the same date.)

Next to Yom Kippur (a biblical holiday), Tisha B'Av (a post-biblical holiday) is the most important fast day in the Jewish calendar. It marks the final day of a three-week period of intense national mourning for the events that led to the loss of Jewish independence with the destruction of the holy shrines of Jewish life.

Aside from these two major historical events, other happenings in Jewish history have been said to have occurred on the ninth of Av. These include the fall of Betar (the last Jewish stronghold during the Bar Kochba rebellion against Rome) in 135 C.E. and the beginning of the expulsion of the Jews from Spain in 1492. The importance of Tisha B'Av as a fast day was emphasized in the Talmud (Taanit 30b), where the comment is made: "He who eats or drinks on the ninth day of Av must be considered as guilty as one who has eaten on Yom Kippur." The fast of Tisha B'Av, like Yom Kippur, begins at sunset and ends the next evening with the appearance of three stars.

Why are the first nine days of Av considered a period of intense mourning?

Although the three weeks prior to Tisha B'Av are days of

mourning, the nine days prior to the ninth of Av are observed more intensely. The Mishna notes (Taanit 4:7) that in commemoration of the destruction of the Temple, during these nine days one should not cut his hair or wash his clothes (except on Thursdays to honor the coming Sabbath). During these days of mourning, weddings and other festivities are not held.

Why are meat and wine not served during the first nine days of Av?

Except on the Sabbath, wine and meat are not consumed during the first nine days of Av (called "the Nine Days") because this period has been designated in Jewish life as one of national mourning over the destruction of the Temples. Since meat and wine are traditionally served on festive occasions, they are banned during the Nine Days. Dairy foods are commonly eaten during this period, and many people eat fowl as well.

Why do Jews sit in the synagogue barefooted and on low benches on Tisha B'Av?

As stated above, Tisha B'Av is a day of mourning for the destruction of the Temples. Sitting on low benches and removing one's shoes are signs of mourning, actions performed by mourners during the week of *Shiva*.

Why does the final meal before the fast on Tisha B'Av consist principally of hard round rolls, bagels, and eggs? And why are the eggs sometimes sprinkled with ashes?

Food that is round-shaped has long been associated with

mourning because of its symbolic connection with eternal life: that which is round is conceived of as eternal, with no beginning and no end. Upon returning from the cemetery after a funeral, round foods are traditionally served to the mourners. (See page 63.)

As stated above, on Tisha B'Av some of the customs observed by mourners are followed. Sprinkling ashes on eggs as a sign of mourning is observed in some communities, but it is not a popular practice.

Why is the Fast of Gedalia observed?

The Fast of Gedalia (Tzom Gedalia) is a minor fast day that falls on the third of Tishri, which follows the second day of Rosh Hashana.

Gedalia was a Jewish official appointed by King Nebuchadnezzar of Babylonia to govern the Jews who remained in Palestine after the destruction of the First Temple in 586 B.C.E. Gedalia, considered a traitor by some Jews, was assassinated on the third day of Tishri. In retaliation, Nebuchadnezzar inflicted reprisals on the Jewish people.

Gedalia's effort to rebuild Jewish life was not fully appreciated in his lifetime, but in death he was mourned as a hero, and now the day of his assassination is observed as a minor fast day in the Jewish calendar. The fasting begins at sunrise on the third of Tishri and ends when the stars appear in the evening.

Why is Asara B'Tevet observed as a fast day?

Asara B'Tevet, the tenth day of Tevet (the month after Chanuka), is observed as a minor fast day in commemoration of the beginning of the siege of Jerusalem in 588 B.C.E. After almost two years of struggle (in 586), King Nebuchadnezzar of Babylonia destroyed the First Temple, which had been built by King Solomon. Asara B'Tevet thus became a day of national mourning and fasting. As with other minor fast days, the fast begins at dawn and ends with the appearance of the evening stars.

Why is Chamisha Asar B'Shevat observed as a holiday?

Hillel and his disciples declared Chamisha Asar B'Shevat a semiholiday. They called it "Rosh Hashana L'Ilanot" (New Year for Trees) because by this day in Israel the annual rains have ended and a new annual cycle of tree growth begins.

Also called Tu B'Shevat (*tu* is an acronym consisting of the Hebrew letters *tet* and *vav,* and has the combined numerical value of fifteen), Chamisha Asar B'Shevat is celebrated on the fifteenth day of Shevat by the eating of various fruits, especially those grown in Israel. In modern Israel this day, also known as "Arbor (Tree) Day," is celebrated by schoolchildren who go out into the fields and plant trees. *Bokser*— carob—has long been a popular holiday treat.

Why is the thirteenth day of Adar observed as a fast day?

The thirteenth day of Adar (the Fast of Esther) was fixed as a fast day in the eighth century. It is not designated as a fast day in the Book of Esther, written centuries earlier. The Bible (Esther 9:18) speaks of the thirteenth day of Adar only as a day of assembly for battle. The Rabbis interpreted the word "assembly" to mean "assembly for prayer and fasting," and the day became known as "Taanit Esther" (the Fast of Esther).

Why is Holocaust Day celebrated?

Holocaust Day ("Yom Ha-shoa" in Hebrew) is a special day in the Jewish calendar. It falls on the twenty-seventh day of Nissan and is celebrated as a minor holiday to commemorate the martyrs and heroes who died under Nazi oppression. There are wreath-laying ceremonies at Yad Vashem (the Jerusalem memorial to Nazi victims), and all Jewish places of entertainment in Israel are closed.

Chapter 16

General Questions

Why do Jewish texts use B.C.E. and C.E. in place of B.C. and A.D. in their system of dating?

B.C., meaning "before Christ," and A.D., meaning *"Anno Domini"* (Latin for "in the year of the Lord"), are abbreviations used by Christians. Their use implies the acceptance of Jesus Christ as divine, a concept rejected by Jews. Hence, in Jewish scholarship B.C.E., meaning "before the Common Era," and C.E., meaning the "Common Era," were introduced to draw a distinction between Christian and Jewish belief.

Why are some Jews averse to using the designation "New Testament"?

As with the use of B.C. and A.D., described above, some Jews believe that to refer to a *New* Testament is to give credence to the Christian idea that the New Testament is the fulfillment of the promises and teachings of the Jewish Bible. In fact, Jews often refrain from using the term "Old Testament" because it implies a *New* Testament.

Why according to the Jewish calendar does the day begin at sundown?

The custom of reckoning days in this fashion is based on the system used in the Book of Genesis. At the end of each day of Creation, Genesis 1 says: "And God saw that it was good. And it was evening and it was morning. . . ." Leviticus 23:32 says: ". . . from evening unto evening shall you keep your Sabbath."

Each twenty-four-hour period begins in the evening at sundown. Thus, the Sabbath begins at sundown on Friday evening and continues for the next twenty-four hours—until nightfall on Saturday.

Why is the English date on which a Jewish holiday falls different each year?

The English date on which a Jewish holiday falls is different each year because the Jewish calendar is a lunar calendar whereas the civil (secular) calendar is solar. In the Jewish calendar there are twenty-nine or thirty days in a month compared to thirty and thirty-one in the civil calendar. The Jewish calendar was adjusted to harmonize with the civil calendar by adding an extra month (Adar II) seven times in each nineteen-year period and by reducing or increasing the number of days in the months Cheshvan and Kislev. The number of days in Adar I and II are also adjusted in leap years. (See the Introduction for further discussion of the calendar.)

Why do some months in the Jewish calendar have twenty-nine days and some thirty days?

The Jewish calendar is a lunar calendar, that is, it is based upon the moon making one revolution around the earth every twenty-nine and one-half days. Since using half-days in the calendar was impractical (one could not very well begin a new day in the middle of another day), and since it was necessary to harmonize the lunar and solar calendars, some months in the Jewish calendar were assigned twenty-nine days and others thirty days. (See the Introduction for a further discussion of the calendar.)

Why does the Bible call Nissan the "first" month of the year, rather than Tishri, which is the month in which Rosh Hashana (New Year) falls?

Nissan is considered the first month of the Jewish year because it is during this month that the Exodus from Egypt took place. During Nissan, when the holiday of Passover falls, the earth reawakens and begins a new cycle of growth.

Tishri, the seventh month in the Jewish calendar, is when Rosh Hashana is celebrated. Tishri falls at the end of summer, when the forces of nature have begun to slow down, and with the beginning of the New Year holiday comes an emphasis on spiritual growth and accountability. (See also page 226.)

Why are some Jewish holidays celebrated for more days in the Diaspora than in Israel?

As explained earlier, the Bible dictates the number of days each of the following holidays is to be celebrated: Passover, seven days; Sukkot, seven days; Shavuot, one day; Shemini Atzeret, one day. In the Diaspora, Orthodox and most Conservative congregations add an extra day of observance to these holidays.

The extra day of observance was added to the holidays because of the uncertainty of the calendar in early times. Not until the middle of the fourth century C.E. was a fixed calendar established by the Sanhedrin. Before that time the arrival of each month had to be attested to by two witnesses who would appear before the Sanhedrin, the supreme judicial body in Jewish life. The witnesses would testify that they personally had seen the crescent of the New Moon. If accepted as truth by the Sanhedrin, this information was transmitted by torch signals from community to community throughout Palestine. Jews in distant places (e.g., Babylonia, Egypt) were informed by messenger of the New Moon's arrival.

The messenger system was not reliable. Travel was difficult and uncertain, and distant communities were often reached a day late. When this occurred, and Rosh Chodesh was not celebrated on the proper date, there was the possibility that holidays falling in that month would be celebrated on the wrong dates. To avoid this possibility, the communities of the Diaspora added one day to the observance of the major holidays. These communities could then be reasonably sure that even if an error in transmission were made, one of the two days on which they celebrated a given holiday would be the actual holiday. This second day of observance became known as the Second-Day Festival of the Diaspora ("Yom Tov Sheni Shel Galuyot").

Why is there a chief rabbi in England and other countries but not in the United States?

According to the United States Constitution there is to be strict separation between Church and State. In many European countries (for example, England and Denmark) where there is an established state religion, a chief rabbi, approved by the government, is the spokesman for the Jewish community.

In the United States, each community is autonomous, and each congregation elects its own rabbi without needing the sanction of the local, state, or federal government.

Why is "God" often spelled "G-d"?

The third of the Ten Commandments reads: "Thou shalt not take the name of the Lord thy God in vain" (Exodus 20:7). But what is God's name? The biblical reference to God as *Yehova* (Jehova), spelled out with the Hebrew characters *yad, hay, vav, hay,* is generally considered the "authentic" name of God, a name never to be pronounced (except by the High Priest when officiating on Yom Kippur) or written out.

Over the centuries other names for God, such as *Adonai* (also pronounced *Adonoy*), "Lord," were given the same status. *Adonai* was (and still is) used only in prayer. On other occasions *ha-Shem* or *Adoshem* were used in its stead. *Ha-Shem* means "the Name." *Adoshem* is a contraction of *Adonai* and *ha-Shem,* and its usage is considered by some to be disrespectful.

In the last few decades, a new practice has come into vogue: that of not writing out in full the *English* names "God" or "Lord." Most authorities consider this to be without foundation and no more than a passing fad.

Why is the word *goy* considered derogatory?

The word *goy* (plural, *goyim*) is a common biblical word meaning "nation" or "people." It carried no other meaning at first, but in time it became a popular synonym for "gentile." Mistakenly, the word was construed as being derogatory.

Why do the Hebrew letters *bet, hay* and also *bet, a-yin, hay* appear on top of Hebrew documents and in the correspondence of Jews?

Bet, hay is an abbreviation for *baruch ha-Shem,* "praised is God." *Bet, a-yin, hay* is an abbreviation for *b'ezrat ha-Shem,* meaning "with the help of God." Both forms are employed by religious people who are constantly cognizant of God's role in the world.

Why are the words *shaygetz* and *shiksa* used?

Shaygetz and its feminine counterpart, *shiksa,* are derogatory words for "non-Jew." They are distorted forms of the Hebrew rootword *sheketz,* which appears in the Bible four times and refers to the flesh of a tabooed animal. Hence, anything taboo or abominable became known as *sheketz.* Since intermarriage with non-Jews is taboo, this term was applied to them. *Sheketz,* the masculine form, is pronounced *shaygetz* in the vernacular and *shiktza,* the feminine form, is pronounced *shiksa* in the vernacular.

Why are Jews not eager to proselytize among non-Jews?

In principle, Jews are not averse to receiving willing converts. In fact, the Talmud refers to a convert as "a child newly born" (Yevamot 48b).

There were periods in Jewish history when Jews actively sought to win converts to Judaism. In the Bible, Ruth the Moabite was welcomed into the Jewish fold with open arms. In fact, she is revered in Jewish history as the ancestor of King David, from whom the Messiah would be descended. The talmudic sage Simeon ben Gamliel said, "When a prospective proselyte shows an interest in Judaism, extend to him a hand of welcome" (Leviticus Rabba 2:9).

However, from the time of the Bar Kochba rebellion against Rome (135 C.E.) onward, Jews began to regard proselytes cautiously, realizing that much of the hatred toward, and persecution of, Jews was initiated by converts to Judaism who spied on Jews and reported them to the authorities.

Why must male and female converts visit a ritual bath before conversion, and why must the male convert subject himself to circumcision?

When an individual converts to Judaism, he or she is expected to demonstrate through positive action the desire to change religions. For both women and men, immersion in a ritual bath *(mikva)* has been a longstanding requirement. The Bible speaks of immersion as the action required for an impure person to be restored to the state of purity. Many Orthodox Jews visit a *mikva* in preparation for the Sabbath and holidays.

Circumcision for male converts became mandatory because since the days of Abraham it has been the "sign of the Covenant [*ot brit*]" between God and Israel (Genesis 17:2). It is *the* act symbolizing acceptance of Judaism. When Shechem ben Chamor wanted to marry Jacob's daughter, Dinah, her brothers did not permit it: "We cannot do this thing to give our sister to one that is uncircumcised. . . . Only on this condition will we consent: be as we are [circumcised]" (Genesis 34:14-15).

Why does a Jew sometimes change his or her first name?

In talmudic times the heathen practice of husband and wife exchanging names at night as protection against demons was condemned by the Rabbis. But in post-talmudic times, especially among Franco-German Jews, when names of the sick were changed to confuse the evil spirits bent on harming the individual, the practice was condoned and was eventually widely accepted among Jews. It was usual for Jews to assume the new name Chayim (for a male) and Chaya (for a female), both meaning "life."

Jews developed an informal name-changing ceremony. In the presence of a *minyan* (quorum of ten adults), the ark was opened and a prayer recited in which the heavenly authorities were notified that the ill person was now to be called "_____ son [or daughter] of _____" and that he or she was no longer to be identified with his or her original name. Those witnessing the ceremony gave charity ("charity delivers from death").

Why do most Jews consider Jerusalem the eternal capital of Israel?

Jewish history and Jewish tradition is linked to Jerusalem more than to any other place on earth. From about 1000 B.C.E., when David captured the city from the Jebusites (of whom there is no longer any trace) and set it up as his capital, Jerusalem has been sacred to Jews. When Solomon built the First Temple there, it became a holy city, often called "the Eternal City." Jews lived in Jerusalem and prayed for its well-being for 1,000 years before there were Christians on the face of the earth, and for 1,600 years before Islamic nations came into being.

Why did many Jews of earlier generations walk stooped, with hands folded behind their backs?

There is a talmudic ban against walking more than four cubits (about six feet) in a jaunty, insolent, upright position—b'koma zekufa—which may account for the development of the posture assumed by many Jews of earlier generations. In the sixteenth century, renowned talmudist Solomon Luria condemned his fellow Jews who ignored the talmudic ban but "[are] very particular with regard to keeping their heads covered which, after all, is not a law but a mere custom."

Why is the Bible sometimes referred to as *Tanach*?

Tanach is an acronym from the three Hebrew words *Tora, Neviim,* and *Ketuvim,* which are the three parts of the Bible: *Tora* (Five Books of Moses or Pentateuch), *Neviim* (Prophets), *Ketuvim* (Holy Writings).

Why is the Talmud also referred to as *Shas*?

Shas is an acronym from the two Hebrew words *shisha sedarim,* meaning "six orders." The Talmud is divided into six main divisions:

1. *Zeraim,* dealing with the subject of tithes, Temple offerings, and agricultural matters
2. *Moed,* dealing with the subject of holidays of all types
3. *Nashim,* dealing with questions of marriage and divorce
4. *Nezikin,* dealing with legal matters
5. *Kodashim,* dealing with the sacrificial system in the Temple
6. *Tohorot,* dealing with questions of ritual purity.

Bibliography

Arzt, Max. *Justice and Mercy*. New York: Holt, Rinehart and Winston, 1963.

Barish, Louis. *High Holiday Liturgy*. New York: Jonathan David, 1959.

Berkovits, Eliezer. *God, Man and History*. New York: Jonathan David, 1959.

Blackman, Philip. *The Mishna*. 7 volumes, translated with notes. London: Mishna Press, 1951.

Chill, Abraham. *The Minhagim*. New York: Sepher-Hermon Press, 1979.

Cohen, A., ed. *The Soncino Books of the Bible*. 14 volumes. London: Soncino Press, 1947 and following.

Danby, H. *The Mishnah*. London: Oxford University Press, 1933.

Donin, Hayim. *To Be a Jew*. New York: Basic Books, 1972.

———. *To Raise a Jewish Child*. New York: Basic Books, 1977.

Dresner, S. *The Dietary Laws*. New York: Burning Bush Press, 1959.

Eisenstein, J.D. *Otzar Dinim Uminhagim*. New York: Hebrew Publishing Co., 1938.

Epstein, Isidore. *The Faith of Judaism*. London: Soncino Press, 1954.

———. *The Babylonian Talmud with Introduction and Commentary*. Volumes 1-36. London: Soncino Press, 1935-1952.

Finkelstein, Louis, ed. *The Jews, Their History, Culture and*

Religion. 4 volumes. Philadelphia: Jewish Publication Society, 1949.

Freedman, H., and Simon, Maurice, ed. *Midrash Rabbah.* Volumes 1-10. London: Soncino Press, 1939.

Ganzfried, Solomon, and Goldin, Hyman E. *Code of Jewish Law.* New York: Hebrew Publishing Co., 1963.

Garfiel, Evelyn. *Service of the Heart.* New York: Thomas Yoseloff, 1958.

Gaster, T.H. *Purim and Hanukkah in Custom and Tradition.* Boston: Beacon Press, 1950.

Goodman, Philip, ed. *Hanukkah Anthology.* Philadelphia: Jewish Publication Society, 1976.

——. *Passover Anthology.* Philadelphia: Jewish Publication Society, 1961.

——. *Purim Anthology.* Philadelphia: Jewish Publication Society, 1949.

——. *Rosh Hashanah Anthology.* Philadelphia: Jewish Publication Society, 1970.

——. *Shavuot Anthology.* Philadelphia: Jewish Publication Society, 1975.

——. *Sukkot and Simhat Torah Anthology.* Philadelphia: Jewish Publication Society, 1973.

——. *Yom Kippur Anthology.* Philadelphia: Jewish Publication Society, 1971.

Goodman, Philip, and Goodman, Hannah. *The Jewish Marriage Anthology.* Philadelphia: Jewish Publication Society, 1965.

Gordis, Robert. *Love and Sex: A Modern Jewish Perspective.* New York: Farrar, Strauss & Giroux, 1978.

Halevi, Judah. *Book of Kuzari.* Translation by H. Hirschfeld. New York: Pardes Publishing Co. 1946.

Hertz, Joseph H. *The Authorized Daily Prayerbook.* London: Soncino Press, 1948.

——. *The Pentateuch and Haftorahs.* London: Soncino Press, 1960.

Jacobs, Louis. *Jewish Law.* New York: Behrman House, 1968.

The Jewish Encyclopedia. 12 volumes. New York: Funk and Wagnalls, 1912.

Kaplan, Mordecai. *Questions Jews Ask.* New York: Reconstructionist Press, 1956.

Kaploun, Uri, ed. *The Synagogue.* Philadelphia: Jewish Publication Society, 1966.

Kayser, Stephen. *Jewish Ceremonial Art.* Philadelphia: Jewish Publication Society, 1959.

Kertzer, Morris. *What Is a Jew?* (revised edition). New York: Macmillan, 1969.

Kinderlehrer, Jane. *Cooking Kosher: The Natural Way.* New York: Jonathan David, 1980.

Kolatch, Alfred J. *The Family Seder.* New York: Jonathan David, 1967.

———. *The Name Dictionary.* New York: Jonathan David, 1967.

Lamm, Maurice. *The Jewish Way in Death and Mourning.* New York: Jonathan David, 1972.

———. *The Jewish Way in Love and Marriage.* San Francisco: Harper & Row, 1980.

Lauterbach, Jacob Z. "Burial Practices" in *Studies in Jewish Law, Customs and Folklore.* New York: Ktav, 1976.

Levy, Isaac. *The Synagogue: History and Functions.* London: Vallentine, Mitchell and Co., 1963.

Millgram, Abraham. *Jewish Worship.* Philadelphia: Jewish Publication Society, 1971.

———. *Sabbath: The Day of Delight.* Philadelphia: Jewish Publication Society, 1944.

Moore, George Foot. *Judaism.* 3 volumes. Cambridge, Massachusetts: Harvard University Press, 1954.

Roth, Cecil, ed. *Encyclopaedia Judaica.* 16 volumes. Jerusalem: Keter, 1972.

Routtenberg, Lilly S., and Seldin, Ruth R. *Jewish Wedding Book: A Practical Guide to the Tradition and Social Customs of the Jewish Wedding.* New York: Shocken Books, 1969.

Schauss, Hayyim. *The Jewish Festivals.* New York: Union of American Hebrew Congregations, 1938.

———. *The Lifetime of a Jew.* New York: Union of American Hebrew Congregations, 1950.

Siegel, Seymour, ed. *Conservative Judaism and Jewish Law.* New York: The Rabbinical Assembly, 1977.

Steinberg, Milton. *Basic Judaism.* New York: Harcourt Brace Jovanovich, 1947.

Stern, Chaim, ed. *Gates of Prayer, The New Union Prayer Book* (Reform). New York: Central Conference of American Rabbis, 1975.

Trepp, Leo. *The Complete Book of Jewish Observances.* New York: Behrman House, 1980.

Waxman, M. *A History of Jewish Literature* (second edition). New York: Thomas Yoseloff, 1960.

Wouk, Herman. *This Is My God.* New York: Doubleday, 1959.

Index

Bar Mitzva.
B'not Mitzva (sing., Bat Mitzva). *See*
Bat Mitzva.
Boaz, 35, 217
Bokser (carob), 289
Book of Death, 232
Book of Esther. *See* Esther, Book of.
Book of Life, 232, 238
Booth. *See* Sukka.
Bowing, 153
Breast-beating, 159, 243
Breastplates, 128-29
Bride, 28, 31. *See also* Marriage.
covering face at wedding, 36
fasting on wedding day, 34
position under canopy, 38
Brit. *See* Circumcision.
Broiling meat, 92-93
Burial. *See also* Cemetery *and*
Funeral.
coffins, 54
of holy objects, 83
in Israel, 55
in kittel, 53
in shrouds, 52, 53
of suicide, 56
in talit, 103, 105
within three days, 50
within 24 hours, 57
Burning bush, 142

Caesarean section, 21
Cairo geniza, 83. *See also* Geniza.
Calendar, Civil (Gregorian), 8-10, 292
Calendar Council, 8
Calendar, Jewish, 8-12, 292-94
English dates and, 292
New Moon, 281
solar calendar and, 292-93
uncertainty of, 185, 217, 227
Candelabrum. *See* Menora.
Candlelighting
Chanuka, 263
Sabbath, 163, 167-70
Shemini Atzeret, 256
Canopy. *See* Chupa.
Cantor, 131, 141, 146
kneeling, 153
repeating Amida, 155
wearing a talit, 101
Capernaum, 118
Caro, Rabbi Joseph, 6
Carob, 289
Carrots, 236
Casket. *See* Coffins.
Catholics, 262

C.E. (Common Era), 291
Cemetery, 62. *See also* Burial *and*
Funeral.
return from, 63
serving food, 77
Ceremony of Water Libation. *See*
Simchat Bet Hasho'ayva.
Chad Gadya, 198, 209
Chag Ha-bikurim, 211, 213
Chag Ha-katzir, 211, 213
Chag Ha-matzot, 183
Chag Ha-pesach, 183
Chag Ha-shavuot, 211
Chai, 100, 118
Chair of Elijah, 20
Chalalim, 30
Chalav Yisrael, 91
Chaldeans, 41
Challa (pl., challot)
decorations
birds, 240
hand, 256
key, 209
ladder, 218
dipping in salt, 174
for Hoshana Rabba, 256
long and braided, 276
for Purim, 276
for Rosh Hashana, 234
round shapes, 234
for Sabbath, 167, 172-74, 193
for Se'uda Shelishit, 178
showbreads, 193
taking challa, 174
Challef, 89
Chametz, 95, 182, 184ff. *See also*
Passover.
removal of, 187
selling of, 188
Chamisha Asar B'Shevat. *See* Tu
B'Shevat.
Chanuka, 12, 34, 259-68
card-playing, 267
Christian influence, 266
foods, 267-68
gift-giving, 259
Maccabees, 261
menora, 259, 262-63
oil, 262
origin, 259-60
prayers, special, 265
Tora reading on, 134, 265
Charity, 118, 298
Charms, 118-19
Chassid (chasid). *See* Chassidim.
Chassidim, 2, 36

Cooking
  on holidays, 164
  on Sabbath, 164
Costume. *See* Dress; Garb; *and* Mas-
  querading.
Court, Jewish religious, 27, 46, 48
Creation, 31, 172, 175, 292
Cremation, 49, 56
Crepe. *See* Blintzes.
Crown. 129
Crusades, 81, 257
Cucumber, 199
Cup of Elijah, 206
Custom(s). *See also* Law, Jewish.
  introduction of new, 17
  local, 3,5

Dairy products, 89-90. *See also*
  Dietary laws.
David, King, 3-4, 181
  house of, 261
  Jerusalem and, 298
  Ruth and, 217
Day of Atonement. *See* Yom Kippur.
Day of Judgment. *See* Yom Kippur.
Days of Awe. *See* High Holiday.
Death (and dying). 49-83. *See also*
  Burial; Cemetery; Funerals; *and*
  Mourning.
  angel of, 65
  attending to the body, 51
  care of the dead, 51
  recitation of Psalms, 51
  respect for the dead, 49
  spices and, 58
  viewing the dead, 54
Decalogue. *See* Ten Commandments.
Deer, as a kosher animal, 88
Demons. *See also* Superstition *and*
  Evil spirits.
  breaking wedding glass, 43
  burial of the dead, 62
  charms as safeguards against, 118
  circumcision, 17
  Shalom Zachar, 14
  Tashlich ceremony, 233-34
Depilatories. *See* Shaving.
Diaspora, 5, 7, 11, 294-95
  Birkat Kohanim and, 157
  extra days of holiday observance,
    185, 196, 217
  Yom Haatzmaut, 282
  Yom Tov Sheni, 11, 185, 194, 257
Dietary laws, 84-98, 184, 220
  arguments against, 87
  blood, 88, 92-93

cheeses, 91, 95
dairy products, 89-90
dishes, separation, 90, 98
fish, 89, 94
health contention, 84
holiness, 84-86
meat products, 89-90
Passover, 95, 184ff.
salting and soaking, 92
survival and, 86
unifier of Jewish people, 85
waiting time between meat and
  dairy, 91
Dinah, 297
Dipping of food, 205-206
Dishes. *See also* Dietary laws.
  Passover, 19
  separation of, 90
Dishwasher, 98
Divorce (get), 30, 46-48
  civil, 47
  civil marriage and, 117-18
Doorposts. *See* Mezuza.
Doughnuts on Chanuka, 267
Draydel (dreidel), 266
Dress, 2, 3, 7. *See also* Garb *and*
  Masquerading.
Duchan. *See* Bima.
Dumplings. *See* Kreplach.
Dutch Jews, 91

Early years, 13ff.
Eastern European Jews, 91, 175, 218
Eastern Jewry. *See* Sephardic Jews.
Ecclesiastes, 257, 273
Echad Mi Yodaya, 198
Education of boys, 23
  of girls, 23-24
Egg(s), chopped herring and, 176
Egypt, Egyptians, 2, 140, 260
  bridal ring and, 41
  embalming in, 52-54
  Passover and, 182, 184, 186
  redemption from, 162, 173, 182
  Sukkot and, 274
  tefilin and, 106
Eighteen Benedictions, 153-54
Eighth Day of Solemn Assembly. *See*
  Shemini Atzeret.
Elijah the Prophet
  chair of, 20
  cup of, 206
  Seder guest, 207
  as the Tishbite, 206
Elul, 10-11, 80, 221, 224
Embalming, 49, 52

Pittom, 251
Piyyutim (sing., piyyut), 147
  on Rosh Hashana and Yom Kippur, 233
  on Shavuot, 216
  Poems. *See* Piyyutim.
Pomegranates, 235
Pontshkes (latkes), 267
Pool of Siloam, 248
Poor man's bread (lechem oni), 190
Pork, 84, 86
Potato, 199
Potato pancakes (latkes), 267
Prague, 119
Prayer(s), 145-160. *See also* Blessings *and* Grace After Meals.
  amen, 152-53
  Amida, 155-56
  Barchu, 154
  beracha levatala (l'vatala), 236
  covering eyes during, 155
  covering head during, 122
  daily services, 148
  facing east, 149
  Hallel, 154, 254
  Kaddish, 149
  Kedusha, 156
  kissing objects during, 151
  kneeling during, 150, 153
  Musaf, 148
  Priestly Benediction, 157-58
  Rabbi Akiba and, 153
  Shehecheyanu, 236
  the Shema, 155
  standing position during, 154
  swaying during, 151
  tefilin during, 106-112
  Umipnay Chata'aynu, 147
  waving objects during, 150
  Prayerbook(s)
  language of, 147
  Machzor, 146
  Siddur, 146
  Star of David, 119
  Ten Commandments, 159
Prayershawl. *See* Talit.
Priest(s). *See* Kohayn.
Priestly Benediction, 75, 125, 142, 157-58
Promised land, 106, 247
Pronunciation, guide to, 12
Prophetic reading. *See* Haftara.
Proselyte(s), 90. *See also* Conversion to Judaism.
Proselytizing, 296
Prostration, 153

on High Holidays, 232
when Tachanun recited, 150
Protestants, 262
Psalms
  for Kaparot ceremony, 239
  recited by shomer, 51
Ptolemy, 260
Pulpit. *See* Bima.
Pumpedita, 5
Pur, 269
Purim, 269-79
  Adloyada, 278-79
  aliyot awarded on, 134
  celebration, of, 272
  date of, 12
  fast of bride and groom on, 34
  Fast of Esther, 271-72
  foods, 275-78
  gift-giving, 270, 274
  masquerading, 279
  noisemakers, 270, 277
  origin, 270-71
  prayers, special, 265, 273
  prohibitions, 272
  se'uda, 270, 273, 275
  Shiva on, 273
  in walled cities, 270, 272

Quill, 114, 119

Rabbenu (Jacob) Tam, 6, 110-11
Rabbi, 131, 146. *See also* Judah the Prince.
Rabbi of Bachrach, 201
Rabbina. *See* Rabina.
Rabina (Ravina), 5, 43
Rachel, 45, 74
Rama. *See* Rema.
Rambam. *See* Maimonides.
Ramban. *See* Nachmanides.
Ram's horn. *See* Shofar.
Rashi, 5-6, 81
  on cemetery procedure, 61
  kittel and, 197
  style of tefilin, 110-11
  on women's obligation to light candles, 169
Rava, 278
Raydle, 192
Razor, use of, 122-23. *See also* Shaving.
Rebecca, 36-37
Redemption of Firstborn. *See* Pidyon Haben.
Reform belief and practice, 7
  Bar Mitzva, 24

Se'uda, Purim, 270, 273, 275
Se'uda Shelishit, 177
Se'udat Havra'a. See Meal of Condo-
lence.
Seven Benedictions. See Sheva
Berachot.
Seventeenth of Tammuz. See Shiva
Asar B'Tammuz.
Sevivon. See Draydel.
Sexton. See Shamash.
Shabbes (Shabbat) goy, 166
Shaatnez, 104
Shacharit. See Shacharit.
Shadchan. See Matchmaker.
Shaddai
mezuza, 114-16
tefilin, 109
Shalachmones. See Purim (gift-
giving).
Shalashudis (Shaleshudes). See
Se'uda Shelishit.
Shaliach tzibbur, 146
Shalom Alaychem, 171
Shalom Zachar, 14-15
Shalosh Se'udos. See Se'uda She-
lishit.
Shamash
on Chanuka menora, 264
synagogue sexton, 131
Temple menora and, 126-27
Shammai, 4
Shankbone (zeroa), 199-200
Shas, 299. See also Talmud.
Shaving, 65, 122-23
Shavuos. See Shavuot.
Shavuot, 11, 25, 32-33, 211ff.
as agricultural holiday, 213
aliyot, 134
Confirmation, 218
Festival of First Fruits, 211
foods, 219-20
funerals on, 58
greenery, 220
Mount Sinai, 214, 216
Passover associated with, 214
Pentecost, 215
Priestly Benediction, 157
Ruth, Book of, 212, 217
study, 216
Ten Commandments, 214
Shaygetz, 296
Shaytl, 120. See also Headcovering.
Shechita, 88-89, 97
on Chanuka, 265
on Rosh Hashana, 235
on Shemini Atzeret, 256

Shehecheyanu, 235-36, 256, 265
Shekel (pl., shekalim), 20-22
Sheloshim, 79
Shema, 102, 110
on mezuza parchment, 114
recitation
before brit, 18
covering eyes, 155
posture during, 154
on tefilin parchment, 107
type of lettering, 155
Shemini Atzeret, 246ff.
Shemoneh Esray, 153-54. See Silent
Devotion.
Shemura matza. See Matza.
Sheva Berachot, 43
and minyan, 45-46
Shevarim, 230
Shevat, 10-12
Shevut, 165
Shiksa, 296
Shisha Sedarim. See Mishna.
Shiva. See also Mourning.
period of, 60, 63-64
visiting during, 50, 67, 68
Shiva Asar B'Tammuz, 11, 33-34,
285-86
Shiva call. See Condolence call.
Shloshet Yemay Hagbala, 214
Shmoneh Esrei (Esray). See Silent
Devotion.
Shochet, 88-89, 97
Shoes
removal in synagogue, 142-43
on Tisha B'Av, 281
on Yom Kippur, 242
Shofar, 2
blowing pattern, 229-30
during Elul, 221, 224
hundred blasts, 231
ram's horn used, 228
on Rosh Hashana, 225
on Sabbath, 2, 228
in the Temple, 281
Shofrot, 230
Shomer, 51
Shomronim. See Samaritans.
Shoshanta (pittom), 251
Showbreads (shewbreads) in Temple,
173
Shroud, 52-53
Shtreiml, 2
Shuckling. See Swaying.
Shulchan Aruch (Code of Jewish Law), 6-
7, 13. See also Law, Jewish.
Shushan, 270, 272